HISTORICAL DICTIONARIES OF LITERATURE AND THE ARTS

Jon Woronoff, Series Editor

1. *Science Fiction Literature*, by Brian Stableford, 2004.
2. *Hong Kong Cinema*, by Lisa Odham Stokes, 2007.
3. *American Radio Soap Operas*, by Jim Cox, 2005.
4. *Japanese Traditional Theatre*, by Samuel L. Leiter, 2006.
5. *Fantasy Literature*, by Brian Stableford, 2005.
6. *Australian and New Zealand Cinema*, by Albert Moran and Errol Vieth, 2006.
7. *African-American Television*, by Kathleen Fearn-Banks, 2006.
8. *Lesbian Literature*, by Meredith Miller, 2006.
9. *Scandinavian Literature and Theater*, by Jan Sjåvik, 2006.
10. *British Radio*, by Seán Street, 2006.
11. *German Theater*, by William Grange, 2006.
12. *African American Cinema*, by S. Torriano Berry and Venise Berry, 2006.
13. *Sacred Music*, by Joseph P. Swain, 2006.
14. *Russian Theater*, by Laurence Senelick, 2007.
15. *French Cinema*, by Dayna Oscherwitz and MaryEllen Higgins, 2007.
16. *Postmodernist Literature and Theater*, by Fran Mason, 2007.
17. *Irish Cinema*, by Roderick Flynn and Pat Brereton, 2007.
18. *Australian Radio and Television*, by Albert Moran and Chris Keating, 2007.
19. *Polish Cinema*, by Marek Haltof, 2007.
20. *Old Time Radio*, by Robert C. Reinehr and Jon D. Swartz, 2008.
21. *Renaissance Art*, by Lilian H. Zirpolo, 2008.
22. *Broadway Musical*, by William A. Everett and Paul R. Laird, 2008.
23. *American Theater: Modernism*, by James Fisher and Felicia Hardison Londré, 2008.
24. *German Cinema*, by Robert C. Reimer and Carol J. Reimer, 2008.
25. *Horror Cinema*, by Peter Hutchings, 2008.
26. *Westerns in Cinema*, by Paul Varner, 2008.
27. *Chinese Theater*, by Tan Ye, 2008.
28. *Italian Cinema*, by Gino Moliterno, 2008.
29. *Architecture*, by Allison Lee Palmer, 2008.
30. *Russian and Soviet Cinema*, by Peter Rollberg, 2008.
31. *African American Theater*, by Anthony D. Hill, 2009.
32. *Postwar German Literature*, by William Grange, 2009.
33. *Modern Japanese Literature and Theater*, by J. Scott Miller, 2009.

Contents

Editor's Foreword

For the modern literature of most countries in this series, the term *modern* is often a necessary, if flimsy, construct used to artificially distinguish the literature of the past century or so from what went before. Many times, especially in the West, the modern has proceeded largely from its immediate past. The situation of Japanese literature, however, is quite different, with a rather sharp—if not always clean—break from the past. "Modern" is often a euphemism for "Western," or what in Japan passes for that, and modern Japanese writers, poets, and playwrights often negotiated a clean break from most of what went before in order to create something new. There were, of course, continuities, traces of earlier literary themes, styles, and predilections (including violence and the supernatural), and obviously they were still writing in Japanese, but even the language, along with the economy, political system, social mores, and much else underwent radical changes as Japan opened its doors to the world after centuries of isolation. Ironically, while to the Japanese this was very much a "new" literature, enough remained of the "old" to fascinate outsiders mesmerized by *japonisme* in the 19th century. This innovative propensity continues to the present day when the Japanese, still revolutionary in certain respects, have turned *manga* into a popular art form and gone high tech with cell phone novels (leading some to wonder just how to define literature).

Such an unusual situation explains why, in some ways, this *Historical Dictionary of Modern Japanese Literature and Theater* has a broader scope than others in the series: It is necessary to weave the nation's political history into that of its literature and vice versa. Thus, the chronology is not just a progression of authors, titles, and styles, but it also mentions the historical events that influenced some of them so strongly. The dictionary section obviously includes entries, quite numerous indeed, on notable writers, memorable works, recurrent themes, and the proliferation of literary journals and awards. But it also says something about the succession of eras and emperors, warfare and militarism, Buddhism and Christianity, nationalism and militarism, the war and the atomic bomb, democracy and pacifism. Literature is defined very broadly, including novels and short stories, poetry and theater, but also adaptation and translation. The introduction traces Japan's literary history, charting the sweeping changes but also revealing some of what has remained, showing why the final result is a literature that can move its readers very deeply in the original while still, in many cases, impress those who read only in translation. The bibliography is quite extensive and designed to point readers in the right direction if they want to understand Japanese literature and, especially, read more of it.

This volume was written by J. Scott Miller, who has spent almost a quarter of a century studying and teaching Japanese literature, including over seven years accumulated time living in Japan. After studying at Princeton University he taught at Colgate University before moving to Brigham Young University in 1994. Over this period, in addition to teaching, he has written books and articles on Japanese literature, with an emphasis on the 19th and 20th centuries. Dr. Miller has contributed to various encyclopedias and reference works prior to writing this one of his own. Japanese literature, like many things Japanese, is particularly difficult to grasp, let alone explain, but this volume will help readers both understand and enjoy it.

Jon Woronoff
Series Editor

Acknowledgments

I am indebted to many people for assistance with this project. I learned fundamental editing and historiographical skills from my graduate school mentors Professors Marius B. Jansen and Earl Miner of Princeton University. Although both are now deceased, their positive influence lives on in ways too numerous to list. I am grateful to my Brigham Young University (BYU) colleagues in the Asian and Near Eastern Languages department as well as the Humanities, Classic and Comparative Literature department for their interest in and support of this project. Special thanks go to my Japanese studies colleagues Van Gessel, Robert Russell, and Jack Stoneman who have offered well-timed assistance and advice. I have benefited from the resources provided by a Ludwig-Weber-Siebach professorship awarded by the BYU College of Humanities and an Alcuin Fellowship awarded by Undergraduate Education at BYU. And I am pleased to have received the help of undergraduate student researchers Maurine Mayhew, Brandon Jahner, and Tyler Ransom, whose diligence and patience have added immensely to the accuracy of this work. I bear sole responsibility for its shortcomings and faults. And, most of all, I thank my wife, Judy, for her patience and encouragement throughout this project, and my children Michela and Joseph for being willing to forgo the occasional Saturday morning of fun while I worked on "the dictionary."

Reader's Note

The purview of this historical dictionary is modern Japanese literature and theater. Although there are good reasons to view the history of Japanese literary arts in terms of a "long" 19th century, beginning in the 1780s and ending after World War I, I have chosen to begin the "modern" with the restoration of the Emperor Meiji to ruling power in 1868. This is, in part, because the Meiji Restoration presents a convenient watershed event from which to begin. It also follows the practice of many Japanese literary historians, who note a general and rapid decline of literary production as the Tokugawa period drew to a close and see the revolutionary changes of the Meiji period offering an infusion of strength to a waning tradition.

I define "Japanese" literature generally as that written in the Japanese language. Other possible definitions, which are explored in part in some of the articles herein, include literature written by Japanese in other languages (such as that in English by Booker Prize–winning author Kazuo Ishiguro), and literature written in Japanese by non-Japanese writers (such as Japan-resident Korean [*zainichi*] authors). Although the definition of "literature" follows general conventions as well (poetry, drama, and narrative fiction), I also include the oral tradition of professional storytelling (*rakugo* and *kôdan*) that played an important role in the emergence of modern literary style.

Compiling a historical dictionary on a Japanese subject is not an easy task. The various sources from which material has been gleaned for this volume do not subscribe to the same editorial conventions. Because the Japanese language uses a different and complex writing system, even the simple task of converting the Japanese terms into roman letters presents a challenge because there have been various systems invented over the years to do so, each with its own idiosyncrasies. Likewise, written Japanese does not place breaks between words, which can create ambivalence about where words begin and end. Also, there is nothing resembling capitalization in Japanese. Although styles for editing Japanese in English-language publications have evolved into a general set of conventions, there is still great variety in usage. I have sought for simplicity and consistency herein.

Regarding proper names, Japanese custom dictates that surnames (Kawabata) be mentioned first, followed by given names (Yasunari). I have followed this practice throughout the work, listing all authors by surname first, alphabetically, in both the dictionary and in the bibliography (in the latter I have listed surnames in ALL CAPS for clarity). To complicate matters, in critical discourse most modern Japanese writers are referred to by their first, rather than last, name, particularly when they possess a fairly common surname. If the reader is unsure, try both names, just to be safe.

Japanese contains lengthened vowels, which are usually represented by a macron above the vowel (*nô* theater, for example). Although these lengthened vowels matter significantly and change the very meaning of the word when not included, I have nevertheless chosen to pretend they do not exist when it comes to alphabetizing the entries. Accordingly, the author Ôba Minako will precede, rather than follow, Oda Sakunosuke.

Within the articles themselves are several simplifying conventions. When a term has an entry of its own, it appears in **boldface** on the first occurrence within the article. Japanese language titles are followed by parentheses that contain the year of publication as well as the title in English translation. The notation "tr." before the italicized English title indicates that the work has been published in English with that title, and the year of first translation immediately follows. Example: *Nobi* (1951; tr. *Fires on the Plain*, 1957). Otherwise, if not italicized, the English translations are my own approximations. Example: *Setchûbai* (Plum Blossoms in the Snow, 1886). (In some cases I have opted to provide more accessible than correspondent translation titles or more recent translations.)

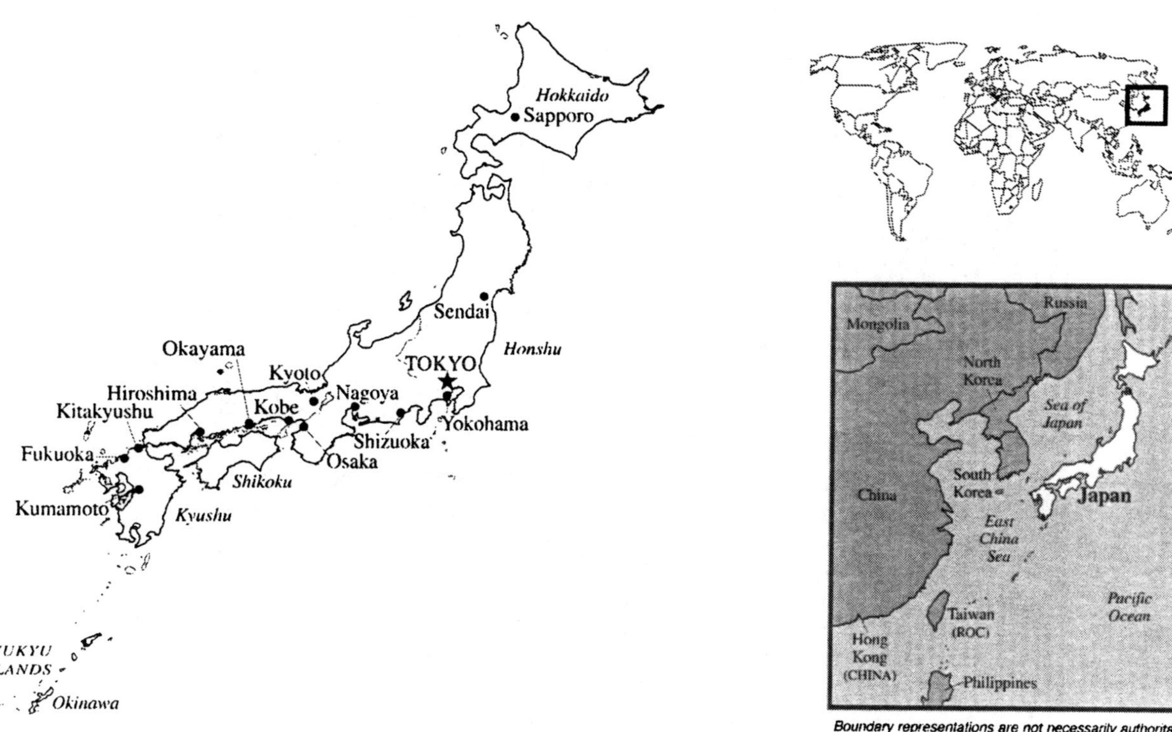

Map provided courtesy of CultureGrams. (c) 2009 ProQuest LLC and Brigham Young University.

Hayashi Fumiko

Higuchi Ichiyo

Mori Ôgai

Natsume Sôseki

Yosano Akiko

Chronology

1600–1868 The Tokugawa period of relative Japanese isolation witnesses rapid urbanization, the growth of mass markets for an explosion of printed literary works, the flowering of *nô* theater, the rise of *haiku* poetry, the emergence of *kabuki*, and the blossoming of a vibrant professional storytelling tradition.

1854 The U.S. fleet under Commodore Matthew Perry forces the Japanese government to open several ports for trade, leading to an influx of foreign traders and goods into Japan.

1868 Transfer of rule from the Tokugawa shogunate to the Emperor Meiji begins the Meiji Era (through 1912).

1870 Kanagaki Robun's illustrated, serialized tale *Seiyôdôchû hizakurige/Shank's Mare to the Western Seas* depicts two Japanese travelers roaming the globe.

1871 Various grassroots organizations put pressure on the Meiji leaders for a constitution and representative government, paralleling the rise of political novels. Another Kanagaki Robun tale, *Aguranabe/The Beefeater*, parodies Japanese fascination with Western fashion and culture. Nakamura Masanao publishes a loose translation of Samuel Smiles' *Self Help* as *Saikoku risshi hen/Success Stories from Western Countries*.

1872 Fukuzawa Yukichi publishes *Gakumon no susume/An Encouragement of Learning*, advocating Japanese mass education and self-reliance.

1878 Despite government suppression, the Freedom and People's Rights Movement serves as a catalyst for many reforms. Niwa Jun'ichirô publishes *Karyû shun'wa/A Springtime Tale of Blossoms and Willows*, an adaptation of Edward Bulwer-Lytton's *Ernest Maltravers*, beginning a decade of adaptive translations of Western fiction. Kawashima Chûnosuke also publishes an adaptation of Jules Verne's *Around the World in Eighty Days* as *Hachijûnichikan sekai isshû*.

1882 *Shintai shishô/Collection of New-Style Poems*, an anthology of translated Western poetry, gives new writers a venue for stylistic experimentation.

1883 The government opens an elaborate Western-style guesthouse, the Rokumeikan (Deer Cry Pavilion), that symbolizes Japan's commitment to modernization.

1884 The invention of Japanese shorthand by Takusari Kôki allows transcription and publication of oral narrative, in particular the serialized ghost tales and stories of professional raconteurs, such as San'yûtei Enchô.

1885 Ozaki Kôyô and colleagues found the Ken'yûsha literary group, with its coterie magazine *Garakuta bunko/Library of Trash*, which grows to become Japan's first literary journal. Tsubouchi Shôyô publishes his groundbreaking critique *Shôsetsu shinzui/The Essence of the Novel* as well as a fledgling novel *Tôsei shosei katagi/The Character of Modern Students*. Tôkai Sanshi publishes his nationalistic narrative *Kajin no kigû/Strange Encounters with Beautiful Women*.

1886 Against the backdrop of calls for unification of writing and speech, realist experimental narrative first appears in the works of Suehiro Tetchô (*Setchûbai/Plum Blossoms in the Snow*), Yamada Bimyô (*Musashino/Musashi Plains*), and Futabatei Shimei (*Ukigumo/The Drifting Clouds*).

1887 Tokutomi Sohô founds the influential periodical *Kokumin no tomo/Nation's Friend*.

1889 Mori Ôgai publishes *Omokage/Vestiges*, another anthology of translated poetry, and helps establish the Romanticist literary journal *Shigarami-zôshi/The Weir*. Romanticism permeates works by Ozaki Kôyô, Kôda Rohan, Yamada Bimyô, and other experimental writers.

1890 The Meiji Constitution, establishing a Prussian-style government and promulgated in 1889, becomes operative. Mori Ôgai publishes two short stories, *Maihime/The Dancing Girl* and *Utakata no ki/A Sad Tale.*

1891 Tsubouchi Shôyô founds the literary journal *Waseda bungaku/ Waseda Literature.* Kitamura Tôkoku publishes *Horaikyoku/Song of Paradise*, a Byronesque poetic drama.

1893 Shimazaki Tôson and colleagues found the literary journal *Bungakkai/The Literary World.*

1894 Sino-Japanese War begins (through 1895). Female author Higuchi Ichiyô, writing in the classical style of Ihara Saikaku, publishes her novel *Ôtsugomori/The Last Day of the Year.* Poet Yosano Tekkan writes a critical manifesto titled *Bôkoku no ne/Sounds Ruinous to the Country*, urging reform of *tanka.*

1895 Tsubouchi Shôyô publishes his play *Kiri hitoha/A Pawlonia Leaf*, a fusion of traditional and Western dramatic conventions. Izumi Kyôka publishes *Yakôjunsa/The Patrolman*, the first of his "problem novels" that address social issues. Poet Masaoka Shiki publishes *Haikai taiyô/Essentials of Haikai (haiku).*

1896 Ozaki Kôyô publishes his novel *Tajô takon/Passions and Regrets.*

1897 Masaoka Shiki founds the haiku magazine *Hototogisu/The Cuckoo.* Shimazaki Tôson publishes his anthology of poems in the modern style *Wakanashû/Collection of Young Herbs.* Ozaki Kôyô publishes his novel *Konjiki yasha/The Gold Demon.*

1898 Kunikida Doppô publishes his narrative sketches *Musashino.*

1900 Yosano Tekkan founds the literary journal *Myôjô/Venus.* Izumi Kyôka publishes gothic novella *Kôya hijiri/The Kôya Priest.* Tokutomi Rôka publishes a series of sketches (*Shizen to jinsei/Nature and Life*) and a semiautobiographical novel (*Omoide no ki/Footprints in the Snow*).

1901 Yosano Akiko publishes *Midaregami/Tangled Hair*, a feminist poetry collection in the *waka* style. Kunikida Doppô publishes *Gyûniku to jagaimo/Beef and Potatoes.* Shimazaki Tôson publishes a poetry collection *Rakubaishû/Fallen Plum Blossoms.*

1902 Nagai Kafû publishes his realist novel *Jigoku no hana/The Flowers of Hell.*

1904 Russo-Japanese War begins (through 1905). Kinoshita Naoe publishes his vernacular antiwar novel *Hi no hashira/Pillar of Fire.* Yosano Akiko publishes her antiwar poem *Kimishini tamau koto nakare/Brother, Do Not Give Your Life!*

1905 Natsume Sôseki publishes the novel *Wagahai wa neko de aru/I am a Cat.* Ueda Bin publishes *Kaichôon/The Sound of the Tide*, a collection of translations of Western poetry. Tsubouchi Shôyô is finally able to stage his play *Kiri hitoha/A Paulownia Leaf.*

1906 Tsubouchi Shôyô forms the *Bungei kyôkai* to perform translated versions of Shakespeare and other Western dramas. Shimazaki Tôson publishes the naturalist novel *Hakai/The Broken Commandment.* Natsume Sôseki publishes both *Botchan/Master Darling* and *Kusamakura/The Three-Cornered World.*

1907 Tayama Katai publishes his autobiographical, naturalist novel *Futon/The Quilt.* Futabatei Shimei publishes the novel *Heibon/Mediocrity.*

1908 Itô Sachio founds the literary journal *Araragi/The Yew.* Nastume Sôseki publishes his humorous novel *Sanshirô.* The tenets of naturalism are articulated by Shimamura Hôgetsu in the journal *Waseda bungaku.* Masamune Hakuchô publishes the novel *Doko e/Whither?*

1909 Osanai Kaoru and Ichikawa Sadanji II form the modern theater group *Jiyû gekijô/Free Theater.* Mori Ôgai and Ueda Bin establish the literary journal *Subaru/Pleiades*, in which *tanka* poet Kitahara Hakushû publishes his lyric debut *Jashumon/Heretics.* Nagai Kafû publishes the novel *Sumidagawa/River Sumida.* Iwano Hômei publishes the autobiographical novel *Tandeki/Debauchery.*

1910 Japanese annexation of Korea. Literary journal *Mita bungaku/Mita Literature* founded at Keiô University. Young writers found *Shirakaba/White Birches* literary magazine. Natsume Sôseki publishes *Mon/The Gate.* Mori Ôgai publishes *Seinen/Youth.* Shimazaki Tôson publishes his novel *Ie/The Family.* Tanizaki Jun'ichirô writes *Shisei/The Tatooer.* Poet reformer Ishikawa Takuboku publishes a collection of modern *tanka* titled *Ichiaku no suna/A Handful of Sand*. Yoshii Isamu also publishes *Sakahogai/Revelry*, his first collection of new *tanka*. Nagatsuka Takashi publishes the long novel *Tsuchi/The Soil*, describing the hardships of agricultural life.

1911 Mori Ôgai publishes *Gan/The Wild Geese*. Natsume Sôseki publishes a critical essay titled *Gendai Nihon no kaika/The Enlightenment of Modern Japan*. Kitahara Hakushû publishes a collection of lyric modern poems titled *Omoide/Recollections*. Playwright Okamoto Kidô completes a new *kabuki* drama *Shûzenji monogatari/Tale of Shûzen Temple*. Hiratsuka Raichô founds the feminist literary journal *Seitô/Bluestockings*.

1912 Death of Emperor Meiji. His son assumes the throne, beginning the Taishô period (through 1926). Natsume Sôseki publishes two novels, *Higan-sugi made/To the Equinox* and *Kôjin/The Wanderer*. Ishikawa Takuboku dies, and his innovative collection *Kanashiki gangu/A Sad Toy* is published posthumously. Shimazaki Tôson publishes his *Chikumagawa sukettchi/Chikuma River Sketches*.

1913 Shimamura Hôgetsu establishes the *Geijutsu-za/Art Theater*. Mori Ôgai publishes the historical novel *Abe ichizoku/The Abe Clan*. Miki Rofû publishes a collection of Symbolist poems titled *Shiroke te no ryôjin/The White-Handed Hunter*. Saitô Mokichi publishes *Shakkô/Red Lights*, a collection of modern *tanka*. Naka Kansuke publishes the memoir-like novel *Gin no saji/The Silver Spoon*.

1914 Japan joins Allied forces in World War I. The literary journal *Shinshichô/New Trends of Thought* is founded. Natsume Sôseki publishes his novel *Kokoro/The Heart* and an essay on criticism *Watakushi no kojin shugi/My Individualism*. Sculptor Takamura Kôtarô publishes *Dôtei/Journey*, a collection of poems. Nagai Kafû publishes *Sangoshû/Coral Anthology*, a collection of translated poetry. Kume Masao produces the modern drama *Gyûnyûya no kyôdai/The Milkman's Brother*. Nagatsuka Takashi publishes a *tanka* collection *Hari no gotoku/Like a Needle*.

1915 Natsume Sôseki publishes his quasi-autobiographical novel *Michikusa/Grass on the Wayside*. Mori Ôgai publishes the historical novel *Sanshô dayû/Sanshô the Baliff*. Akutagawa Ryûnosuke publishes

Rashômon/Rashô Gate. Tokuda Shûsei publishes *Arakure/Rough Living*, a novel about a young seamstress.

1916 Natsume Sôseki dies, leaving his final novel *Meian/Light and Darkness* unfinished. Nagai Kafû publishes *Udekurabe/Geisha in Rivalry*. Kurata Hyakuzô publishes his Buddhist play *Shukke to sono deshi/The Priest and the Disciples*.

1917 Shiga Naoya writes *Kinosaki nite/At Kinosaki* and *Wakai/Reconciliation*. Arishima Takeo publishes novel *Kain no matsuei/The Descendants of Cain*. Poet Hagiwara Sakutarô publishes a collection of colloquial free verse poetry *Tsuki ni hoeru/Howling at the Moon*. Kikuchi Kan writes a stage play *Chichi kaeru/The Father Returns*.

1918 Rice riots occur as a result of World War I inflation, leading to several years of agricultural depression. The children's literary magazine *Akai Tori/Red Bird* is founded. Akutagawa Ryûnosuke writes *Jigokuhen/The Hell Screen*. Arishima Takeo publishes the novel *Umare izuru nayami/The Anguish of Creation*. Satô Haruo writes the prose poem *Den'en no Yûutsu/Rural Melancholy*. Shimazaki Tôson publishes *Shinsei/A New Life*. Poet Murô Saisei publishes *Jojô shokyokushû/Short Lyrical Songs*. Kasai Zenzô publishes the story *Ko wo tsurete/With Children on My Hands*.

1919 Arishima Takeo's novel, *Aru onna/A Certain Woman*, portrays a new kind of heroine resistant to conventional female stereotypes. Mushanokôji Saneatsu writes *Kôfukumono/A Happy Man*, a novel based on the communal village he founded in 1918. Kikuchi Kan writes the novel *Onshû no kanata ni/The Realm Beyond*. Uno Kôji writes the novel *Kura no naka/In the Storehouse*.

1920 Yamamoto Yûzô publishes the play *Eijigoroshi/Infanticide*. Arishima Takeo publishes the essay *Oshiminaku ai wa ubau/Love, the Ruthless Plunderer*. Mushanokôji Saneatsu publishes his most popular novel, *Yûjô/Friendship*.

1921 Ômi Komaki founds the leftist journal *Tanemakuhito/The Sower*. Shiga Naoya publishes *An'ya kôro/A Dark Night's Passing*. Satô Haruo publishes a collection of poetry *Junjôshi-shû/Romantic Poems*. Kurata Hyakuzô publishes the critical essay *Ai to ninshiki to no shuppatsu/The Beginning of Love and Understanding*.

1922 Satomi Ton begins serialized publication of his long novel *Tajô-busshin/Passions and Piety.*

1923 The Great Kantô Earthquake devastates Tokyo and Yokohama. Yokomitsu Riichi publishes *Nichirin/The Sun*, which propels him into the modernist limelight. Ibuse Masuji publishes *Sanshôuo/The Salamander.* Nagayo Yoshirô publishes *Seidô no Kirisuto/The Bronze Christ.* Hagiwara Sakutarô publishes a collection of modernist poetry *Aoneko/The Blue Cat.*

1924 *Tsukiji Shôgekijô/Tsukiji Little Theater* established by Osanai Kaoru and Hijikata Yoshi. Literary journals *Bungei sensen/Literary Front* (proletarian) and *Bungei jidai/Literary Times* (neo-perceptionist) are founded. Tanizaki Jun'ichirô publishes *Chijin no ai/Naomi.* Miyazawa Kenji publishes free verse poems as *Haru to Shura/Spring and Asura.* Miyamoto Yuriko publishes the novel *Nobuko.* Iwata Kunio's play *Chiroru no aki/Tyrol Autumn* is performed.

1925 Kajii Motojirô publishes *Remon/The Lemon.* Horiguchi Daigaku publishes his translation of contemporary French poetry as *Gekka no ichigun/A Moonlit Gathering.* Kishida Kunio publishes his drama *Kamifûsen/Paper Balloon.*

1926 Emperor Taishô dies. His son, Hirohito, assumes the throne, beginning the Shôwa period (through 1989). Kawabata Yasunari publishes *Izu no odoriko/The Izu Dancer.* Hayama Yoshiki writes the proletarian novel *Umi ni ikuru hitobito/Life on the Sea.* Poet Itô Sei writes *Yuki akari no michi/A Road in Snowlight.*

1927 Akutagawa Ryûnosuke publishes the dystopian novella *Kappa/Water Sprite*; commits suicide. Writer and labor organizer Fujimori Seikichi writes proletarian drama *Nani ga kanojo wo sô saseta ka/What Caused Her to Do That?* Hirabayashi Taiko publishes the proletarian short story *Seryôshitsu nite/At the Charity Ward.*

1928 Two literary journals appear: *Shi to shiron/Poetry and Poetics* (modernism) and *Ashibi/Andromeda* (progressive *haiku*). Yamamoto Yûzô publishes novel *Nami/Waves.* Hayashi Fumiko publishes breakthrough bestseller *Hôrôki/Diary of a Vagabond.* Tanizaki Jun'ichirô publishes the novel *Tade kuu mushi/Some Prefer Nettles.*

1929 Great Depression affects Japan. Hijikata Yoshi founds the *Shin-Tsukiji gekidan/New Tsukiji Theater Troupe*. Shimazaki Tôson publishes *Yoakemae/Before the Dawn*. Kobayashi Takiji publishes *Kanikôsen/The Factory Ship*, a scathing indictment of capitalist nationalism. Tokunaga Sunao publishes a highly successful proletarian novel, *Taiyo no nai machi/The Street without Sunlight*. Critic Kobayashi Hideo publishes *Samazama naru ishô/All Manner of Designs*.

1930 Yokomitsu Riichi publishes the novel *Kikai/Machine*. Hori Tatsuo publishes *Seikazoku/The Saintly Family*. Miyoshi Tatsuji publishes the free verse anthology *Sokuryôsen/Surveying Boat*.

1931 Manchurian Incident expands Japanese military control in China and at home. Nagai Kafû publishes *Tsuyu no atosaki/After the Rains*.

1932 Tomoda Kyôsuke and Tamura Akiko found the Tsukiji Theater. Kishida Kunio founds the drama journal *Gekisaku/Playwriting*. Poet Maruyama Kaoru publishes the anthology *Ho, rampu, kamome/Sail, Lamp, Seagull*.

1933 Founding of the journals *Shiki/The Seasons* (poetry) and *Bungakkai/Literary World* (literature). Tanizaki Jun'ichirô publishes a novella, *Shunkinshô/A Portrait of Shunkin*, and an essay of cultural criticism, *In'ei raisan/In Praise of Shadows*. Nishiwaki Junzaburô publishes the poetry collection *Amubaruwaria/Ambarvaria*. Ozaki Kazuo publishes his autobiographical novel *Nonki megane/Rosy Glasses*.

1934 Maruyama Tomoyoshi and other Marxist dramatists form the *Shinkyô gekidan/New Cooperative Theater*. Murô Saisei publishes the story *Ani imoto/Older Brother Younger Sister*. Nakahara Chûya publishes a poetry collection *Yagi no uta/Poems of the Goat*.

1935 Journals *Rekitei/The Traveled Path*, *Nihon Roman-ha/Japanese Romantics*, and *Tama* (a *tanka* journal) founded. Kawabata Yasunari publishes *Yukiguni/Snow Country*. Nakano Shigeharu publishes the proletarian novel *Mura no ie/House in a Village* as well as a collection of poetry. Itô Shizuo publishes a lyric anthology *Waga hito ni atauru aika/Laments Addressed to My Beloved*. Yokomitsu Riichi publishes an essay *Junsui shôsetsu-ron/On Pure Literature*. Kobayashi Hideo publishes his groundbreaking essay *Watakushi-shôsetsu ron/On the I-Novel*. Ishikawa Tatsuzô publishes the historical novel *Sôbô/The*

Emigrants, which receives the first Akutagawa Prize, established, along with the Naoki Prize, by writer/publisher Kikuchi Kan.

1936 Abe Tomoji publishes the novel *Fuyu no yado/A Place to Winter*. Hori Tatsuo publishes the novel *Kaze tachinu/The Wind Rises*.

1937 Marco Polo Bridge Incident leads to all-out war with China. Tomoda Kyôsuke founds the *Bungaku-za/Literary Theater*. Kubo Sakae's Marxist play *Kazanbaichi/Land of Volcanic Ash* is first performed to wide acclaim. Nagai Kafû publishes *Bokutô kitan/Tales from East of the River*. Shimaki Kensaku writes *Seikatsu no tankyû/The Quest for Life*. Yokomitsu Riichi publishes the long novel *Ryoshû/Travel Sadness*. Tachihara Michizô issues a collection of sonnet-metered poems *Wasuregusa ni yosu/To the Day Lilies*.

1938 Hino Ashihei publishes the novel *Mugi to heitai/Wheat and Soldiers*, which eventually sells 1.2 million copies. Nakahara Chûya publishes the poetry collection *Arishihi no uta/Poems from Bygone Days*. Critic Miki Kiyoshi writes *Jinsei ron nooto/Notes on Life*.

1939 Nakano Shigeharu pens the novel *Uta no wakare/Leaving Songs Behind*. Murano Shirô issues a poetry collection *Taisô shishû/Poems on Exercise*. Ono Tôsaburô publishes an anthology of poems titled *Ôsaka*.

1940 Dazai Osamu publishes *Hashire Merosu/Run, Melos!* Itô Sei publishes an autobiographical novel *Tokunô Gorô no seikatsu to iken/The Life and Opinions of Tokunô Gorô*.

1941 Pacific War starts with Pearl Harbor attack. Takamura Kôtarô publishes poetry collection *Chieko shô/Chieko's Sky*. Masamune Hakuchô pens the essay *Sakkaron/On Authors*.

1942 Nakajima Atsushi publishes the novella *Sangetsuki/Tiger-Poet*. Sakaguchi Ango writes the essay *Nihon bunka shikan/A Personal View of Japanese Culture*.

1943 Nakajima Atsushi publishes the novel *Riryô*. Critic Karaki Junzô publishes *Ôgai no seishin/The Spirit of Ôgai*.

1944 Dazai Osamu publishes *Tsugaru*, an autobiographical novel based on a trip to his remote birthplace. Poetess Nakamura Teijo publishes collection *Teijo kushû/Teijo's Verse Anthology*.

1945 Japan surrenders after atomic bombing and is occupied by Allied forces. Miyamoto Yuriko and colleagues form the Shin-Nihon bungakkai/New Japan Literary Association. Morimoto Kaoru completes the commissioned play *Onna no isshô/A Woman's Life*.

1946 A new Japanese constitution is promulgated under the Occupation. New journals *Shin Nihon bungaku/New Japanese Literature*, *Kindai bungaku/Modern Literature*, and *Yakumo/Eight Clouds* are founded. Noma Hiroshi pens *Kurai e/Dark Pictures*. Haniya Yutaka writes *Shirei/Death Spirit*. Nakamura Shin'ichirô publishes *Shi no kage no moto ni/In the Shadow of Death*. Umezaki Haruo writes *Sakurajima/Sakura Island*. Miyamoto Yuriko writes *Banshû heiya/Banshû Plain*. Oda Sakunosuke publishes *Doyô fujin/Madam Saturday*. Sakaguchi Ango publishes a novel, *Hakuchi/The Innocent*, and an essay, *Darakuron/On Decadance*. Kuwabara Takeo writes an essay *Daini geijutsu: gendai haiku ni tsuite/Second-Class Art: On Modern Haiku*. Kobayashi Hideo writes an essay *Mujô to iu koto/On Transcience*.

1947 Dazai Osamu publishes the novel *Shayô/The Setting Sun*. Takeda Taijun writes *Shinpan/The Judgment* and *Mamushi no sue/This Outcast Generation*. Shiina Rinzô writes *Shin'ya no shuen/Midnight Banquet*. Ishikawa Jun publishes *Yakeato no Iesu/The Jesus of the Ruins*. Noma Hiroshi writes *Seinen no wa/Ring of Youth*. Kobayashi Hideo writes the essay *Motsuaruto/Mozart*. Niwa Fumio publishes the short story *Iyagarase no nenrei/The Hateful Age*.

1948 Tanizaki Jun'ichirô completes his long novel *Sasame Yuki/The Makioka Sisters*. Ôoka Shôhei publishes his first novel, *Furyoki/A POW's Memoirs*. Dazai Osamu publishes the novel *Ningen shikkaku/No Longer Human*. Shiina Rinzô writes *Eien naru joshô/The Eternal Preface*. Poet Kaneko Mitsuharu publishes the collection of antiwar poems *Rakkasan/Parachute*.

1949 Kawabata Yasunari publishes *Yama no oto/The Sound of the Mountain* and *Senbazuru/Thousand Cranes*. Mishima Yukio publishes his first novel, *Kamen no kokuhaku/Confessions of a Mask*. Mushanokôji Saneatsu writes a comeback novel *Shinri sensei/A Teacher of Truth*. Inoue Yasushi publishes *Tôgyû/Bullfighting*. Shimao Toshio publishes *Shutsukotô-ki/A Tale of Leaving a Lonely Island*. Kinoshita

Junji's play *Yûzuru/Twilight Crane* is first performed. Tamiya Torahiko publishes the long story *Ashizuri misaki/Ashizuri Promontory.*

1950 Korean War begins. Ibuse Masuji publishes satirical novel *Yôhai taichô/Lieutenant Lookeast.* Abe Kôbô publishes the short story *Akai mayu/Red Cocoons.* Critic Nakamura Mitsuo pens polemical essay *Fûzoku shôsetsu-ron/On the Novel of Manners.*

1951 Abe Kôbô publishes *Kabe: S. Karuma-shi no hanzai/The Crime of S. Karuma.* Hotta Yoshie writes the novel *Hiroba no kôdoku/Solitude in the Public Square.* Ôoka Shôhei publishes the novel *Nobi/Fires on the Plains.*

1952 The Allied Occupation of Japan ends. Noma Hiroshi publishes *Shinkû chitai/Zone of Emptiness.* Kobayashi Hideo writes the essay *Gohho no tegami/Van Gogh's Letters.*

1953 First commercial television broadcasts begin. Yasuoka Shôtarô publishes *Warui nakama/Bad Company.*

1954 Yoshiyuki Junnosuke publishes *Shû'u/Sudden Shower.* Kojima Nobuo writes *Amerikan sukûru/American School.* Shôno Junzô publishes the award-winning story *Pûrusaido shôkei/Evenings at the Pool.*

1955 Endô Shûsaku pens *Shiroi hito/The White Man.* Ishihara Shintarô publishes *Taiyô no kisetsu/Seasons in the Sun.* Kôda Aya writes *Nagareru/Flowing.* Agawa Hiroyuki publishes the novel *Kumo no bohyô/Burial in the Clouds.*

1956 Japan becomes a member of the United Nations. Mishima Yukio publishes *Kinkakuji/The Temple of the Golden Pavilion.* Fukazawa Shichirô writes *Narayamabushi-kô/Ballad of Narayama.* Etô Jun publishes his groundbreaking study *Natsume Sôseki.* Critic Katô Shûichi pens his essay *Zasshu bunka/Hybrid Culture.*

1957 Ôe Kenzaburô publishes *Shisha no ogori/Lavish Are the Dead.* Kaikô Takeshi writes *Panikku/Panic.* Enchi Fumiko publishes *Onnazaka/The Waiting Years.* Mishima Yukio's commissioned play *Rokumeikan/The Deer Cry Pavilion* is staged by the Bungaku-za. Nakamura Mitsuo publishes a study titled *Futabatei Shimei-den/Life of Futabata Shimei.* Inoue Yasushi publishes the novel *Tempyô no iraka/Rooftiles of Tempyô.*

1958 Ôe Kenzaurô publishes *Shiiku/The Catch.*

1959 Ariyoshi Sawako publishes *Kinokawa/Ki River.* Yasuoka Shôtarô writes *Kaihen no kôkei/A View by the Sea.*

1960 The U.S.–Japan Security Treaty crisis (*Anpo*). Miura Tetsuo writes *Shinobukawa/Shame in the Blood.* Kita Morio writes *Yoru to kiri no sumi de/The Corner of Night and Fog.* Kurahashi Yumiko writes the controversial political satire *Parutai/Partei.* Yamamoto Shûgorô publishes *Aobeka monogatari/This Madding Crowd.* Shimao Toshio publishes *Shi no toge/The Sting of Death.*

1961 Minakami Tsutomu publishes *Gan no tera/The Temple of the Wild Geese.*

1962 Takahashi Kazumi publishes *Hi no utsuwa/Vessel of Sadness.* Kita Morio writes *Nireke no hitobito/The House of Nire.* Abe Kôbô pens *Suna no onna/Woman in the Dunes.*

1963 Yoshiyuki Junnosuke publishes *Suna no ue no shokubutsu-gun/Vegetable Garden in the Sand.* Inoue Mitsuharu writes *Chi no mure/People of the Land*, a novel about Nagasaki atomic bomb victims. Tsuji Kunio publishes *Kairô nite/In the Corridor.*

1964 Summer Olympics, held in Tokyo, mark Japan's reemergence as a global industrial nation. Ôe Kenzaburô publishes *Kojinteki na taiken/A Personal Matter.* Shibata Shô publishes the novel *Saredo warera ga hibi/Anyway, That Was Our Time.* Takami Jun publishes a poetry collection *Shi no fuchi yori/By the Abyss of Death.* Shôno Junzô publishes the novel *Yûbe no kumo/Evening Clouds.*

1965 Takahashi Kazumi publishes *Jashûmon/Heretical Faith.* Ibuse Masuji writes *Kuroi ame/Black Rain.* Kojima Nobuo publishes *Hôyô kazoku/Embracing Family.*

1966 Endô Shûsaku publishes *Chinmoku/Silence.* Ariyoshi Sawako writes novel *Hanaoka Seishû no tsuma/The Wife of Hanaoka Seishû.*

1967 Absurdist playwright Betsuyaku Minoru writes *Matchiuri no shôjo/The Little Match Girl.* Ôe Kenzaburô publishes the novel *Man'en gan'nen no futtobôru/The Silent Cry.*

1968 Kawabata Yasunari is awarded the Nobel Prize for Literature. Kôno Taeko pens *Fui no koe/A Sudden Voice.* Oba Minako writes the story *Sanbiki no kani/The Three Crabs.* Critic Yoshimoto Takaaki publishes *Kyôdô gensô ron/A Theory of Collective Fantasy.*

1969 Kuroi Senji publishes *Jikan/Time.* Experimental writer Kurahashi Yumiko publishes *Sumiyakisuto Q no keiken/The Adventures of Sumiyakisuto Q.* Critic Karatani Kôjin writes the essay *Ishiki to shizen/Consciousness and Nature.*

1970 Furui Yoshikichi publishes *Yôko.* Abe Akira writes *Shirei no kyûka/The Commander's Holiday.* Etô Jun writes the essay *Sôseki to sono jidai/Sôseki and His Time.* Mishima Yukio writes the novel *Hôshô no umi/Sea of Fertility* and then commits ritual suicide after calling for a national coup d'etat.

1971 Ôba Minako publishes *Tsuga no yume/Hemlock Dreams.* Ôoka Shôhei publishes the historical novel *Reite senki/Record of the Battle of Leyte.*

1972 Normalization of Japanese relations with China. Critic Yamazaki Masakazu publishes *Ôgai tatakau kachô/Ôgai: Combative Patriarch.* Karatani Kôjin writes the essay *Ifu suru ningen/Human in Awe.* Ariyoshi Sawako publishes the novel *Kôkitsu no hito/The Twilight Years.*

1973 Oil crisis affects Japanese industry and economy. Abe Kôbô publishes *Hako otoko/The Box Man.*

1975 Nakagami Kenji publishes *Misaki/The Cape.* Sata Ineko publishes a short story about her atomic bomb victimization, *Matsuri no ba/Ritual of Death.*

1976 Yamazaki Masakazu publishes *Fukigen no jidai/The Age of Ill Humor.* Ôe Kenzaburô publishes the novel *Pinchi rannaa chôsho/Pinch Runner Memorandum.* Murakami Ryû publishes the novel *Kagirinaku tômei ni chikai buruu/Almost Transparent Blue.*

1977 Miyamoto Teru publishes *Doro no kawa/Muddy River.* Nakagami Kenji writes *Kareki nada/Sea of Kareki.* Minakami Tsutomu publishes the novel *Kinkaku enjô/The Burning of the Golden Pavilion.* Yoshiyuki Junnosuke publishes the novel *Yûgure made/Until Evening.*

1979 Ôe Kenzaburô publishes *Dô jidai geemu/Contemporaneity Game*. Korean writer Lee Hoesung (Ri Kaisei) publishes the novel *Mihatenu yume/Unfulfilled Dream*.

1980 Murakami Ryû publishes *Koin rokkaa beibiizu/Coin Locker Babies*. Ishikawa Jun publishes novel *Kyôfûki/Tale of a Mad Wind*. Endô Shûsaku writes the novel *Samurai/The Samurai*. Tanaka Yasuo publishes the postmodern novel *Nantonaku, kurisutaru/Somewhat Like Crystal*.

1981 Inoue Hisashi writes the satirical novel *Kirikirijin/The Kirikirians*. Shiba Ryôtarô writes *Hitobito no Ashioto/People's Footsteps*.

1982 Critic Maeda Ai publishes the theory treatise *Toshi kûkan no naka no bungaku/The Spirits of Abandoned Gardens*.

1983 Tsushima Yûko publishes *Hi no kawa no hotori de/By the River of Fire*. Hikari Agata publishes *Uhohho tankentai/The 'Ahem!' Expedition Team*. Critic Isoda Kôichi publishes *Rokumeikan no keifû/Pedigree of the Deer Cry Pavilion*. Nakagami Kenji publishes the novel *Chi no hate, shijô no toki/The Ends of the Earth, the Supreme Time*.

1984 Abe Kôbô publishes the novel *Hakobune sakura-maru/The Ark Sakura*.

1985 Critic Katô Norihiro publishes *Amerika no kage/The American Shadow*. Nogami Yaeko publishes the novel *Mori/The Forest*. Hino Keizô publishes the novel *Yume no shima/Dream Island*.

1986 Masuda Mizuko publishes *Shinguru seru/Single Cell*. Ôe Kenzaburô publishes the novel *M/T to mori no fushigi no monogatari/M/T and Wonder Tales of the Forest*.

1987 Yoshimoto Banana publishes *Kitchin/Kitchen*. Murakami Ryû publishes *Ai to gensô no fashizumu/Fascism in Love and Fantasy*. Murakami Haruki publishes *Noruwei no mori/Norwegian Wood*. Poet Tawara Machi publishes the *tanka* collection *Sarada kinenbi/Salad Anniversary*.

1988 Yoshimoto Banana publishes *TUGUMI/Goodbye Tsugumi*.

1989 Emperor Shôwa dies. His son Akihito assumes the throne, beginning the Heisei Era. Inoue Yasushi publishes the novel *Koshi/Confucius*.

Yamada Eimi publishes the novel *Hôkago no kiinooto/After-School Keynote.*

1990 Kaikô Takeshi's novel *Shugyoku/The Jewel* is published posthumously. Nakagami Kenji publishes *Sanka/Songs of Praise.* Tsutsui Yasutaka publishes *Bungakubu Tadano kyôju/Professor Tadano of the Literature Department.*

1993 Endô Shûsaku publishes his last novel, *Diipu ribaa/Deep River.*

1994 Ôe Kenzaburô receives the Nobel Prize for Literature and publishes *Moeagaru midori no ki/A Green Tree with Glittering Flame.* Critic Kawamura Minato publishes *Nan'yo Karafuto no nihon bungaku/Japanese Literature of the South Sea Islands and Sakhalin.*

1995 The Great Hanshin Earthquake hits Kobe. Aum Shinrikyô sect launches Sarin gas attack in the Tokyo subway. Murakami Haruki publishes the novel *Nejimaki-dori kuronikuru/The Wind-Up Bird Chronicle.*

1996 Korean writer Yu Miri publishes the novel *Furu hausu/Full House.* Murakami Ryû publishes the novel *Hyûga Uirusu/Hyûga Virus.*

1997 Journal *Araragi/The Yew* shuts down. Tawara Machi publishes the *tanka* collection *Chokoreeto kakumei/Chocolate Revolution.* Murakami Haruki publishes a collection of accounts of the Aum Shinrikyô attacks as *Andaaguraundo/Underground: The Tokyo Gas Attack and the Japanese Psyche.*

1999 Ôe Kenzaburô publishes a novel based on Aum attacks, *Chûgaeri/Somersault.* Poet Maruya Saiichi publishes *Shin shinhyakunin isshu/The Second New Collection of One Hundred Poems by One Hundred Poets.*

2000 Korean writer Hyeon Wol (Gen Getsu) wins the Akutagawa Prize for *Kage no sumika/Where the Shadows Reside.* Murakami Haruki publishes *Kami no kodomotachi wa mina odoru/After the Quake.* Murakami Ryû publishes the novel *Kibô no kuni no ekusodasu/Exodus from a Country of Hope.*

2001 The Women's Literature Prize is renamed the Fujin Kōron Literary Prize. Tsushima Yûko publishes the novel *Warai-ôkami/The Laughing Wolf.*

2002 Higuchi Ichiyô's portrait appears on the new ¥5,000 bank note. Censor-confiscated Occupation-period works by Ibuse Masuji and other postwar writers are identified in an American library. Works by contemporary women writers, such as Yamada Eimi, begin to replace male Meiji authors, such as Mori Ôgai, in secondary textbooks. Author Yu Miri indicted for libel in an I-Novel. Kôno Taeko awarded the Kawabata Prize for *Han-shoyûsha/Half Owner.*

2003 Mizumura Minae awarded the Yomiuri Prize for *Honkaku shôsetsu/A Real Novel.* Voice recording made by Kikuchi Kan in 1939 is discovered. UNESCO proclaims the Bunraku Puppet Theater as one of its Masterpieces of the Oral and Intangible Heritage of Humanity.

2004 Akutagawa Prize winners 19-year-old Wataya Risa's *Keritai senaka/Kick Me* and 20-year-old Kanehara Hitomi's *Hebi ni piasu/ Snakes and Earrings* are the youngest recipients to ever win the prize. A 1921 documentary film showing Mori Ōgai is discovered.

2005 Literary journal *Waseda Bungaku*, established in 1891, changes format from commercial to "free paper." Kôdansha established the Ôe Kenzaburô Prize. The Yahoo Japan Prize for literature is also established, with selection made by online voting. Murakami Ryū wins the Noma Prize for Literature for his novel *Hantō o deyo/Leave the Peninsula.*

2006 Murakami Haruki wins Frank O'Connor International Short Story Award for his collection *Buraindo wirô, suriipingu wuuman/ Blind Willow, Sleeping Woman.* Unpublished manuscript by Endō Shūsaku is discovered in a former editor's library.

2007 Historic first performance of *kabuki* at the Paris Opera House. The 23-year-old author Aoyama Nanae is awarded the Akutagawa Prize for *Hitoribiyori/On My Own.* Five of the 10 bestsellers of the year are cell-phone novels.

2008 A large number of previously unpublished *tanka* composed by Terayama Shûji are discovered and published. Growing economic distress in Japan leads to proletarian novelist Koyanashi Takiji's 1929 novel *Kanikôsen/The Factory Ship* becoming a bestseller, appearing as text and in graphic novel format.

Introduction

What, one might ask, is distinctively Japanese about Japanese literature? Several key features distinguish Japanese literary sensibilities within the context of world literature. First, one cannot overstate the importance of lyric in the Japanese literary tradition. Even as drama and mimesis played a key role in the development of Western literary arts, lyric is at the center of Japanese literary origins. Prior to the arrival of a writing system, Japanese literature consisted of an oral tradition that placed great emphasis on poetry. When the Chinese writing system came to Japan in the fifth through seventh centuries, Japanese soon used the sounds of Chinese characters to transcribe whole collections of poetry from the preliterate age, such as those found in the eighth-century *Man'yôshû* (Ten Thousand Leaves). During the Heian period (794–1186), Chinese was used as the language of the court and for composing formal literature in Chinese, but the adaptation and stylization of Chinese characters (*kanji*) to represent the syllabic phonemes of Japanese led to a new alphabet, called *kana*, that was employed to write poetry, diaries, narratives, and songs in Japanese.

Over time both *kana* and *kanji* came to be used together, allowing writers to imbue their writing with layers of depth that worked because Japanese contains many homophones that offer the possibility of multiple interpretations. For example, one common pun that has been employed in Japanese for centuries is the term *matsu*, which includes the meanings "wait," "pine (tree)," "final," "grind," and "depend upon," among others. The particular meaning of each use of the word *matsu* is clear when writers use the respective *kanji*. However, when a writer employs the phrase *matsu* using only *kana* (which have been stripped of their specific meaning through stylization), any or all of the meanings may be implied. This gives all forms of Japanese literature richness and depth, even as it adds to the difficulty of translating into foreign languages. Hence, playfulness and lyric richness is a major characteristic of Japanese literature, both classical and modern.

Another characteristic of Japanese literature is a heightened aesthetic sensibility. Throughout the centuries poetry contests and other forms of literary competition created different schools of judgment and volumes of treatises devoted to determining what defined the essence of beauty in literary art. Numerous factions of critical theory arose, beginning in the Heian period, devoted to classifying and prescribing essential aspects of aesthetic sensibility. A prevailing concern for beauty imbues Japanese literature with both elegance and highly self-conscious aesthetic regard.

That aesthetic regard is often evoked by descriptions of nature, and Japanese literature is rich with allusions to nature and man's relationship to it. To an almost Romantic degree, nature has been employed to reflect the narrator's or poet's internal state. Many natural phenomena, such as the blossoming of cherry trees or the death of vegetation in autumn, become metaphors for life, love, death, and parting. Nature is never very far from the surface in Japanese literature; in even the most urban of stories or plays, the characters make frequent allusions to the changing of the seasons or use other nature metaphors.

Finally, the ongoing themes of Japanese literature reflect the physical and social conditions of Japan. Located in an earthquake and typhoon zone, Japan has always been a place where things could come quickly to an end with little or no warning. This physical insecurity has led to a particular emphasis on the Buddhist notion of *mujô* (impermanence). Life's evanescence, manifest in nature, can also be seen in the fleeting pleasures of the *ukiyo* (floating world), the setting for many urbane narratives and dramas. Socially, Japanese hierarchies based on occupation, gender, rank, and status determine one's course of life and even the very words one may use in communicating, and this social and linguistic stratification is mirrored in the variety of literary genres tailored to the higher and lower classes. A finely balanced social structure is not without its share of tension, and in Japanese literature the class and gender tensions manifest themselves in great contrasts: opposite the reflective, contemplative mode of lyric poetry, one finds the violence of samurai tales; in contrast to verse that describes love and yearning, one finds puppet plays filled with tragic double suicides. These and other characteristics of Japanese literature not only distinguish it from other literatures but also make it attractive to audiences both within Japan and around the world.

JAPAN'S LITERARY HERITAGE

The literary heritage of Japan runs long and deep. During the Heian period (794–1185), the cultural arts flourished in present-day Kyoto, yielding a rich collection of literary works, including the *Tale of Genji* (ca. 1008), seen by some as the world's first novel of psychological depth. Civil war shattered the peace of the Heian period and the subsequent unrest lasted for centuries, throughout which stories describing the military valor of both the noble and the nameless made their way from oral tale into the literary canon. Ghost stories were also a popular genre during this time of warring clans, reflecting the decay of order and the fears that reigned among the populace. Buddhism, which brought solace to many, also created the archetype of the wandering poet-monk that added a rich lyric dimension to Japanese literature. Portuguese missionaries landing in Japan in the 16th century opened up new worlds with both Christianity and technology that, in turn, led to the consolidation of power in the hands of one reigning clan.

As order was restored to Japan with the founding of the Tokugawa shogunate (1603), the subsequent peace and urban development allowed a new kind of cultural flowering, one that was intensified by the expulsion of Christians from Japan in the early 17th century. With Japan adopting a policy of isolation from the West and the Tokugawa family shifting the capital from Kyoto to Edo (present-day Tokyo), the literary focus shifted as well to the urban space. A rising merchant class, eager to enjoy the privileges of nobility, used their growing wealth to refine themselves culturally, in the process subsidizing artists, playwrights, storytellers, and writers who created a constant flow of new books, plays, prints, and stories about and for the city dwellers. Theaters and *yose* variety halls catered to a booming population, lending libraries and bookstores distributed the latest serialized illustrated novels, and schools of poetry flourished around the country. Chinese novels, imported through Nagasaki, were published as wildly popular Japanese adaptations. The government, from time to time, sought to rein in the excesses of the age, forbidding, for example, the depiction of contemporary events in the theater or in print. Writers and playwrights quickly circumvented the restrictions by resetting their stories in earlier times and changing the names of the characters. Occasionally an author's flouting the law led to his being manacled or fined, but overall the Tokugawa period was a time of great literary flourishing.

MODERN JAPANESE LITERATURE

In the middle of the 19th century, as the Tokugawa regime grew more and more complacent and ineffective, the Western powers, with sights set on Asian empire, posed a serious threat to Japan. The whisper of information about the West entering Japan through the Dutch trading post in Nagasaki spoke volumes about the superiority of Western technology and military strength and described in alarming detail the fate of Japan's Asian neighbors. The looming visage of colonization threatened Japan, precipitating a series of internal struggles that resulted in Japan opening its ports to Western trade in the 1850s and a complete change of government in the 1860s. This political development led, in turn, to widespread social and cultural changes over the following decades that had a profound impact on the literature of Japan, bringing about a sea change in how literature was perceived, created, and consumed. Modern Japan was born.

The restoration of the Meiji sovereign to political rule in 1868 signaled Japan's entrance into the modern, global world. Although much of the change was gradual, particularly in cultural matters, within one decade the opening of Japan to trade with the West had changed a trickle of information and cultural influence into a torrent. Western merchants settled in trading ports in Japan, bringing with them not only technological artifacts, such as telegraphs and trains, but also their families, books, and music. They established newspapers, which helped spawn Japan's own newspaper industry. Their Victorian novels and poems were adapted and translated into Japanese versions. Their amateur productions of Shakespeare were soon copied on the Japanese stage. And over time Japanese traveled to the West, bringing back language skills and firsthand knowledge of current Western artistic and literary tastes.

Often the influence of the West on Japanese literature is seen as a one-way flow, but the West developed an equally passionate interest in Japan as well. As Japanese craftsmen and performers made their way to the grand expositions of late 19th-century Paris, London, and

Chicago, they fueled a movement called *japonisme*, which brought elements of Japanese culture to art, music, literature, fashion, and dance. Westerners, in turn, traveled to Japan seeking new perspectives, themes, and insights. Some, such as Frank Lloyd Wright, returned home and exercised a great influence on modernist art. Others, such as Lafcadio Hearn, remained in Japan and helped nurture Japanese appreciation for traditional culture.

As Japan modernized, its literature modernized as well, and not solely by imitating Western models. Even as some avant-garde writers and playwrights sought inspiration in the works of Western realism and modernism, other writers, such as Higuchi Ichiyô, found their muse in the writings of Heian- and Tokugawa-period authors. These works, written in the style and language of classical Japanese, were elegant but largely inaccessible to the masses, whose colloquial speech had deviated from the written form of Japanese centuries before. One of the central challenges, then, for a modernizing Japanese literature specifically, and culture in general, was how to unify the written and spoken languages. This so-called *genbun itchi* (unification of speech and writing) debate reached an impasse when intellectuals who were exploring the issue realized that the divide paralleled that of class and education and saw language reform as a huge challenge.

This challenge was met, however, and surmounted when young writers turned to the storytelling stage for a style of literary language that was both accessible and flexible enough to be used for casual and formal purposes. The Japanese storytelling tradition had a rich repertoire of memorized tales that were performed nightly in theaters across Japan, improvised to suit their audiences by skilled raconteurs who had undergone years of apprenticeship and training. The style of language was deferential at times, as befits a performer before an audience, but it also imitated a host of stock characters as it sought linguistic realism within the performance of the stories. In 1884, *Kaidan Botandôrô* (The Ghost Tale of the Peony Lantern) became the first of these stories to be transcribed, using Japanese shorthand (another Meiji period innovation), and subsequently published as a very successful serialized novel. Writers then had a pattern of written language, both formal and informal, that allowed them to create literature that mirrored contemporary speech and could be read by the masses. The result was a host of new novels to usher in the 20th century. Among these experimental products of the new Japanese literature were both works of mass appeal, echoing those from the Tokugawa period boom, as well as works of philosophical and aesthetic depth, reflecting high-minded intellectual tradition and imported Western writing.

THE 20TH CENTURY

As the 20th century began Japan was in between two important wars. In 1894–95, Japan fought and defeated China over control of Korea and other territories, and in 1904–5 Japan fought and defeated Russia over control of Manchuria. Both victories earned Japan the respect, if not the fear, of Western powers and set in motion aggressive industrial and military development that had a profound effect on society and culture for the first half of the century. In the literary realm, Japanese writers sought to meet or better their Western peers as well. In rapid succession, Japanese writers and playwrights experimented with Realism, Naturalism, Symbolism, and free verse poetry. Women writers formed the Seitô (Bluestockings) Society, from which emerged a nascent feminist movement. Humanist writers joined together into the Shirakaba (White Birch) Society, and others focused on perception or consciousness. The more politically minded authors took inspiration from Russian authors and the Bolshevik Revolution, and Marxism found an outlet among proletarian writers.

During the 1920s Japan's rising militarism led to new government clashes with writers who spoke out against strong-arm policies and censorship. When Japan entered into conflicts with China in the 1930s, an effectual curtain eventually fell on the literary stage as writers were either imprisoned or coerced into cooperating with the war effort. The growing anti-Western sentiment fostered by the military was echoed in a strongly nationalist literary output marking a dark period for Japanese literature.

When the war ended, Japan entered a new era of literary productivity. Within a decade, four distinct "generations" of writers were publishing a variety of novels, short stories, poetry, and drama dealing with the war and its aftermath. The Allied Occupation, like the merchant trading posts of the Meiji Era, introduced new, primarily American, cultural influences to Japan, and soon the imports and impacts reverberated into novels, plays, and the cinema. Authors wrote of the challenges of living in postwar poverty, of the tensions of occupation, and of the effects of the atomic bomb. In the 1950s, Japan's film industry, led by such directors as Kurosawa Akira, produced international award-winning films, many of them based on literary works. The popularity of these films abroad, combined with a growing cadre of Japanese-speaking Westerners, led to the first wave of English translations of Japanese literature and the establishment of Japanese studies programs at universities in the English-speaking world.

In the 1960s some writers saw Japan as a phoenix rising from the ashes of defeat, best symbolized by the successful hosting of the Tokyo Olympics in 1964. Others focused on the unrest, where Japanese college students staged protests and campus sit-ins over the renewal of the U.S.-Japan Security Treaty (*Anpo*). Marxism was the dominant ideology of literary critics, and some writers, such as Abe Kôbô, incorporated existentialist philosophy into their works. A growing number of atomic bomb victims documented their stories in narrative, poetry, and drama, and an underground theater movement thrived. Owing in part to an increasing number of English-language translations of Japanese literature, the author Kawabata Yasunari became the first Japanese to win a Nobel Prize for Literature, signaling the arrival of Japanese literature on the global stage.

The 1970s opened with nationalist author Mishima Yukio staging a failed coup and committing ritual suicide inside a Japan Self Defense Forces office. The move shocked writers and critics alike and underscored a penchant for suicide among Japanese writers. The country continued to grow economically, and the social and environmental consequences of rapid and unpredictable growth found their way into literature as well. The oil shortages of 1973 sent tremors throughout society, undermining a growing sense of economic security. Underclass (*burakumin*) writer Nakagami Kenji wrote of the prejudice suffered by his fellow untouchables.

By the 1980s, as Japan's economy and influence burgeoned, many writers were questioning the growing Japanese sense of global superiority. A renewed interest in things Japanese led to the growth of Japanese studies programs in America, Europe, and Australia. When the real estate bubble burst at the end of the decade, writers articulated strong disenchantment with the Meiji-born dream of a Japan dominating the world stage. Postmodernism emerged in Japan as well, and such writers as Murakami Ryû and Yamada Eimi wrote of the fallout of the Occupation and a prolonged U.S. military presence in Japan. The decade ended with the death of the Shôwa emperor and a reevaluation of his role in World War II. During the final decade of the 20th century, author Ôe Kenzaburô won the 1995 Nobel Prize, and Murakami Haruki's apathetic protagonist from his magical realist novels found widespread appeal among readers in Japan and, as the century turned, among a global audience.

THE PRESENT

In recent years, Japanese literature and theater have continued to undergo transformation and change. The impact of postmodernism, with its blurring of generic boundaries, is obvious in some developments, such as the emergence of hypertext novels. Some of the changes have technological roots, such as the cell-phone novels that have taken hold among younger readers. Graphic novels (*manga*) also grow more and more popular, and many works of modern literature, such as Kobayashi Takiji's 1929 proletarian novel *The Factory Ship*, have been redone in comic book form. Foreign authors writing in Japanese constitute a growing presence on the literary scene, and Japanese literature finds a wider distribution abroad as more and more works are translated into English and other languages. Many literary critics today, as in years past, fear they are witnessing the final days of Japanese literature. Others find new hope for the future in the playful fusion of forms and genres. Historically, modern Japanese literature has weathered storms and sustained challenges before. At the dawn of the Meiji period there was also a perception of literary decline that found, in the chaotic transformations of the time, an infusion of strength and innovation. That heritage should guarantee a vibrant, if unpredictable, future for modern Japanese literature.

The Dictionary

– A –

ABE AKIRA (1934–1989). Abe Akira was a novelist, essayist, and literary critic from Hiroshima. He grew up in Kanagawa Prefecture and attended Tokyo University. He became involved in student theater productions while there, and in 1959 began work as a radio and television broadcast director, writing in his spare time. He won the ***Bungakkai*** Newcomer Prize for *Kodomobeya* (*Children's Room*, 1962) and with his later work *Shirei no kyûka* (*The Commander's Holiday*, 1970) garnered critical attention. He continued writing throughout the 1970s, penning the much-acclaimed short story "*Momo*" (*Peaches*, 1972). Many of his works were turned into plays, and his novels were centered on life experiences with his military-veteran father and mentally retarded brother and son. He also wrote **literary criticism**. He died of acute heart failure.

ABE KÔBÔ (1924–1993). Abe Kôbô was a writer, playwright, and inventor born in Tokyo and raised in Manchuria. His father was a physician, and although Abe graduated from Tokyo University with a medical degree, he never practiced medicine. He began publishing **poetry**, followed by his first novel, the story of an opium addict, *Owarishi michi no shirube ni* (The Road Sign at the End of the Street, 1948), that established his reputation. He worked as an avant-garde novelist and playwright, but it was not until he published ***Suna no onna*** (1962; tr. *The Woman in the Dunes*, 1964) that he won widespread international acclaim. The novel was turned into an award-winning film. In 1973, he founded an acting studio in Tokyo and continued to write and publish novels, including *Tanin no kao* (1959; tr. *The Face of Another,* 1966), *Moetsukita chizu* (1967; tr. *The Ruined Map*,

1969), and *Hakobune sakura maru* (1984; tr. *The Ark Sakura*, 1988). Abe's surreal and often-nightmarish explorations of the individual in contemporary society earned him comparisons to Franz Kafka, and his influence extends well beyond Japan. *See also* MODERN THEATER; SCIENCE FICTION; UTOPIAN LITERATURE.

ABE TOMOJI (1903–1973). Abe Tomoji was a novelist, translator, and scholar from Okayama Prefecture. He attended Tokyo University where he studied ***tanka***, English literature, Tolstoy and Anton Chekhov, and published his first novel, *Kasei* (Metamorphosis) in a campus magazine. Upon graduation, he taught English literature at Meiji and Tôhoku universities. He subsequently published a novel titled *Fuyu no yado* (A Place to Winter, 1936) and many Japanese **translations** of English literature, including *Moby-Dick*, *Treasure Island*, *The Adventures of Sherlock Holmes*, and *Wuthering Heights*.

ADAPTATION. Adaptation (*hon'an*) is a term that was used throughout the **Tokugawa** period to refer to translated literary works, in contrast to *hon'yaku*, which was reserved for medical and scientific texts. Though adaptations often parallel the original works in many ways, they do not correspond to the work but alter such elements as the setting, characterization, or plot. Historically adaptations have been highly regarded in Asia, seen more as homage than plagiarism. During the early **Meiji** period, adaptation was the dominant mode of literary transmission from the West into Japan, with works as diverse as *Aesop's Fables*, Jean-Jacques Rousseau's *Social Contract* and *1001 Arabian Nights*, and the science fiction of Jules Verne making their first Japanese appearance as adaptations rather than literal **translations**. By the early 20th century, correspondent translation had eclipsed adaptation as the dominant mode of literary transmission in Japan. *See also* ADAPTIVE TRANSLATIONS; *BUNGEI EIGA*; FREE VERSE; KAWATAKE MOKUAMI; KAWATAKE SHINSHICHI III; *MANGA*; *RAKUGO*.

ADAPTIVE TRANSLATIONS. During the **Tokugawa** period, works of foreign literature, especially popular Chinese novels, were in great demand as both **translations** and **adaptations**. During the **Meiji** period, the term *hon'anmono*, or adaptive translation, was applied to works of imported literature that were loosely translated and given Japanese characteristics. Between 1872 and 1900, dozens of Western novels and stories, such as *Gulliver's Travels*, *Robinson Crusoe*, and Edgar Allan Poe's *The Black Cat*, appeared as Japanese adaptations. These adaptations, often serialized in newspapers and magazines, were not translations in the strictest sense, often being reset in Japan with the main characters given Japanese names and identities. Although later disparaged for their lack of correspondence or originality, these adaptive translations were a key means of introducing the canon of Western literature into Japan. *See also RAKUGO*; SAN'YÛTEI ENCHÔ.

AESTHETICISM. *Yuibi shugi* or *tanbi shugi* (aestheticism) is a term used to describe the narrow aesthetic focus of late 19th-century Western **Romanticism** (and later **modernism**) that found its way to Japan. Embodied in the phrase "art for art's sake," aestheticism focused on sensual pleasure over moral or sentimental ideas. Meiji writer Takayama Chogyû, who edited influential journals, such as *Teikoku Bungaku* (Imperial Literature) and *Taiyô* (The Sun), blended aesthetics with Romantic individualism and philosophical self-realization. **Mori Ôgai** reflects this trend in both the journal ***Shigarami Zôshi*** (*The Wier*) and his novel ***Maihime*** (1890; tr. *The Dancing Girl*, 1948). Aestheticism also plays into the works of **Mishima Yukio** and **Tanizaki Jun'ichirô**. *See also SHUGI.*

AGAWA HIROYUKI (1920–). Agawa Hiroyuki is a writer of historical fiction and **I-Novels** and a **literary critic**. Agawa was born in Hiroshima, became interested in the works of **Shiga Naoya** during high school, and began writing novels after serving in the Japanese navy following his graduation from Tokyo University. His novel *Haru no shiro* (1952; tr. Citadel in Spring, 1990) won the **Yomiuri Prize**, and he has subsequently won the **Noma Prize** (1994), the **Order of Cultural Merit** (1999), and the **Kikuchi Kan Prize** (2007). His historical novels often deal with World War II. *See also* ATOMIC BOMB LITERATURE.

AIDA MITSUO (1924–1991). Aida Mitsuo was a poet-calligrapher who published a number of works exploring the preciousness of life. A practicing Zen **Buddhist**, Aida published *Ningen damono* (Because I'm Human, 1984), *Okagesan* (Our Debt to Others, 1987), and *Inochi ippai* (Live a Full Life, 1991), each of which reveals his personal, open philosophy of life and his mastery of brush and ink calligraphy. Some of his **poetry** has been translated into English. He died of a brain hemorrhage.

AIKOKUSHIN. *See* NATIONALISM.

AINU LITERATURE. The term Ainu refers to an indigenous people who once occupied the northern islands of Hokkaido, Sakhalin, and the Kurils and who are now largely assimilated into the Japanese population, although there are still remnants in parts of Hokkaido. Their language, which uses the word *ainu* for "people," is unrelated to Japanese or Korean and had no written script, but contains a rich oral tradition that uses repetition and alliteration to create a sense of flow and harmonic intonation in dialogue. The primary oral narrative form is the *yukar*, an epic genre that features a hero, usually a boy or human but sometimes an animal. The Ainu practiced shamanism, and their stories often contain elements of spirit possession. Although a government policy of forced assimilation from the **Meiji** era on did much to eliminate Ainu culture, Japanese and Western ethnographers collected and published a number of *yukar* and other stories during the early 20th century. In recent years, the Japanese government has reversed its policy and made funds available for the preservation of Ainu language and culture, and a series of English translations of the narratives have recently begun appearing. A contemporary Ainu novelist is Uenishi Haruji (1925–).

AKAI TORI. *Akai Tori* (Red Bird) was a children's magazine established by Suzuki Miekichi (1882–1936) in 1918. It ran continuously for 198 issues (aside from a hiatus between 1929 and 1931). Seeking to foster the purity of children, Suzuki established the magazine in reaction to the government's hard-line approach to childhood. The magazine attracted the support of and contributions by a number of literary luminaries, such as **Akutagawa Ryûnosuke**, **Arishima Takeo**, **Izumi Kyôka**, **Kitahara Hakushû**, **Tokuda Shûsei**, and other acclaimed writers, poets, and artists. Its long-lived success started the so-called Akai Tori movement in **children's literature** as well as a nursery rhyme boom in the 1920s. In 1984, the Japan Nursery Rhyme Association declared July 1 (the date of publication of the first issue of *Akai Tori*) Nursery Rhyme Day.

AKIYAMA SHUN (1930–). Akiyama Shun is a **literary critic** from Tokyo who graduated from Waseda University in French literature. He worked for a newspaper and then as a university professor. In 1967, he published *Naibu no ningen* (The Inner Man, 1967), and in 1996 his critical study of Oda Nobunaga was a bestseller and won the **Yomiuri Prize.** An **I-Novel** advocate, Akiyama has served on the selection committee of many notable **literary awards.**

AKUTAGAWA RYÛNOSUKE (1892–1927). Akutagawa Ryûnosuke was born in Tokyo, the son of a milkman. His mother went insane shortly after his birth, so he was adopted and raised by his maternal uncle. He began writing while at Tokyo University studying English literature, where he published his first short story, "***Rashômon***" (1915; tr. *Rashômon*, 1952), in a literary magazine. This story and his "*Yabu no naka*" (1921; tr. *In a Grove*, 1952) were combined in Kurosawa Akira's (1910–1998) award-winning film *Rashômon* (1950). He married Tsukamoto Fumi in 1918 and had three children. Opposing **naturalism**, Akutagawa borrowed many themes from old tales, giving them a complex modern interpretation. A stressful 1921 trip to China led to deteriorating physical and mental health, and he subsequently began suffering visual hallucinations and anxiety over his psychological state. He finally committed **suicide** at the age of 35. **Kikuchi Kan** established the prestigious **Akutagawa Ryûnosuke Prize** in his honor (1935). *See also AKAI TORI*; CHILDREN'S LITERATURE; DAZAI OSAMU; *KAKURE KIRISHITAN*; KIKUCHI KAN; KUME MASAO; *MIKAN*; MURÔ SAISEI; PSYCHOLOGICAL LITERATURE; SAITÔ MOKICHI; UNO KÔJI; UTOPIAN LITERATURE; YAMAMOTO YÛZÔ.

AKUTAGAWA RYÛNOSUKE PRIZE. The Akutagawa Ryûnosuke Prize (*Akutagawa Ryûnosuke shô*) is Japan's most prestigious **literary award.** Established by **Kikuchi Kan** in 1935 in memory of writer **Akutagawa Ryûnosuke**, it is sponsored by the **Association**

for the Promotion of Japanese Literature and is awarded semiannually to the best story of a purely literary nature published in a newspaper or magazine by a new or rising author. The judges include contemporary writers, literary critics, and former winners of the prize. Winners receive a pocket watch, cash sum of one million yen, and considerable media attention and often go on to fill the ranks of the ***bundan*** (writer's guilds). Notable prize recipients include **Ishikawa Jun**, who received it for *Fugen* (1936, tr. *The Bodhisattva, or, Samantabhadra*, 1990) and **Inoue Yasushi** for *Tôgyû* (The Bullfight, 1949). The list of prizewinners forms a veritable "who's who" among modern writers.

ANGURA ENGEKI. *See* MODERN THEATER.

ANTINATURALISM. Antinaturalism (*hanshizen shugi*) developed in opposition to the **naturalism** of **Shimazaki Tôson** and **Tayama Katai**. Seen as a progression of the **Meiji** period *yoyûha* (leisure school) founded by **Masaoka Shiki**, **Mori Ôgai**, and **Natsume Sôseki**, antinaturalism played a subsequent role in the *Subaru* (Pleiades) and *Mita Bungaku* (Mita Literature) movements and the writings of **Tanizaki Jun'ichirô**. *See also SHUGI.*

AN'YA KÔRO. Originally published in installments in the **literary journal** *Kaizô*, *An'ya kôro* (1921–37; tr. *A Dark Night's Passing*, 1976) is author **Shiga Naoya**'s only full-length novel, upon which he toiled for a quarter century. Although Shiga's style is linked with the **I-Novel** genre, *An'ya kôro* is only a partial reflection of his life and contains many fictional elements. The story deals with the inner struggles of Kensaku, a man who learns that his grandfather is actually his father. The subsequent alienation and torment he feels from this revelation, combined with his wife's unfaithfulness and his own illness, lead him into deep despair. Finally, in a moment of enlightenment on a mountaintop at dawn, he discovers the inner serenity that allows him to face his impending death in peace. *See also* BUDDHIST LITERATURE.

AOZORA. *Aozora* (Blue Sky) was a coterie magazine established by **Kajii Motojirô**, Nakatani Takao (1901–95), and Tonomura Shigeru

(1902–61) in 1925. Kajii's first novel, *Remon* (The Lemon, 1925), graced the first issue, but the magazine was short-lived, ceasing publication in 1927. Contributors included Yodono Ryûzô (1904–67) and Takeda Rintarô (1904–46). *See also* LITERARY JOURNALS.

AOZORA BUNKO. The Aozora Bunko (Open Air Library) is a digital library founded in 1997 by Tomita Michio (1952–) with the goal of making Japanese and **translated** English literature available in an electronic format free of charge. The library contains over 7,000 titles and includes early modern literature by such authors as **Mori Ôgai** and **Akutagawa Ryûnosuke** as well as more modern works by **Nakajima Atsushi** and **Hayashi Fumiko**, among others. Recently Aozora Bunko has run into a potential dilemma because most of the Western world holds that copyright is in effect until 70 years after an author's death. Most of the content in the Aozora Bunko, though in harmony with current Japanese copyright law, would violate this time constraint should Japan's copyright law be brought into line with Western law. Hence, a petition was circulated in 2007 to lobby for reform in Japanese copyright law. As of December 2008, no clear-cut decision had been made. *See also* DIET LIBRARY; MUSEUM OF MODERN JAPANESE LITERATURE; NATIONAL INSTITUTE OF JAPANESE LITERATURE.

ARAI MOTOKO (1960–). Arai Motoko is a Japanese **science fiction** and fantasy writer from Nerima, Tokyo. She graduated from Rikkyô University in 1983. Her first novel received an award in 1977 when she was still in high school. Her novels include *Gureen rekuiemu* (1980; tr. *Green Requiem*, 1984) and *Hoshi e yuku fune* (1980; tr. *Ship to the Stars*, 1984). She received the Seiun Award in 1981–82 for short fiction, and the Japan Science Fiction Grand Prize (akin to the Nebula Award) for her novel *Chigurisu to yûfuratesu* (Tigris and Euphrates, 1996–98).

ARISHIMA TAKEO (1878–1923). Arishima Takeo was a novelist, short-story writer, and essayist born in Tokyo of wealthy samurai lineage. He became a Christian following a failed **suicide** attempt in college, but left Christianity for socialism while studying in the United States. He became acquainted with such authors as **Shiga**

Naoya and **Mushanokôji Saneatsu**, with whom he formed a group named after their **literary journal**, ***Shirakaba***. His best-known work, *Aru Onna* (1909; tr. *A Certain Woman*, 1951), deals with a woman's place in **Meiji** society. Arishima committed double suicide after being discovered by the husband of a lover he took after his wife's death. *See also AKAI TORI*; SATOMI TON.

ARIYOSHI SAWAKO (1931–1984). Ariyoshi Sawako was a best-selling novelist, playwright, and director from Wakayama. She attended Tokyo Woman's Christian University and studied English literature, but after a long absence graduated with a two-year degree. An aspiring theater critic, she contributed to a theater journal just after graduating college. She was a candidate for the **Akutagawa Ryûnosuke Prize** in 1956 and shortly thereafter published her first major novel *Kinokawa* (1959; tr. *The River Ki*, 1980). She divorced her first husband in 1964 and then published what is widely considered her best novel, *Hanaoka Seishû no tsuma* (1966; tr. *The Wife of Hanaoka Seishû*, 1978). She followed that with another bestseller, *Kôkitsu no hito* (1972; tr. *The Twilight Years*, 1984). She died at age 53 of heart failure, in the prime of her career. *See also* FEMINISM; WOMEN IN LITERATURE.

ASAHI SHIMBUN. *See* Newspapers.

ASSOCIATION FOR THE PROMOTION OF JAPANESE LITERATURE. The Association for the Promotion of Japanese Literature (*Nihon Bungaku Shinkôkai*) is a juridical foundation that conducts selection and awarding of five major **literary awards**: the **Akutagawa Ryûnosuke Prize**, **Naoki Prize**, Ôya Nonfiction Prize, Matsumoto Seichô Prize, and **Kikuchi Kan Prize**. The association was established by **Kikuchi Kan** in 1937 and is a public service corporation under the jurisdiction of the **Ministry of Education**. Its offices are located in Tokyo.

ATÔDA TAKASHI (1935–). Atôda Takashi is a writer from Tokyo who graduated from Waseda University and worked as a librarian in the **Diet Library** while writing essays and short stories. His debut novel was *Reizoko yori ai wo komete* (Love from the Refrigerator,

1953), and he won the **Naoki Prize** for *Napporeon kyô* (1979; tr. *Napoleon Fever*, 1985).

ATOMIC BOMB LITERATURE. The shock and devastation of the nuclear bombings of Hiroshima and **Nagasaki** in August 1945 affected many Japanese, both directly and indirectly. Many postwar authors, such as **Inoue Mitsuharu** and **Ôe Kenzaburô**, used the bombings symbolically in their writings, finding in the deep pathos and tragedy a symbol for the confusion of the modern world. Other writers, such as **Ibuse Masuji**, found hope for humanity in the stubborn resilience of both the victims and nature. Authors emerged as well from among the victims themselves, who compiled anthologies of stories, **poetry**, diaries, essays, and dramas, establishing a genre of literature dubbed *hibakusha bungaku* (literature of the bombed) that has grown to many volumes of published writing. Among the notable *hibakusha* writers are novelists Ôta Yôko (1903–63) and Hayashi Kyôko (1930–) and poets Tôge Sankichi (1917–53) and Shôda Shinoe (1910–65). *See also* MILITARISM; NATIONALISM; WAR LITERATURE.

AWARE. *Aware*, or *mono no aware*, is a classical Japanese term used to describe the **Buddhist** notion of the transience of things and is often used in situations where one is moved (*aware*) upon seeing tangible things (*mono*) come to an end. *Aware* was articulated as a term of literary analysis during the Edo period, when critic Motoori Norinaga (1730–1801) noted that *aware* is the crucial emotion moving readers of *Genji monogatari* (*The Tale of Genji*, ca. 1008) and framed it as a particularly Japanese sensibility. Modern writers have often incorporated *aware* in fiction and **poetry**, both as an emotion experienced by characters as well as a structuring device; hence the paucity of "happy endings" in modern Japanese literature.

– B –

BENSHI. Commercial cinema came to Japan in the 1900s, and early on theaters employed professional narrators called *benshi* (silent film narrators), stationed on the side of the audience, to describe the action and imitate the dialogue taking place on the silent screen. Narrative mediation or performance, a commonplace in traditional Japanese theater and puppet plays, served to enhance the experience and often provided Japanese filmmakers with more latitude in edits and scene transitions. The *benshi* were often professional storytellers (*see KÔDAN; RAKUGO*) who by the 1910s found ***yose*** variety theaters, their standard source of income, in decline. Because professional storytelling involved a great deal of improvisation, they made an easy transition to the role of *benshi*. Before a film screening, they would often give background information on the film, and during the show they would even give their own opinions or break into chanted poetry during scenes with no dialogue, coordinating their roles with the live orchestra, if the theater employed one. *Benshi* were so popular (theaters employed over 6,000 *benshi* during the late 1920s) that the silent film era lasted nearly a decade longer in Japan than in other countries. Although *benshi* have been extinct from mainstream entertainment for decades, there are still several actively practicing *benshi* today, as well as a movement to revive their art in an effort to find new frontiers in film. *See also BUNGEI EIGA*.

BETSUYAKU MINORU (1937–). Betsuyaku Minoru is a playwright and children's author born in Manchuria when it was a Japanese colony. As an infant he lost his father and moved back to Japan with his mother after World War II. He attended Waseda University after high school, was introduced to theater activists there, and joined the *jiyû butai* (free theater) group. Betsuyaku dropped out of Waseda for financial reasons, however, and began life as a salaryman, writing plays in coffee shops. His hard work paid off, as he was awarded the **Kishida Kunio** Prize for Drama in 1963 for *Matchi uri no shôjo* (The Little Match Girl) and *Akai tori no iru fûkei* (A View with Red Birds). Betsuyaku's collaboration with leading actors kept him in the mainstream, and he has been working for the Japan Playwrights Association from the 1990s and since 2003 has worked for the *Pikkoro shiataa* (Piccolo Theater) in Hyôgo Prefecture. Betsuyaku is also known for establishing the Theater of the Absurd in Japan after reading Irish playwright Samuel Beckett's works. *See also* CHILDREN'S LITERATURE; MODERN THEATER.

BLACK LIZARD. *See KUROTOKAGE.*

BLACK RAIN. *See KUROI AME.*

BOTCHAN. One of the most beloved novels by author **Natsume Sôseki**, *Botchan* (1906; tr. *Botchan: Master Darling*, 1947) mirrors Sôseki's personal experiences of leaving Tokyo for the first time and working as a provincial schoolteacher. The protagonist, referred to as Botchan (young master), a deferential term of endearment, is a recent college graduate sent from Tokyo to teach mathematics at a middle school on the island of Shikoku. His interactions with the students, his conversations and battles with colleagues, and his rebellious attitude toward corrupt authorities in this often-humorous novel explore the changes Japan was undergoing following the **Meiji Restoration.**

BROKEN COMMANDMENT, THE. *See HAKAI.*

BUDDHIST LITERATURE. Although Western philosophy and style underscore many works of modern Japanese literature, Buddhism, which came to Japan in the sixth century, continues to exercise a profound influence on prose and poetry. Thematically, many important modern novels deal with Buddhist concepts, such as *mujô* (the ephemerality of things) and karma. The novels of **Minakami Tsutomu** and Itsuki Hiroyuki (1932–), for example, are replete with Buddhist settings and allusions. Likewise **Shiga Naoya**'s novel ***An'ya kôro*** (1921–37; tr. *A Dark Night's Passing*, 1976) is explicitly Buddhist in structure and theme. Contemporary writer **Setouchi Jakuchô**, who has completed a modern Japanese translation of *The Tale of Genji* (ca. 1008), is a Tendai Buddhist nun. *See also AWARE*; CHRISTIAN LITERATURE; KITAMURA TÔKOKU; KURATA HYAKUZÔ; MIYAZAWA KENJI; NIWA FUMIO; OKAMOTO KANOKO; YASUOKA SHÔTARÔ.

BUNDAN. The term *bundan* (literature group) refers to a type of unofficial literary guild that has connected many of Japan's writers for over a century. The term was first coined in 1889 by **Tsubouchi Shôyô** to describe the cohesion of the **Ken'yûsha** as it successfully lobbied for and controlled literary publication in the *Yomiuri* newspaper. As that group dissolved, **naturalists** and other writers took up the cause, and *bundan* played an important role in representing writers' rights and pressuring publishers to pay decent fees for stories. In the 1920s, **Kikuchi Kan** served as the de facto head of *bundan* and, in his capacity as a publisher, brought greater security to writers and helped further solidify the structure of *bundan* by establishing **literary awards** that brought new respect to the writing profession.

The *bundan* are self-regulating entities that are also highly exclusive, for example, eschewing scholars who also write novels. From the beginning, there were writers (such as **Natsume Sôseki** and **Mori Ôgai**) who did not join *bundan*, and even today **Murakami Haruki** remains aloof. Nevertheless, while *bundan* have changed and nearly expired several times, over the years their influence and power continue to shape the world of Japanese literature in very direct ways. *See also* AKUTAGAWA RYÛNOSUKE PRIZE; JAPAN P.E.N. CLUB; NAKA KANSUKE; PUBLISHING HOUSES.

BUNGAKKAI. *Bungakkai* (Literary World) describes two separate **literary journals**, one from the **Meiji** period and the other in current publication. **Shimazaki Tôson** and **Kitamura Tôkoku** founded the first *Bungakkai* in 1893, but it ceased publication five years later. The journal was one of the main venues for **Romantic** literature during the Meiji period. In 1933, **Kobayashi Hideo** and Hayashi Fusao (1903–75) reestablished *Bungakkai* as a platform for their advocacy of "art for art's sake." It was banned, however, in 1938 for publishing **Ishikawa Jun**'s antiwar story "*Marusu no uta*" (The Song of Mars). Editor-in-chief Kawakami Tetsutarô was fined, but **Kikuchi Kan** paid in his stead and the magazine then came to be under the jurisdiction of the **Bungei Shunjû** Publishing Company, which has subsequently continued to publish the journal. A monthly, it is currently one of the big five literary journals and sponsors the *Bungakkai Shinjinshô* (Bungakkai Newcomer Award). *See also* KOBAYASHI HIDEO; KURAHASHI YUMIKO; LITERARY AWARDS; NAKAMURA MITSUO; ODA SAKUNOSUKE PRIZE.

BUNGAKU SHÔ. *See* LITERARY AWARDS.

BUNGEI EIGA. The term *bungei eiga* (literary films) denotes a genre that includes both strict and liberal film **adaptations** of literary works. Adaptation has long been popular in Japanese culture, and soon after the advent of the cinema in Japan **film** studios began to adapt popular foreign films for Japanese audiences. Literary works soon followed, and these literary films were particularly popular during the 1930s since, as adaptations of established, well-known works, they could avoid **censorship** because they need not claim the attitudes of the original author. Early *bungei eiga* include **Kawabata Yasunari**'s ***Izu no odoriko*** (1926; tr. *The Izu Dancer*, 1964), which appeared as a silent film in 1933, and **Tanizaki Jun'ichirô**'s *Shunkinshô* (1932; tr. *A Portrait of Shunkin*, 1963) that appeared as a "talkie" in 1935. During the 1950s, as Japanese cinema matured and began to capture world notice, many of the most renowned films, such as Kurosawa Akira's (1910–98) *Rashômon*, Mizoguchi Kenji's (1898–1956) *Sanshô dayû* (*Sansho the Bailiff*), and Ichikawa Kon's (1915–2008) *Nobi* (*Fires on the Plains*), were adaptations of stories by modern Japanese writers. In the 1960s, director Hiroshi Teshigahara made award-winning films from **Abe Kôbô**'s novels ***Suna no onna*** (1962; tr. *Woman in the Dunes,* 1964) and *Tanin no kao* (1959; tr. *The Face of Another*, 1966). Literary films also include adaptations of non-Japanese literary works; several films by Kurosawa, for example, are adaptations of Shakespeare plays. *See also BENSHI.*

BUNGEI SHUNJÛ. *Bungei shunjû* (Literary Chronicle) is a monthly **literary journal** established by **Kikuchi Kan** in 1923 and published by the Bungei Shunjû **publishing house**. The magazine is representative of current style, tradition, and characteristics of Japan and covers topics in politics, economics, management, sports, education, history, military affairs, the Imperial household, and medicine. Each issue has about 30 pieces, ranging from opinion articles to scholarly theses. The magazine is traditionally antileftist and rarely, if ever, publishes material from the Japan Communist, Social Democratic, or other left-wing parties. *Bungei shunjû* announces the winners of various **literary awards** each year, including the **Akutagawa Ryûnosuke Prize** (March and September issues), Matsumoto Seichô Prize (July), and the **Kikuchi Kan Prize** (December). *See also BUNGAKKAI*; NAOKI PRIZE; NAOKI SANJÛGO; YAMAMOTO SHÛGORÔ; YOKOMITSU RIICHI.

BUNGEI ZASSHI. *See* LITERARY JOURNALS.

BURAKUMIN* LITERATURE.** From ancient times, Japanese society has been stratified into many layers, and among the lowest ranks has existed an "untouchable" class called the *eta*. Historically they were families living in outlying communities (*buraku*) composed of those working in "polluted" trades that put them in contact with death or ritual impurity (such as executioners, undertakers, or leather workers). Although they were legally liberated in 1871 and given the designation "new commoner" (*shin-heimin*), discrimination continues to this day in certain areas of Japan. The oppression experienced by *burakumin* in Japan was the subject of a **Meiji** novel, **Shimazaki Tôson**'s ***Hakai (1906; tr. *The Broken Commandment*, 1956). Despite educational disadvantages that *burakumin* have suffered historically, writers, such as **Nakagami Kenji** and Sumii Sue (1902–67), have recently emerged from among the *burakumin* to tell their stories.

– C –

CELL-PHONE NOVELS. Cell-phone novels (*keitai shôsetsu*) represent an emerging genre of literature in modern Japan. Often written by nonprofessional authors using only first names, cell-phone novels are crafted in a diary style with short sentence structure, simple melodramatic story lines, and mild characterization. Cell-phone novels are often first distributed via cell-phone text messaging and then are published as hard copy texts. The first cell-phone novel appeared in 2003, written by a young online writer using the name Yoshi. *Deep Love*, the story of a teenage prostitute in Tokyo, became so popular online that it was soon published as a book, with 2.6 million copies sold in Japan, then spun off into a television series, a ***manga***, and a movie. Subsequent cell-phone novels incorporate elements of sex, violence, and young tragic love. Websites featuring low-cost downloads have expanded authorship, although payouts to authors come only after the novels become published works. In 2007, five of 10 Japanese bestsellers originated as cell-phone novels.

CENSORSHIP. Censorship in modern Japan has served as both a political expedient wielded by government as well as a self-regulating tool used by the **publishing houses**. In 1869, the first publishing regulations were enacted, followed in 1875 by regulations for newspapers. Under the **Meiji** Constitution, these regulations were modified and intensified, focusing not only on treasonable materials but also on anything deemed "injurious to public morals." Publishers learned quickly what would and would not pass the government censors and often used self-censorship to avoid the scandal of official censure.

The inevitable clash between writers and censorship laws came early and often through the end of World War II, in part because of the kind of freedoms of expression the new narrative styles allowed and encouraged. With the rise of Communism and **proletarian literature** in the 1920s, the police were particularly severe in enforcing the Peace Preservation Act of 1925, which outlawed groups that sought to alter the system of government or to abolish private ownership. This act was broadly interpreted and was often used to censor literary publication. As Japan's war with China escalated, writers were forced to either produce propaganda or not write at all. **Tanizaki Jun'ichirô** was particularly affected by wartime censorship, as both his modern translation of *The Tale of Genji* (ca. 1008) and his novel ***Sasameyuki*** (1943–48; tr. *The Makioka Sisters*, 1957) were subjected to censorship.

Following the war, the Allied **Occupation** force set up its own censorship system, which came to an end with the Occupation and the establishment of Article 21 of the Japanese Constitution prohibiting censorship. Although Japanese literature has been free of censorship ever since, there have been subsequent obscenity trials focusing on the translation of works by D. H. Lawrence and the Marquis de Sade. *See also* ITÔ SEI; MARXISM; MILITARISM; SHIBUSAWA TATSUHIKO; THOUGHT POLICE.

CENTRAL REVIEW. *See CHÛÔ KÔRON.*

CHILDREN'S LITERATURE. The **Tokugawa** period publishing boom expanded Japanese readership in new directions. Cheap woodblock printing allowed mass marketing of books, resulting in a proliferation of works written for wider audiences. By the **Meiji** period, children were reading, or being read, literature that, like the *otogizôshi* fairy tales of earlier centuries, were written primarily with them in mind. As was the case with Japanese popular fiction, children's literature established itself as a dominant genre in the 1910s. The **literary journal** ***Akai Tori*** (*Red Bird*), appearing first in 1918 and running nearly without break until 1936, was pivotal in establishing children's literature as a legitimate genre. The monthly magazine featured traditional and modern literature for young readers written by both amateur and serious writers, including luminaries, such as **Akutagawa Ryûnosuke**, **Arishima Takeo**, **Izumi Kyôka**, **Kitahara Hakushû**, and **Tokuda Shûsei**. Its success spawned other children's magazines, such as *Kane no fune* (*Golden Ship*) in 1919 and *Dôwa* (*Fairy Tale*) in 1920.

During the prewar period, writers such as **Yamamoto Yûzô** and **Miyazawa Kenji** wrote many stories and books for children, and in the **postwar** period the role of children's literature shifted from didacticism to entertainment, in part because of the emergence of ***manga*** and the influence of children's television programs. By the later part of the 20th century, children's literature was a thriving business in Japan, with a number of series (including the *Harry Potter* franchise in **translation**) selling over a million copies. Notable contemporary children's authors include Eiko Kadono (1935–), author of *Majo no takkyūbin* (1985; tr. *Kiki's Delivery Service*, 2003), and Takagi Toshiko (1932–), author of *Garasu no usagi* (1977; tr. *The Glass Rabbit*, 1986). Both works of children's literature have been made into **films**. *See also* BETSUYAKU MINORU; DETECTIVE NOVELS; DIET LIBRARY; *GENBUN ITCHI*; HAKUBUNKAN; KANEKO MISUZU; KURAHASHI YUMIKO; MIKI ROFÛ; MODERN THEATER; ÔBA MINAKO; ONO TÔSABURÔ; UNO KÔJI; YAMAMOTO SHÛGORÔ.

CHINMOKU. *Chinmoku* (1966; tr. *Silence*, 1969), for which author **Endô Shûsaku** received the **Tanizaki Jun'ichirô Prize**, is an epistolary novel that portrays a young Portuguese Jesuit, Rodrigues, in early 17th-century Japan. The priest voyages to Japan in search of a former mentor who has left the faith and now works as an anti-Christian propagandist for the **Tokugawa** government. His discovery along the way of the blind faith of hidden Christians and his own inner doubts underscore the profound differences between passive and active belief. Rodrigues finds his own faith challenged as God remains silent to the cries of believers who suffer brutal persecution. The work mirrors Christian Endô's own struggles with his faith in the face of **postwar** religious discrimination. *See also* CHRISTIAN LITERATURE; *KAKURE KIRISHITAN*.

CHRISTIAN LITERATURE. Japan's 16th-century contact with the West occurred through the vector of Jesuit missionaries, ushering in a "Christian century" that witnessed entire fief conversions and the translation of scriptures and other religious texts into Japanese. With the subsequent outlawing of Christian practice by the **Tokugawa** regime, practicing lay Christians went underground, to reappear only during the **Meiji Restoration** (*see KAKURE KIRISHITAN*). Anti-Christian sentiment during the Tokugawa period effectively kept Japanese readers free from Christian contamination, but with the opening to the West, some of the first foreigners to settle in Japan were Christian missionaries. Young Japanese eager to study Western ways often attended Christian academies where they learned English, and along the way many were converted, some remaining faithful while others moved away from Christian ideology toward the philosophies of **naturalism** or **Marxism**.

Many early modern writers, such as **Kitamura Tôkoku**, were influenced by doctrines of Christianity, in particular a focused sense of self-consciousness and guilt that were relatively absent in Buddhism. Although the period of intense **nationalism** during World War II led most Christian writers to eschew the faith, a number of the postwar generation of writers found their way to Christianity. Notable among these are **Endô Shûsaku**, **Shiina Rinzô**, and **Shimao Toshio**. Today a disproportionately large percentage of Japanese writers have ties with Christianity. *See also* ARISHIMA TAKEO; *CHINMOKU*; FUKUNAGA TAKEHIKO; *HI NO HASHIRA*; KINOSHITA NAOE; KUNIKIDA DOPPÔ; MIKI RÔFU; MIURA AYAKO; NAGASAKI; NAKAMURA MASANAO; SHIGA NAOYA; TOKUTOMI ROKA.

CHÛÔ KÔRON. *Chûô Kôron* (Central Review) is a popular monthly Japanese **literary journal** established during the **Meiji** period and continuing to this day. Published by the Chûô Kôron **publishing**

house, the journal was founded in 1887 under the title *Hanseikai zasshi* in Kyoto by the Hanseikai (Reflection Society), a literary group of professors and students of Ryûkoku University. In 1899, the journal changed its name to *Chûô Kôron* and soon became one of Japan's foremost general-interest magazines with an ongoing influence on Japan's intellectual community. **Shiba Ryôtarô** noted that the journal's history corresponds to that of modern Japan itself. It publishes a wide variety of material, including novels, photographs, and reports based on various philosophical, economic, political, cultural, and social topics. Noteworthy contributors to the magazine include **Tanizaki Jun'ichirô, Shimazaki Tôson**, and **Kajii Motojirô**. *See also* MURÔ SAISEI; TANIZAKI JUN'ICHIRÔ PRIZE.

COLONIAL LITERATURE. Following Japan's victories in the Sino-Japanese and Russo-Japanese wars, the territories of Korea, Formosa (Taiwan), Manchuria, and the Sakhalin, Kuril, and various South Pacific islands were made effectual colonies of Japan, and this state of empire lasted through the end of World War II. Japanese expatriates settled in these new colonies, and many Japanese authors, including **Abe Kôbô, Endô Shûsaku**, and **Nakajima Atsushi**, wrote of their experiences there. The colonized Imperial subjects were taught Japanese language, and a number of them wrote literary works in Japanese. For example, in Taiwan, some writers, such as Lü Heruo (1914–51; Japanese: Ro Kakujaku) and Chen Huoquan (1908–99; Japanese: Chin Kasen), wrote stories in Japanese. These stories contain elements of resistance as well as the tensions that come from assimilation and colonization. Japan's neglected colonial literary heritage is beginning to receive scholarly attention in Japan. *See also* MILITARISM; NATIONALISM; RYÛKYÛ LITERATURE; *ZAINICHI* LITERATURE.

COMIC BOOKS and COMICS. *See MANGA*.

CRITICISM. *See* LITERARY CRITICISM.

CROSS-EYED DEN. *See HEMEDEN.*

– D –

***DAISAN NO SHINJIN*. See** THIRD GENERATION.

***DANCING GIRL, THE*. *See MAIHIME*.**

***DARK NIGHT'S PASSING, A*. *See AN'YA KÔRO*.**

DAZAI OSAMU (1909–1948). Dazai Osamu, given name Tsushima Shûji, was born in northern Japan, the child of a wealthy landowner. An excellent boarding school student, he began neglecting his studies after his idol **Akutagawa Ryûnosuke** committed **suicide**. Much of his career was marked by attempted suicides, addictions, extramarital affairs, divorce, and even an arrest for involvement with the Communist Party. He never graduated from university, but connections with **Ibuse Masuji** enabled him to get his works published. He first used his pen name Dazai Osamu in the short story *Ressha* (Train, 1933), an early experiment using first-person autobiographical style that became his trademark. He remained a productive writer during World War II and published his best-known work, ***Shayô*** (1947; tr. *The Setting Sun*, 1956), shortly after the end of the war. Dazai abandoned his children and second wife and finally succeeded in double suicide with a mistress in 1948, leaving his final work, *Guddo bai* (Goodbye), unfinished. *See also* DAZAI OSAMU PRIZE; MARXISM; ODA SAKUNOSUKE; POSTWAR LITERATURE; TSUSHIMA YÛKO.

DAZAI OSAMU PRIZE. The Dazai Osamu Prize (*Dazai Osamu shô*), founded in 1964 in honor of author **Dazai Osamu**, is awarded annually for an unpublished short story by a previously unrecognized author. (The work may have appeared in a coterie magazine.) The winner receives a commemorative gift and a cash award of one million yen. After being discontinued in 1978, the award was revived in 1999 and is now sponsored by the Mitaka city government. Prize recipients include **Miyamoto Teru**, who received it for *Doro no kawa* (Muddy River, 1977). *See also* LITERARY AWARDS.

DETECTIVE NOVELS. The Japanese detective novel (*tantei shôsetsu* or *suiri shôsetsu*) was born in the 1890s and flourished during the 1920s. The movement's key author, **Edogawa Rampô**, was an admirer of Edgar Allan Poe, Arthur Conan Doyle, and Maurice Leblanc and founded the Detective Story Club in Japan in the 1940s. **Matsumoto Seichô**'s story of social and political corruption, *Kao* (1957; tr. *Face*, 1980), injected **realism** to detective literature. Since the 1980s, detective fiction has evolved to include elements of intellectual reasoning and introspection. Detective fiction also recently expanded to include ***manga*** (visual novels), most notably the weekly **children's** publication *Meitantei Konan* (*Case Closed*), established in 1994. *See also* MINAKAMI TSUTOMU; OKAMOTO KIDÔ; SAKAGUCHI ANGO; YAMAMOTO SHÛGORÔ.

DIET LIBRARY. The National Diet Library (*Kokkai Toshokan*, abbreviated NDL) was created in June 1948 to help members of the Diet in researching matters pertaining to public policy. The library was formed from two preexisting libraries: the libraries of the two branches of the former Imperial Diet (established in 1890) and the Imperial Library (established in 1872). The NDL consists of two buildings in Tokyo (the second being built in 1961) and one in Kyoto Prefecture (called the *Kansai-kan*, built in 2002). The primary responsibilities of the NDL are to assist the Diet members in their public service duties and to provide library services for the other branches of government, as well as the general public. In addition to the main collection, the NDL is made up of an International Library of **Children's Literature**, an Oriental Library (*Tôyô Bunko*), and 26 branch libraries in the executive and judicial branches of government. *See also* AOZORA BUNKO; MUSEUM OF MODERN JAPANESE LITERATURE; NATIONAL INSTITUTE OF JAPANESE LITERATURE.

DRIFTING CLOUDS. *See UKIGUMO.*

– E –

EDO PERIOD LITERATURE. *See* TOKUGAWA LITERATURE.

EDOGAWA RAMPÔ (1894–1965). Edogawa Rampô, pen name of Hirai Tarô, was an author and critic famous for his **detective**

novels featuring protagonist Akechi Kogorô. Edogawa's pseudonym is a Japanese transcription of the name Edgar Allan Poe (*Edogaa Aran Pô*), whom Edogawa admired. He also idolized Sir Arthur Conan Doyle, as reflected in Akechi Kogorô's similarity to Sherlock Holmes. Edogawa was born in Mie Prefecture and grew up in Nagoya before going to Waseda University in 1912 to study economics. After graduating in 1916, he held numerous odd jobs, including selling soba noodles as a street vendor. His debut in the genre of mystery novel came with *Nisen dôka* (The Two-Sen Copper Coin, 1923). *Nisen dôka* is widely considered to be the first original Japanese modern mystery novel. By the end of his life, he had published over 40 full-length mystery novels, many of which have been translated into English. Edogawa also founded the Japan Mystery Writer's Club. A detective novel **literary award** is named in his honor.

ENCHI FUMIKO (1905–1986). Enchi Fumiko was a female writer famous for exploring female psychology and sexuality. Of poor health as a child, Enchi was educated through private tutors and introduced to the Japanese classics by her grandmother. Her literary career began in the 1920s when she wrote stage plays sympathizing with the **proletarian literature** movement. She won an award from the Society of Women Writers for her novel *Himojii tsukihi* (Days of Hunger, 1954) and the **Noma Prize** for *Onnazaka* (1957; tr. *The Waiting Years,* 1971). She was awarded the **Order of Cultural Merit** in 1985 and died of a heart attack in 1986. *See also* FEMINISM; MODERN THEATER; WOMEN IN LITERATURE.

ENDÔ SHÛSAKU (1923–1996). Endô Shûsaku, a Catholic author, was one of the postwar **Third Generation** writers. Endô was born in Tôkyô in 1923, but soon moved with his family to Japan-occupied Manchuria. When his parents divorced in 1933, Endô returned to Japan with his mother to live in Kobe. Endô's mother converted to Catholicism when Endô was a small child. His books reflect many of his childhood experiences, and his Catholic faith and ambivalence about it permeate his writing. Works, primarily **I-Novels**, include *Shiroi hito* (1955; tr. *White Man,* 1976), for which he won the **Akutagawa Ryûnosuke Prize,** ***Chinmoku*** (1969; tr. *Silence,* 1969), which won the 1966 **Tanizaki Jun'ichirô Prize,** and his final novel, *Deepu ribaa* (1993; tr. *Deep River,* 1994). *See also* CHRISTIAN

LITERATURE; COLONIAL LITERATURE; *KAKURE KIRISHITAN*; NAGASAKI.

ESSENCE OF THE NOVEL, THE. *See SHÔSETSU SHINZUI.*

– F –

FEMINISM. Feminism (*josei kaihôron*) as a movement began in Japan in the early 20th century. During the **Meiji** period, **women** authors, such as the writer **Higuchi Ichiyô** and the poet **Yosano Akiko**, met with great critical acclaim. In the 1920s, an indigenous Japanese feminist movement, led by Hiratsuka Raichô, resulted in women's suffrage and widened opportunities for professional advancement. Postwar writers, such as **Minakami Tsutomu**, and Japanese feminist writers, such as **Ariyoshi Sawako** and **Hayashi Fumiko**, wrote forcefully of the trials Japanese women face in society. Japanese feminism received a boost from the West's women's liberation movement of the late 20th century, and the ideal of self-determination for women continues through such contemporary Japanese women writers as **Yamada Eimi** and **Hayashi Mariko**. *See also* ENCHI FUMIKO; HIKARI AGATA; KINOSHITA NAOE; LITERARY CRITICISM; MIYAMOTO YURIKO; TAMURA TOSHIKO; THOUGHT POLICE; TSUSHIMA YÛKO; WOMEN IN LITERATURE.

FILM AND LITERATURE. Film and literature have been closely related since film debuted in Japan in the early 20th century. The silent film industry, which lasted well into the 1930s in Japan, employed former professional storytellers as ***benshi***, narrators who added realistic dialogue and gave interpretation and background information to silent film audiences. As film has become more of a mainstream genre, many renowned novels and short stories have been depicted on screen, including ***Yukiguni*** (1948; tr. *Snow Country*, 1956), ***Sasameyuki*** (1943–48; tr. *The Makioka Sisters*, 1957), ***Rashômon*** (1915; tr. *Rashômon*, 1952), ***Maihime*** (1890; tr. *The Dancing Girl*, 1948), ***Kokoro*** (1914; tr. *Kokoro: A Novel*, 1957), and ***Suna no onna*** (1962; tr. *Woman in the Dunes*, 1964). Many of these literary films have received international awards, and others have been converted into television dramas or have been remade as animated films. *See also BUNGEI EIGA*.

FOOTPRINTS IN THE SNOW. *See OMOIDE NO KI.*

FOREIGN AUTHORS WRITING IN JAPANESE. Although the term "Japanese literature" usually denotes Japanese writers writing in Japanese, the modern period has seen the rise of non-Japanese writers who write in Japanese and publish in Japan. Notable authors include Korean-Japanese (***zainichi***) authors who focus on economic and family hardships growing up in Korean neighborhoods in Osaka. In 1970, Lee Hoesung (1935–; Japanese: Ri Kaisei) won an **Akutagawa Ryûnosuke Prize** for *Kinuta o utsu onna* (The Woman Who Scours Cloth, 1970). In 1988, Lee Yangji (1955–92; Japanese: I Yanji) won the same prize for her novel *Yuhi* (1988, tr. *Yuu-Hee*, 1991) about the difficulty in adapting to her ancestral Korean heritage. Yû Miri (1968–) won the **Noma Prize** for her novel *Furu hausu* (Full House, 1996) followed by the Akutagawa Prize for *Kazoku shinema* (Family Cinema, 1997). Hyeon Wol (1965–; Japanese: Gen Getsu) won the Akutagawa Prize for *Kage no sumika* (Where the Shadows Reside, 1999).

Other non-Japanese writers include Chinese-born Yang Yi (1964–; Japanese: Yan Ii), who moved to Japan at age 22 and won the Akutagawa Prize in 2008 for *Toki ga nijimu asa* (A Morning When Time Blurs, 2008), and Ian Hideo Levy (1950–; Japanese: Rîbi Hideo), the first American-born **translator** turned writer to win the Noma Prize for his novel *Seijôki no kikoenai heya* (The Room Where the Star-Spangled Banner Cannot Be Heard, 1992). **Poet** Arthur Binard (1967–; Japanese: Âsâ Binâdo) was the first native English speaker to win the Nakahara Chûya Prize for his collection of poems *Tsuriagete wa* (Catch and Release, 2001). *See also* COLONIAL LITERATURE; HEARN, LAFCADIO.

FREE VERSE. Japanese **poetry** has historically been governed by metric considerations based upon the ***tanka*** tradition. Free verse does away with the strict metrical structure of *tanka*, lending itself to the use of colloquial grammar and vocabulary. When Western examples of free verse entered Japan during the **Meiji** period, some Japanese poets saw free verse as a liberating form, with their **adaptations** and **translations** of Western free verse appearing in several anthologies, including **Ueda Bin**'s ***Kaichôon*** (The Sound of the Tide, 1905). The 20th century witnessed many fine Japanese free verse poets, including **Takamura Kôtarô**, **Ishikawa Takuboku**, and **Hagiwara Sakutarô**. *See also* MIYAZAWA KENJI; MIYOSHI TATSUJI; TACHIHARA MICHIZÔ.

FREEDOM AND PEOPLE'S RIGHTS MOVEMENT. The Freedom and People's Rights Movement (*jiyû minken undô*) was a political and social reform campaign led by Itagaki Taisuke (1837–1919) during the 1870s that sought to create a democracy in Japan and secure civil rights through public orations, political meetings, and pamphleteering, most notably Ueki Emori's (1857–92) *Minken jiyû ron* (On Popular Rights and Liberty, 1879). Although ultimately unsuccessful, the movement's popularity put pressure on the **Meiji** oligarchy that led to the formation of the Diet and the creation of the Meiji Constitution in 1889. The government sought to suppress the movement in various ways. Itagaki eventually helped form the Public Party of Patriots (*Aikoku kôtô*) to promote civil liberties and consequently became the target of an assassination attempt.

One literary outgrowth of the movement was the emergence of *sôshi shibai* (hooligan shows), mass-oriented propaganda performances that developed into a new style of theatrical **adaptation** and had influences on the emergence of ***shinpa*** drama. **Kawakami Otojirô**, one of the "hooligans," incorporated movement themes into political ballads, such as *Itagaki-kun sônan jikki* (Disaster Strikes Itagaki: The True Account, 1891). *See also* MODERN THEATER; THEATER REFORM.

FRIENDS OF THE INK STONE. *See* KEN'YÛSHA.

FUJIMORI SEIKICHI (1892–1977). Fujimori Seikichi was a novelist and playwright from Nagano Prefecture. While attending Tokyo University, he penned the novel *Nami* (Waves, 1914), for which he became widely known. His most famous play was *Nani ga kanojo o sô saseta ka* (What Caused Her to Do That?), which premiered in 1926. Thereafter, he continued to focus on drama, particularly with socialist themes, and founded the first all-Japan **proletarian** arts league. He also ran for office in 1928 as a representative from Nagano Prefecture. After World War II, he continued to be active in literary and relief organizations in Japan. He died tragically in his old age, hit by a truck while taking a walk. *See also* MODERN THEATER.

FUJIN KÔRON LITERARY PRIZE. *See* WOMEN'S LITERATURE PRIZE.

FUKAZAWA SHICHIRÔ (1914–1987). Fukazawa Shichirô was a novelist and guitarist from Yamanashi Prefecture. His first book, *Narayama bushi-kô* (1956; tr. *The Oak Mountain Song*, 1957), was a popular bestseller and has been adapted into **film** twice since then. In 1960, he wrote a controversial satire that was published in ***Chûô Kôron*** (Central Review) that led to a murder in the publisher's household the following year. He suffered a heart attack in 1968 and spent the rest of his life fighting its complications. Fukazawa was awarded the **Tanizaki Jun'ichirô Prize** for *Michinoku no ningyôtachi* (The Dolls of Michinoku, 1981). Three of his novels have been adapted into films. *See also BUNGEI EIGA*.

FUKUNAGA TAKEHIKO (1918–1979). Fukunaga Takehiko was a novelist and poet from Fukuoka Prefecture. He graduated in French literature from Tokyo University in 1945 and published his first novel, *Tô* (The Tower, 1945) the following year, but was hospitalized with pulmonary illness for the next six years. During that time, he formed the literary magazine *Matinée Poétique* with **Nakamura Shin'ichirô** and **Katô Shûichi** and explored the possibility of rhyming fixed form **poetry** in the Japanese language. The three also started a new movement that distanced itself from the First Generation of postwar writers. Fukunaga published *Kusa no hana* (Grass Flowers, 1954), which established his status as a novelist. He taught for many years at Gakushûin University and was an expert on European literature movements. He **translated** many of the works of Charles Baudelaire and also classical Japanese texts into modern Japanese. He was one of three authors to write the story for the **science fiction** film *Mothra*, and became a Christian two years before his death. *See also* CHRISTIAN LITERATURE.

FUKUZAWA YUKICHI (1835–1901). Fukuzawa Yukichi was an author, translator, and political theorist, founder of Keiô University, and one of the foremost thinkers of the **Meiji Restoration**. Fukuzawa studied Dutch in his youth and traveled to Edo to teach the language in 1858. He went to the United States as an envoy of the **Tokugawa** shogunate in 1860 and became an official government English **translator** upon his return. The information he collected as a translator resulted in his work *Seiyô jijô* (Conditions in The West, 1866). Fukuzawa produced numerous other writings that expounded his theories on civilization and current events. His portrait appears on the current 10 thousand yen banknote.

FURUI YOSHIKICHI (1937–). Furui Yoshikichi was an author and **translator** who graduated from Tokyo University with a degree in German literature. He worked as an assistant professor of German literature at Rikkyô University until 1970, when he retired to write full time. His 1971 novella *Yoko* was awarded the **Akutagawa Ryûnosuke Prize**. He also won the 1983 **Tanizaki Jun'ichirô Prize** for *Asagao* (Morning Glory, 1975), and the 1986 **Kawabata Yasunari Prize** for *Nakayama saka* (On Nakayama Hill, 1985).

FUTABATEI SHIMEI (1864–1909). Futabatei Shimei, born Hasegawa Tatsunosuke, was a **realist** author, Russian-Japanese **translator**, and **literary critic**. Futabatei studied Russian at the Tokyo School of Foreign Languages, but quit in protest of administrative restructuring. He then published the literary critique *Shôsetsu sôron* (General Theory of the Novel) in 1886, with the help and encouragement of **Tsubouchi Shôyô**. His later work ***Ukigumo*** (1887; tr. *The Drifting Clouds*, 1967), written in a colloquial narrative style borrowed from that used by storytellers in the ***yose*** theaters, is often called Japan's first modern novel. Futabatei went on to write other novels and died of tuberculosis while returning from an assignment to Russia for the *Asahi* newspaper. *See also GENBUN ITCHI*; PSYCHOLOGICAL LITERATURE; *RAKUGO*; SAN'YÛTEI ENCHÔ; SHORTHAND.

FUTON. *Futon* (1907; tr. *The Quilt*, 1978) is a **naturalist** novel by **Tayama Katai**. Strongly autobiographical and confessional in structure and tone, *Futon* is considered, along with ***Hakai*** (1906; tr.

The Broken Commandment, 1956), to be one of the first **I-Novels.** It describes the forbidden yearnings of a married writer for his young female student. After she takes his advice to follow her heart and runs off with another man, the novel concludes with the pathetic scene of the writer, forever separated from the object of his love, trying to recapture her memory by smelling her bed linen. The novel received intense critical attention for the implied confession it contained of Tayama's own affection for a female pupil.

– G –

GAN. *Gan* (1911–13; tr. *The Wild Geese*, 1951) is a novel by **Mori Ôgai** set in Tokyo in 1881 that underscores the tensions between old and new ways following the **Meiji Restoration.** The story portrays a girl who, out of financial necessity, becomes a mistress to an old bill collector. She falls in love with a medical student upon whom she places her hopes of rescue. The novel realistically portrays the hardships that fill the lives of **women**, students, and the working classes during Japan's period of rapid modernization.

GENBUN ITCHI. Written Japanese, fundamentally standardized by the eighth century, had undergone sporadic and incremental change prior to the Meiji period, evolving into a collection of documentary, epistolary, and narrative styles that were firmly bound in the classical language. The spoken language, on the other hand, which had developed considerably over the centuries, reflected the multiple dialects and complex hierarchies of contemporary Japan. The disparity between writing and speech caused great concern for Meiji leaders, both because learning the written language took a great deal of time and effort and because it was a barrier to mass literacy. Although **Tokugawa literature** contained examples of colloquial dialogue, writers and scholars sought a narrative style that was closer to speech yet flexible enough to be used in formal contexts.

Futabatei Shimei is generally credited with the first successful use of a vernacular style in his novel ***Ukigumo*** (1887; tr. *The Drifting Clouds*, 1967). However, Futabatei gives credit for his model of colloquial narrative to ***rakugo*** storyteller **San'yûtei Enchô**, whose collaboration with **Takusari Kôki** (inventor of *sokki*, Japanese **shorthand**) allowed *rakugo* stories to be published in newspapers. Other writers quickly joined the so-called *genbun itchi* (unification of writing and speech) movement, to which there was opposition through the 1910s. **Publishing houses** adopted the new style in their children's literary journals, such as ***Akai Tori***, and other mass-marketed publications, which led to its widespread adoption. The use of classical written styles continued among some authors, however, for several decades. *See also* KINOSHITA NAOE; *KÔDAN*; LITERARY CRITICISM; NAGATSUKA TAKASHI; TSUBOUCHI SHÔYÔ; YAMADA BIMYÔ.

GIKOTENSHUGI. *See* PSEUDO-CLASSICISM.

GUNDAN. *See* WAR LITERATURE.

GUNKI. *See* WAR LITERATURE.

GUNKOKU SHUGI. *See* MILITARISM.

– H –

HAGIWARA SAKUTARÔ (1886–1942). Hagiwara Sakutarô was a **free verse** poet, essayist, and literary critic from Gunma Prefecture. He was interested in **poetry** at an early age and published ***tanka*** verses in the journal ***Myôjô*** (Venus) in his teens. He enrolled in two universities, but dropped out of both after a combined five semesters. In 1913, Hagiwara published five *tanka* poems in a journal edited by **Kitahara Hakushû**, and Kitahara became Hagiwara's mentor. The following year he joined **Murô Saisei** and Christian minister Yamamura Bochô (1884–1924) in creating a literary journal *Takujô Funsui* (Tabletop Fountain). He later published controversial poetry anthologies, including his **modernist** collection *Aoneko* (1923; tr. *Blue Cat*, 1978), and wrote **literary criticism** focusing on Japanese poetry.

HAIKU. *Haiku* (called *haikai* until the **Meiji** era) is a simplified lyric form derived from traditional ***tanka*** poetry consisting of 17 syllables in the pattern 5–7–5. During the **Tokugawa** period, *haiku* emerged under the guidance and genius of Matsuo Bashô (1644–94) and was further reformed by the poets Yosa Buson (1716–84) and Kobayashi Issa (1763–1827). During the Meiji period, poet **Masaoka Shiki** strongly criticized Bashô, objecting to the gamelike point system *haiku* schools used to grade student compositions and the lack of masculine sophistication in Bashô's work. Conversely, Masaoka held the highest praise for Buson's **poetry** and predicted the demise of *haiku* due to its lack of innovation. Despite Shiki's pessimism, however, both his contemporaries, such as **Natsume Sôseki**, and subsequent poets, such as Taneda Santôka (1882–1940) and Katô Shûson (1905–93), pursued the art, and today *haiku* clubs and circles regularly publish their poems in **literary journals** and newspapers. *See also* FREE VERSE; KUME MASAO; MIKI ROFÛ; NAKAMURA TEIJO; TSUJI KUNIO.

HAKAI. *Hakai* (1906; tr. *The Broken Commandment*, 1956), a **naturalist** novel by **Shimazaki Tôson**, tells of a schoolteacher named Ushimatsu who tries to conceal his identity as a member of the ***burakumin*** untouchable class. When his idol and mentor, an "outed" *burakumin* politician, is murdered, Ushimatsu decides to confess his secret to his students and is fired in disgrace. The novel ends as he departs in the snow, resolved to make a new life for himself in Texas.

HAKUBUNKAN. Hakubunkan **publishing house** was founded by Ohashi Sahei (1835–1901) in 1887. Within two years the company was publishing 10 magazines and in five years had published 500 book titles, eventually reaching 87 magazine and 6,500 book titles. At the turn of the 19th century, Hakubunkan redefined the publishing industry with the lead periodical *Taiyô* (The Sun) and pioneered vertical integration of the printing industry through in-house writers, paper service, and private newswire. Under editor Oshikawa Shunrô (1876–1914), Hakubunkan also initiated mass-oriented **children's literature** and pictorial novels from adventure stories. Extensive national networks allowed Hakubunkan to influence literary and political movements through selective publishing. The extent of its influence, however, led to its being liquidated during the Allied **Occupation**. *See also AKAI TORI.*

HANIYA YUTAKA (1909–1997). Haniya Yutaka was born in Taiwan when it was a Japanese colony. He was initially drawn to anarchism, but joined the Communist Party in 1931 and was arrested and imprisoned. After World War II, he founded the small **literary journal** *Kindai Bungaku* (Modern Literature), which burgeoned into a popular periodical. Through *Kindai Bungaku* Haniya became acquainted with and published author **Abe Kôbô**. Haniya won the **Tanizaki Jun'ichirô Prize** for his collection *Yami no naka no kuroi uma* (Black Horses in the Darkness, 1970). *See also* MARXISM.

HANSHIZEN SHUGI. *See* ANTINATURALISM.

HAYAMA YOSHIKI (1894–1945). Hayama Yoshiki was an author associated with the **proletarian literature** movement. His best-known work is *Umi ni ikuru hitobito* (Men Who Live on the Sea, 1933), a novel about labor conditions on workboats. Hayama spent time in prison for his involvement with the labor movement, but became a **nationalist** during World War II. *See also* MARXISM.

HAYASHI FUMIKO (1903–1951). Hayashi Fumiko was born an illegitimate child in Kyushu and moved around the island with her mother. After graduating high school, Hayashi went to Tokyo with her lover, did odd jobs, and helped launch the **poetry** magazine *Futari* (Two). She then lived with several different men before marrying Tezuka Rokubin (1902–89) in 1926. She published the serialized **I-Novel** *Hôrôki* (1928; tr. *Diary of a Vagabond*, 1951) in a women's magazine, and it became a bestseller for which she wrote two sequels. During World War II, Hayashi joined a journalist group called *Jûgun sakka* (Campaigning Writers) and served in the military in China and French Indochina. After the war, she wrote many novels and essays, including *Bangiku* (1948; tr. *Late Chrysanthemum*, 1956), which was awarded the **Women's Literature Prize** and was later made into a **film**. A prolific writer, **translated** into many foreign languages, Hayashi died in 1951 of a heart attack. *See also* FEMINISM.

HAYASHI MARIKO (1954–). Novelist and essayist Hayashi Mariko was born in Yamanashi Prefecture. After graduating from Nihon

University, she worked as a copywriter. Her professional debut came with the essay collection *Runrun o katte ouchi ni kaerô* (Let's Buy 'Run-run' and Head Home, 1982), which became a bestseller. She was awarded the **Naoki Prize** in 1985 and subsequently has won the **Yoshikawa Eiji Prize** and Shibata Renzaburô Prize. Her novels and essays focus on the challenges women face in their lives. Hayashi is currently on the selection committee of the Naoki Prize. *See also* FEMINISM.

HAYASHI TATSUO (1896–1984). Hayashi Tatsuo was an intellectual and **literary critic** who wrote many books about the history of civilization, culture, and the Occidental mind. He was born in Tokyo but spent his youth in Seattle with his diplomat father. After high school in Kyoto, he studied philosophy under Nishida Kitarô (1870–1945) at Kyoto University. Following his graduation, he became a professor of cultural history at Tôyô University and also taught at Tsudajuku and Hôsei universities and was on the editing committees of philosophical journals. After World War II, Hayashi became chief of the ***Chûô Kôron* publishing house**. Opposed to socialist idealogy, he was awarded the Asahi Cultural Prize in 1973 for his research and writings on the Occidental mind. Hayashi died of old age in Kanagawa Prefecture.

HEARN, LAFCADIO (1850–1904). Lafcadio Hearn (Japanese citizenship name Koizumi Yakumo) was an American newspaper correspondent and Japanese author. He was born in Greece and moved to Ohio in the late 1860s. He worked as a correspondent for the *Cincinnati Daily Enquirer* but later moved to New Orleans. While there he also contributed many publications to national periodicals, such as *Harper's Weekly* and *Scribner's Magazine.*

In 1890, Hearn moved to Japan on assignment and taught school in remote Matsue, Shimane Prefecture. There he married Koizumi Setsu (1868–1932) and became a naturalized Japanese citizen before moving to Kumamoto just over a year later, where he completed his most famous work, *Glimpses of Unfamiliar Japan*, in 1894 (later **translated** into Japanese as *Shirarezu Nihon no omokage*). After a short stint in Kobe at a newspaper, he taught English literature at Tokyo University from 1896–1903, and there penned the books *In*

Ghostly Japan (1899) and *Kaidan* (1904), both collections of Japanese ghost stories. He died of heart failure in Tokyo. His writings had an influence on Japanese writers **Kawabata Yasunari** and **Mishima Yukio**. *See also* FOREIGN AUTHORS WRITING IN JAPANESE; *JAPONISME*.

HEMEDEN. *Hemeden* (Cross-Eyed Den, 1895) was the first novel written by **Hirotsu Ryûrô**. *Hemeden*, followed shortly by Hirotsu's second novel, ***Kurotokage*** (Black Lizard, 1895), established a new Japanese literary genre, the **serious novel**. *Hemeden* captures the gloomy life of Den, a cross-eyed, grotesquely deformed dwarf. Taunted by peers and the world at large, hardworking and amiable Den falls in love with a young girl named Ohama. Ohama's cousin deceives Den into paying him to help Den's chances with Ohama, and Den is eventually driven to commit robbery and murder to pay his debts. Den is sent to the gallows, clinging to the illusion that Ohama loves him.

HI NO HASHIRA. *Hi no hashira* (1903–4; tr. *Pillar of Fire*, 1972) is a novel by author **Kinoshita Naoe** that was published serially in the *Mainichi* newspaper over a 14-month span prior to and during the Russo-Japanese War. The novel depicts tycoons and government purveyors looking to make a large profit off the **war**, covert government repression of the antiwar movement, and the exile of socialist Christians from their churches. It is considered to be one of the first Japanese socialist novels. *See also* MILITARISM.

HIBAKUSHA BUNGAKU. *See* ATOMIC BOMB LITERATURE.

HIDDEN CHRISTIANS. *See KAKURE KIRISHITAN*.

HIGUCHI ICHIYÔ (1872–1896). Higuchi Ichiyô, given name Natsu, is considered to be the first female professional writer of modern Japanese literature. Born in Tokyo, she studied at the Haginoya, a poetry school, but after the deaths of her brother and father worked odd jobs to help make ends meet until she turned to writing at age 20. Her first major work, "***Ôtsugomori***" (1894; tr. *On the Last Day of the Year*, 1981), was followed the next year by "***Takekurabe***" (1895–96;

tr. *Growing Up*, 1956), "*Nigorie*" (1895; tr. *Troubled Waters*, 1953), and "*Jûsan'ya*" (1895; tr. *The Thirteenth Night*, 1960–61). Higuchi died of tuberculosis in 1896 at the age of 23. Her life story has been retold in both **film** and television drama, and her portrait appears on the current five thousand yen note. *See also* FEMINISM; PSEUDO-CLASSICISM; ROMANTICISM; WOMEN IN LITERATURE.

HIJIKATA YOSHI (1898–1959). Hijikata Yoshi was a Tokyo-born theater director who was active in the *shingeki* **theater reform** movement and joined with **Osanai Kaoru** in 1924 to create the Tsukiji Little Theater, the first in the world to use electric illumination. The theater featured foreign plays by such playwrights as Anton Chekov and Maxim Gorky **translated** into Japanese. However, with Osanai's sudden death in 1928, Hijikata was ousted from control, and in 1929 he formed the New Tsukiji Theater Company with the aim to focus on more socialist-**realist** theater. This new company adapted many of the novels of the contemporary **proletarian literature** movement. In 1932, however, government opposition became fierce and Hijikata was arrested. The following year he fled to the Soviet Union and remained there in fear of persecution by the **thought police**. He was deported to Europe in 1937 and stayed for four years before returning to Japan, where he was immediately arrested. After World War II, he was released and joined the Communist Party. *See also* MARXISM.

HIKARI AGATA (1943–1992). Hikari Agata was a novelist from Tokyo. He enrolled at Waseda University but dropped out after his first year and became a copywriter, contributor to a monthly magazine, and freelance writer. He was awarded a new writer prize for his novel *Juka no kazoku* (A Family Party, 1982) and published *Uhohho tankentai* (The 'Ahem!' Expedition Team, 1983), which was an **Akutagawa Ryûnosuke Prize** finalist. Hikari's works centered on themes of **feminism** as well as the degradation of the family in society. His literary career was cut short when he died of stomach cancer. Hikari published 18 novels, four essays, and two **translations** during his lifetime. A few of his works have been turned into **films** or television dramas.

HINO ASHIHEI (1907–1960). Hino Ashihei was a soldier in the Japanese army in China who wrote and published **war** novels about the daily life of soldiers. These include *Mugi to Heitai* (1938; tr. *Wheat and Soldiers*, 1958) and *Fun'nyôtan* (Tales of Excrement and Urine, 1937), for which he received the **Akutagawa Ryûnosuke Prize**, delivered to him in Manchuria by **Kobayashi Hideo**. He took his own life at age 53. *See also* SUICIDE.

HINO KEIZÔ (1929–2002). Hino Keizô was a journalist and novelist from Tokyo. He grew up in Korea when it was still a colony of Japan, but returned to Japan to study and graduated from Tokyo University. He took a job with the *Yomiuri* newspaper and served as a correspondent in Korea and Vietnam, then began writing novels, winning the **Akutagawa Ryûnosuke Prize** for *Ano yûhi* (The Evening Sun, 1974). He was awarded the **Tanizaki Jun'ichirô Prize** for *Sakyû ga ugoku yô ni* (As the Sand Dunes Move, 1986). He also **translated** works from Vietnamese into Japanese.

HIRABAYASHI TAIKO (1905–1972). Novelist Hirabayashi Taiko, given name Tai, was born in Nagano Prefecture. Drawn to socialism in high school, she moved to Tokyo after graduation and lived with anarchist Yamamoto Torazô. Following the Kantô Earthquake, the two were exiled from Tokyo and moved to Manchuria, where she gave birth in Dalian to a baby girl, who died shortly thereafter from malnutrition. That experience was the basis of her **proletarian** novel *Seiryôshitsu nite* (In the Charity Hospital, 1928). Her novel *Kô iu onna* (This Kind of Woman, 1946) received the first **Women's Literature Prize**. Royalties from her long career were used to establish the Hirabayashi Taiko Literary Prize in 1973, and a museum in her honor is located in her hometown of Suwa. *See also* FEMINISM; MARXISM; WOMEN IN LITERATURE.

HIROTSU KAZUO (1891–1968). Hirotsu Kazuo, novelist, **translator** and **literary critic**, was the son of novelist **Hirotsu Ryûrô**. He published the **literary journal** *Kiseki* (Miracle), to which he contributed translations of European literature and short stories. During World War II, he moved to Shizuoka Prefecture near friend **Shiga Naoya**. A critic of nihilism, Hirotsu became part of the **proletarian literature** movement of the 1930s and later wrote **I-Novels**. He won the **Noma Prize** for *Nengetsu no ashiato* (The Footsteps of Time,

1963). He also wrote an extensive defense of the accused Communist saboteurs in the Matsukawa incident, published in two parts, *Izumi e no michi* (Road to the Spring, 1953–54) and *Matsukawa Saiban* (The Matsukawa Trial, 1954–58). *See also* KASAI ZENZÔ; MARXISM; UNO KÔJI.

HIROTSU RYÛRÔ (1861–1928). Hirotsu Ryûrô, given name Naoto, was a **Meiji** novelist famous for his tragic novels. Born in **Nagasaki**, he traveled to Tokyo in 1874 to study German and then turned to writing in 1885 after serving four years in the Ministry of Agriculture and Commerce. Hirotsu joined the **Ken'yûsha** literary group and published two novels, ***Hemeden*** (Cross-Eyed Den, 1895) and ***Kurotokage*** (Black Lizard, 1895), which epitomized the **tragic novel**. His most famous work was *Imado Shinjû* (Double Suicide at Imado, 1896). Retiring in 1908, Hirotsu died of a heart attack 20 years later. He was the father of writer **Hirotsu Kazuo**. *See also* SERIOUS NOVELS.

HISAN SHÔSETSU. *See* TRAGIC NOVELS.

HON'AN. *See* ADAPTATION.

HON'ANMONO. *See* ADAPTIVE TRANSLATIONS.

HON'YAKU. *See* TRANSLATION.

HORI TATSUO (1904–1953). Hori Tatsuo was a writer, **poet**, and **translator** born in Tokyo and graduated from Tokyo University. As a student he helped to translate French poetry for *Roba* (Donkey), a **literary journal**. During his literary career, he wrote a number of novelettes and poems. His early writing was in the spirit of **proletarian literature**, while his later work tended more toward **modernism**. Much of his work, such as his most famous novel *Kaze tachinu* (1936–37; tr. *The Wind Awakes*, 1947), a love story set in a mountain sanitarium, was characterized by the theme of death, reflecting his own struggle with tuberculosis, to which he eventually succumbed at age 49. *See also* MARXISM; NAKAMURA SHIN'ICHIRÔ; NAKANO SHIGEHARU; SATA INEKO.

HORIGUICHI DAIGAKU (1892–1981). Horiguchi Daigaku was a **poet** and French literature **translator** from Tokyo. His first name, which means "university," was given him by his college-student father because he was born near the campus of Tokyo University. He enrolled in Keiô University to study literature, but dropped out. Always an active poet, he was a member of the *Shinshisha* (New Poetry Society) and also contributed ***tanka*** to various **literary journals**. Through his association with **Yosano Tekkan** and **Yosano Akiko** he was persuaded to try his hand at other forms of poetry. At 19 Horiguchi traveled abroad with his diplomat father and spent the next 14 years in Mexico, Belgium, Spain, and Brazil, becoming fluent in French with a particular interest in **symbolism**. His first poetry anthology was titled *Gekkô to piero* (Moonlight and Clowns, 1919). Upon returning to Japan, he published a translation of contemporary French poetry titled *Gekka no ichigun* (A Moonlit Gathering, 1925). He published over 20 books of poetry during his lifetime and was awarded the **Order of Cultural Merit** in 1979.

HOSHI SHIN'ICHI (1926–1997). Hoshi Shin'ichi, novelist and **science fiction** writer, is best known for his "short-short" science fiction stories. Often no more than three or four pages, these works deal with a plethora of topics, and he wrote over a thousand of them during his lifetime. He also wrote mysteries and won the Mystery Writers of Japan Award in 1968. Several of his books and collections of short stories have been **translated** into English, including *Nokku no oto ga* (1965; tr. *There Was a Knock*, 1984), a collection of 15 stories, and *Ki magure robotto* (1966; tr. *The Capricious Robot*, 1986). He won the Japan Science Fiction Grand Prize in 1998. Since 1979, there has been an annual Hoshi Shin'ichi Short-Short Contest, with the winning stories published in an anthology.

HOTOTOGISU. *Hototogisu* (The Cuckoo, 1898), a novel written by **Tokutomi Roka**, received wide acclaim when first published. The romantic story captures the deep affection between valiant young naval officer Takeo and his beautiful and refined wife Namiko. Namiko's jealous stepmother and Takeo's overprotective mother are constant threats to the couple's traditional marriage. Namiko becomes a victim of the unrealistically high expectations and frustrations of her Western-educated stepmother. After Namiko contracts tuberculosis, Takeo's mother suggests that he divorce his wife before her illness sweeps through the family. Takeo's indisputable love for Namiko dramatizes the conflict of love over family and social pressures. *See also* WOMEN IN LITERATURE.

HOTTA YOSHIE (1918–1998). Hotta Yoshie was a novelist from Toyama Prefecture who graduated from Keiô University. While in college he composed poems and worked with the **literary journal** *Hihyô* (Criticism). He worked in Shanghai but returned to Japan after the war and focused on writing novels. In 1956, he traveled to India to participate in an Asian authors conference and published his experiences in the paperback *Indo de kangaeta koto* (Thoughts from India, 1957). This launched his attempt to familiarize the world with Japanese culture and was the impetus for his traveling to various countries. He based many of his subsequent novels on these experiences. Hotta won the **Akutagawa Ryûnosuke Prize** for *Hiroba no kodoku* (1951; tr. *Solitude in the Plaza*, 1955), and his *Hôjôki shiki* (Personal Reflections on the *Hôjôki*, 1971) was also critically acclaimed and is currently being made into an animated **film**.

HYÔRON*. *See LITERARY CRITICISM.

– I –

I AM A CAT*. *See *WAGAHAI WA NEKO DE ARU*.

IBUSE MASUJI (1898–1993). Ibuse Masuji, an author from Hiroshima, studied French literature at Waseda University in Tokyo but left before graduation after an altercation with a professor. He began his own writing career with such works as *Sanshôuo* (1929; tr. *The Salamander*, 1956). By the late 1920s, top **literary critics** began to notice his work. Ibuse worked as a propaganda writer during World War II, but his best-known work, ***Kuroi Ame*** (1965; tr. *Black Rain*, 1968), for which he was awarded the **Noma Prize** and the **Order of Cultural Merit**, reflects a deep empathy for **atomic bomb** victims. *See also* DAZAI OSAMU.

INOUE HISASHI (1934–). Inoue Hisashi is a playwright and comic fiction author. He was born in Yamagata Prefecture and graduated from Sophia University. He has had a prolific career in both theater and literature, for which he has won numerous awards, including the **Naoki Prize** for *Tegusari shinjû* (Handcuffed Double Suicide, 1972), the **Yomiuri Prize** for *Kirikirijin* (The Kirikirians, 1981), and the **Tanizaki Jun'ichirô Prize** for *Shanhai mûn* (Shanghai Moon, 1991). He has his own theater troupe and has served as president of the **Japan P.E.N. Club**. *See also* MODERN THEATER.

INOUE MITSUHARU (1926–1992). Inoue Mitsuharu was a novelist born in Fukuoka Prefecture. A self-taught writer, he was known as a compulsive liar, concocting stories about his Manchurian birth and how he was arrested for lobbying for the independence of Korea. His debut as a writer, *Guadarukanaru senshishû* (Anthology of Guadalcanal War Poetry, 1958), depicted youth during the **war**. His subsequent writings addressed such social issues as **atomic bomb** victims and war crimes committed by Japanese soldiers in the Pacific during World War II. Inoue passed away from liver cancer. *See also* ÔOKA SHÔHEI.

INOUE YASUSHI (1907–1991). Inoue Yasushi, a **poet** and writer of historical fiction, was born in Hokkaido but raised by his grandmother in Shizuoka Prefecture. Inoue attended Kyoto Imperial University where he studied aesthetics and philosophy. In the late 1930s, Inoue temporarily abandoned the writing career he had begun with short stories and poems and became a reporter for the *Sunday Mainichi* newspaper. He returned to writing after World War II and published two short novels in the same year: *Ryôjû* (1949; tr. *The Hunting Gun*, 1961) and *Tôgyû* (The Bullfight, 1949), for which he won the **Akutagawa Ryûnosuke Prize**. His subsequent historical narratives *Rôran* (1959; tr. *Lou-lan*, 1959) and *Tempyô no iraka* (1957; tr. *The Roof Tile of Tempyo*, 1975) encompassed Chinese and Japanese themes, respectively.

I-NOVELS. Although the diary and personal essay have long been a part of Japanese literature, the I-Novel (*watakushi shôsetsu*) is a peculiarly Japanese genre that is now seen to have begun in the early

20th century with the appearance of **Shimazaki Tôson**'s ***Hakai*** (1906; tr. *The Broken Commandment*, 1956) and **Tayama Katai**'s ***Futon*** (1907; tr. *The Quilt*, 1978). The I-Novel is considered a literary development stemming from **naturalism**, which was used by writers as a tool for exploring such social and philosophical issues as poverty and death. Tayama's use of personal confession and experience expanded the potential for literary realism by investigating the psychological issues of consciousness and identity. I-Novels developed several de facto rules: the stories must avoid the fantastic and be completely realistic; the narrator/protagonist must equate with the author; and the writing should not be overly elaborate. Many authors, such as **Shiga Naoya**, wrote I-Novels during the 1910s, and though some writers took a narrow, narcissistic turn, the better examples of the I-Novel demonstrate self-deprecating wit and probing self-inquiry.

Although the I-Novel fell somewhat out of fashion in the early 1920s, the rise of **proletarian literature**, with its amateurish tone and penchant for propaganda, led to reactions from serious writers, as can be seen in **Hayashi Fumiko**'s I-Novel *Hôrôki* (1928; tr. *Diary of a Vagabond*, 1951). Following World War II many writers continued to write autobiographical stories, notable among them **Dazai Osamu**'s ***Shayô*** (1947; tr. *The Setting Sun*, 1956). *Sukyandaru* (1986; tr. *Scandal*, 1987), written by **Endô Shûsaku**, is a modern continuation of the I-Novel, although the genre's popularity steadily declined toward the end of the 20th century. *See also* AGAWA HIROYUKI; AKIYAMA SHUN; *AN'YA KÔRO*; HIROTSU KAZUO; KASAI ZENZÔ; KOBAYASHI HIDEO; KUME MASAO; MIURA TETSUO; MIZUMURA MINAE; NAKAMURA MITSUO; OZAKI KAZUO; PSYCHOLOGICAL LITERATURE; *SHIRAKABA*; TAKAMI JUN; TAMIYA TORAHIKO; TOKUDA SHÛSEI; UNO KÔJI.

INSPIRING TALES OF STATESMANSHIP. *See KEIKOKU BIDAN.*

ISHIGURO KAZUO (1954–). Kazuo Ishiguro is a British novelist of Japanese descent. Born in **Nagasaki**, he moved with his family to England in 1960. Although Ishiguro writes only in English, his style often reflects a Japanese literary focus on intricate character development and the themes of transience and loss. Ishiguro's works include two books in immediate post–World War II settings: *The Remains of the Day* and *An Artist of the Floating World*, the latter set in postwar Japan. *See also* FOREIGN AUTHORS WRITING IN JAPANESE.

ISHIHARA SHINTARÔ (1932–). Ishihara Shintarô is a novelist, politician, and three-term governor of Tokyo. He was born in Kobe and graduated from Hitotsubashi University. He made his debut as an author before graduating from college with his novel *Taiyô no kisetsu* (1955; tr. *Season of Violence*, 1966), which won the **Akutagawa Ryûnosuke Prize** and was later adapted into a **film** in which Ishihara appeared. Ishihara served as a member of the House of Councilors from 1968 to 1972 and as a member of the House of Representatives from 1972 to 1995. In 1999, he was elected governor of Tokyo. He has published over 25 books in his lifetime and continues to be a controversial political figure in Japan, largely for his **nationalism**. *See also* MISHIMA YUKIO.

ISHIKAWA JUN (1899–1987). Ishikawa Jun, given name Kiyoshi, was a modernist author who studied French literature at the Tokyo School of Foreign Languages. Early in his career he worked at Fukuoka University as a professor of French literature. He began his writing career after leaving the university due to controversy over student protest movements. He won the fourth annual **Akutagawa Ryûnosuke Prize** for his story *Fugen* (1936, tr. *The Bodhisattva, or, Samantabhadra*, 1990). Ishikawa became famous for both his nonconformist novels and criticisms and for his biographies. He died of lung cancer while working on his last novel, *Hebi no Uta* (A Song of Snakes, 1987). *See also BUNGAKKAI*; MODERNISM.

ISHIKAWA TAKUBOKU (1886–1912). Ishikawa Takuboku was a writer of ***tanka*** and **free verse poetry**. Ishikawa began his literary career at 13 with a hand-printed booklet "*Chôji-kai*" (Class Trip, 1899). He soon dropped out of middle school to continue writing and contributed to numerous magazines and newspapers during his short lifetime. Ishikawa's major works include two volumes of *tanka* poems, *Ichiaku no Suna* (1910; tr. *A Handful of Sand*, 1947) and *Kanashiki gangu* (published posthumously in 1912; tr. *Sad Toys*, 1962), as well as his diaries. He lived in and wrote of Hokkaido. Ishikawa died of tuberculosis. *See also MYÔJÔ*; YOSANO TEKKAN.

ISHIKAWA TATSUZÔ (1905–1985). Ishikawa Tatsuzô was born in Akita Prefecture and studied literature at Waseda University, but never graduated, leaving instead for Brazil where he worked on a farm. Ishikawa won the inaugural **Akutagawa Ryûnosuke Prize** for *Sôbô* (1935; tr. *The Emigrants*, 1985), a novel based on his experiences in Brazil. He continued to be an active writer during and after World War II, although he was heavily **censored** and arrested for his work *Ikite iru heitai* (1938; tr. *Soldiers Alive*, 2005), an account of atrocities committed in China. In 1969, he won the **Kikuchi Kan Prize** for his literary contributions. *See also* JAPAN P.E.N. CLUB; WAR LITERATURE.

"ISM." *See SHUGI.*

ISODA KÔICHI (1931–1987). Isoda Kôichi was a **literary critic** and scholar of British literature. He was born in Yokohama and studied English literature at Tokyo University. His career as a critic began with a study of **Mishima Yukio**, *Junkyô no bigaku* (Aesthetics of Heresy, 1964). He continued to publish essays on Westernization and the Japanese tradition. His original **Romanticist** viewpoint switched to a more empirical mode after 1978 and he published *Rokumeikan no keifû* (Pedigree of the Deer Cry Pavilion, 1983), which garnered the **Yomiuri Prize**. The following year he started working as a professor, but died shortly thereafter.

ITÔ SACHIO (1864–1913). Itô Sachio, given name Kojirô, was a ***tanka*** poet, **literary critic**, and novelist from Chiba Prefecture. He attended Meiji University but dropped out to become a disciple of the poet **Masaoka Shiki**, and in 1908 established *Araragi* (The Yew), a **literary journal** devoted to *tanka* that remained in circulation until 1997. His most famous work, *Nogiku no haka* (1906; tr. *Nogiku no Haka*, 1979), was published in the literary magazine *Hototogisu* and was later remade as a **film** three times. Poet **Saitô Mokichi** was one of Sachio's students. He died of a brain hemorrhage.

ITÔ SEI (1905–1969). Itô Sei, given name Hitoshi, was a critic, poet, and novelist born in Hokkaido. After graduating from Otaru Commercial College, he was accepted into Hitotsubashi University but later dropped out. In his youth, he wrote an anthology of **poetry** titled *Yukiakari no michi* (Snow-lit Road, 1926), but focused on novels and criticism in his later years. He translated James Joyce's *Ulysses* into Japanese, as well as D. H. Lawrence's *Lady Chatterley's Lover*, the latter of which went to trial in the 1950s in a landmark obscenity case. Many of his novels became bestsellers, and he also received the Japan Art Academy Prize. In memoriam, the first **Itô Sei Prize** was awarded in 1990 and continues to be awarded annually for outstanding novels and **literary criticism**. *See also* CENSORSHIP; MODERNISM.

ITÔ SEI PRIZE FOR LITERATURE. The **Itô Sei** Prize for Literature (*Itô Sei bungaku shô)* was established in 1990 by a group of residents in Itô's hometown of Otaru City, Hokkaido, on the 20th anniversary of his death. The prize is awarded to outstanding works by established novelists and critics. The winner receives a bronze sculpture and a cash award of one million yen. Notable recipients include **Ôe Kenzaburô** and **Tsushima Yûko.**

ITÔ SHIZUO (1906–1953). Itô Shizuo was a **poet** from **Nagasaki** Prefecture who graduated from Kyoto University. His most famous work is *Wagahito ni ataeru aika* (Lamentation to My People, 1935). **Hagiwara Sakutarô** referred to Itô, one of the representative **Romantic** writers of his day, as the "last poet of Japan." He was a contributor to the **literary journal** *Shiki* (Four Seasons) with **Miyoshi Tatsuji, Nakahara Chûya**, and **Tachihara Michizô**. His hometown in Nagasaki awards the Itô Shizuo Prize in his honor.

IWANO HÔMEI (1873–1920). Iwano Hômei was a poet and novelist from Hyôgo Prefecture. He studied at Meiji Gakuin University, Sendai Theological Seminary, and Senshû University. After first making himself known in literary circles writing **poetry**, he began writing novels and joined **Tayama Katai** and **Shimamura Hôgetsu** in establishing the school of **naturalist** writers.

IZU DANCER, THE. *See IZU NO ODORIKO.*

IZU NO ODORIKO. "*Izu no odoriko*" (1926; tr. *The Izu Dancer*, 1955) was **Kawabata Yasunari**'s first widely acclaimed work. This short story, about a young man's attraction to a dancing girl and his subsequent change of emotion upon finding she is still a child, has been translated into English many times. It has also been made into several **films**.

IZUMI KYÔKA (1873–1939). Izumi Kyôka, given name Kyôtarô, was an author of novels, short stories, and *kabuki* plays, who was best known for his style of gothic **Romanticism** influenced by the supernatural elements of earlier literature. Because of his family's impoverished circumstances, Izumi first attended a tuition-free Christian school. He sought and received apprenticeship with **Ozaki Kôyô** in 1891, thereafter relying heavily on Ozaki's mentoring, public support, and personal advice. Izumi's best-known works include "*Gekashitsu*" (1895; tr. *The Surgery Room*, 1996), "*Yakô junsa*" (Night Watchman, 1895), and ***Kôya hijiri*** (1900; tr. *The Kôya Priest*, 1959–60). *See also AKAI TORI*; SATOMI TON; TRAGIC NOVELS; WOMEN IN LITERATURE.

– J –

JAPAN P.E.N. CLUB. The Japan P.E.N. Club (*Nihon Pen Kurabu*) is a nongovernmental organization formed by writers aimed at promoting discussion and expression, protecting freedom of the press, and furthering international cultural exchange. In 1935, Japan's minister of foreign affairs received a request from the International P.E.N. Club to establish a branch in Japan. He then relayed that request to the foremost ***bundan*** (writer's guilds), and **Shimazaki Tôson** was appointed to be the first president. The Club was not active during World War II but was reactivated in 1947 and reinstated as a member of the International P.E.N. Club. In 1957, Tokyo and Kyoto jointly hosted an International P.E.N. Club conference centered on the theme "The Mutual Influence of

Oriental and Occidental Literature." The Japan P.E.N. Club has been politically active throughout the years and has been historically liberal and antiwar in its political orientation. Other notable Japan P.E.N. Club presidents include **Masamune Hakuchô**, **Shiga Naoya**, **Kawabata Yasunari**, and **Ishikawa Tatsuzô**.

JAPONISME. The French term *japonisme* describes the intense interest in things Japanese that swept across Europe and America between 1860 and 1920. Japanese art objects made their way to France as Japan opened trade with the West in the early 1860s, including *ukiyoe* landscapes and portraits that caught the eye of such painters as van Gogh, James McNeill Whistler, Paul Klee, and Claude Monet. In the late 19th century, Japanese entertainers, such as **Kawakami Otojirô**'s theater troupe, performed Japanese music and dance at international expositions, inspiring Claude Debussy and Giacomo Puccini, among others, to incorporate Japanese melodies into their works. Much of the appeal came from the exoticism that surrounded Japan stemming from its isolation during the **Tokugawa** period and its emergence as a new market and cultural landscape. The momentum of *japonisme* allowed writers, such as **Lafcadio Hearn**, who mined the rich folklore of Japan in **translations** and **adaptations**, to flourish as they targeted the Western interest in Japanese life and customs.

JIDÔ ENGEKI. *See* MODERN THEATER.

JIYÛ MINKEN UNDÔ. *See* FREEDOM AND PEOPLE'S RIGHTS MOVEMENT.

JOSEI KAIHÔRON. *See* FEMINISM.

– K –

KABUKI. *See* MODERN THEATER.

KAICHÔON. *Kaichôon* (The Sound of the Tide, 1905) is an anthology of **translated poetry** published by **Ueda Bin**. It appeared in the **literary journals** *Teikoku Bungaku* (Imperial Literature) and ***Myôjô***

(Venus) and incorporated elements of Italian, English, French, and German poetry. The collection includes translations of works by Dante Gabriel Rossetti, Charles Baudelaire, Paul Verlaine, Heinrich Heine, Robert Browning, Dante, Shakespeare, Stéphane Mallarmé, and Gabriele d'Annunzio, among others. It served to introduce French **symbolism** to Japan. Many of its translated poems are still found in Japanese textbooks today.

KAIKÔ TAKESHI (1930–1989). Kaikô Takeshi, given name Ken, was a novelist, essayist, and literary critic in postwar Japan. Kaikô attended Osaka University in the early 1950s and was a contributor to the **literary journal** *Enpitsu* (Pencil). In 1952, he married Maki Yôko, and through her found an ad-writing job in Tokyo working for a brewing company. Kaikô won the **Akutagawa Ryûnosuke Prize** for *Hadaka no ôsama* (1957; tr. *The Naked King*, 1977) and left his job to become a full-time writer. In 1964, he was sent to Vietnam by the *Asahi* newspaper as a special correspondent and was one of 17 survivors of a machine gun raid. Along with the Akutagawa Prize, Kaikô was awarded the Mainichi Literary Prize (1968), the **Kawabata Yasunari Prize** (1979), the **Kikuchi Kan Prize** (1981), and the Japanese Literature Prize (1987). He died at the age of 58 of esophageal cancer. Shûeisha established the Kaikô Takeshi Nonfiction Prize, which honors well-written nonfiction books. *See also* PUBLISHING HOUSES; SHIBATA SHÔ.

KAJII MOTOJIRÔ (1901–1932). Kajii Motojirô, best known for his lyrical short stories, was diagnosed with tuberculosis as a college student. He nonetheless continued attending Tokyo Imperial University, where he helped found the literary magazine ***Aozora*** (Blue Sky), in which he published his most widely recognized story, "*Remon*" (1925; tr. *The Lemon*, 1988). Tuberculosis took his life at age 31. *See also* MARUYAMA KAORU; MIYOSHI TATSUJI.

***KAJIN NO KIGÛ*.** The first two volumes of the eventual 16 that comprised the unfinished novel *Kajin no kigû* (1885–97; tr. *Strange Encounters with Beautiful Women*, 1948) were published soon after author Shiba Shiro returned from studying abroad in the United States. Written under the pen name **Tôkai Sanshi**, Shiba used the semiautobiographical **political narrative** as a pulpit from which to preach his idealistic vision of Japan as a strong, compassionate democracy. *Kajin no kigû* follows the protagonist as he sees and befriends two beautiful American girls in Philadelphia and, through them, meets others from China, Spain, and Ireland. His peregrinations allow the author to explain the curiosities of foreign lands as well as offer possible models for Japan to follow.

***KAKURE KIRISHITAN* (HIDDEN CHRISTIANS).** Following the **Tokugawa** proscription of Christianity in the 17th century, many practicing Japanese Christians took their beliefs underground, and for two centuries secretly practiced a modified form of Catholicism. Their existence became known after Japan opened to the West, when foreign priests discovered and met with them in and around **Nagasaki**. The proscription had not been lifted, however, and Japanese professing to be Christian were imprisoned, tortured, or exiled until 1873 when the ban was officially lifted after Japan encountered fierce pressure from overseas governments. Hidden Christians play an important role in many modern novels. **Akutagawa Ryûnosuke**, **Endô Shûsaku**, and **Shimao Toshio**, among others, write of the *kakure kirishitan* in their stories. *See also CHINMOKU*; CHRISTIAN LITERATURE.

KANAGAKI ROBUN (1829–1894). Kanagaki Robun was the pen name of Nozaki Bunzô, author and journalist whose activity spanned the **Tokugawa** and Meiji periods. Two of his representative works, *Seiyôdôchû hizakurige* (Shank's Mare to the Western Seas, 1870–76) and *Aguranabe* (1871; tr. *The Beef Eater*, 1956), deal with the opening of Japan to the West and the conflicts between tradition and modernization. He continued writing light fiction while enduring criticism during the **Meiji Restoration**. Aside from novels, Kanagaki is known for his illustrated biographies, including an **adapted** biography of Ulysses S. Grant published on the occasion of former U.S. President Grant's visit to Japan in 1879. He also made shop signs in his youth and later joined painter Kawanabe Kyôsai (1831–89) to create Japan's first ***manga*** magazine, *Eshinbun Nihonji* (Illustrated Japan News).

KANEKO MISUZU (1903–1930). Kaneko Misuzu, given name Teru, was a poetess and songwriter from Nagato, Yamaguchi Prefecture, who wrote mainly for children and has been compared to Christina Rossetti. Her hometown was a sardine-fishing village, and scenes of fishing and the sea fill her **poetry**. After the birth of her child, she divorced her husband, who had contracted venereal disease from the pleasure quarters. Subsequent custody battles led her to commit **suicide**, with her final request being that her ex-husband allow Kaneko's mother to rear the child. During her short life, she wrote more than 500 poems, and, though she was forgotten for a time, her poetry was rediscovered in 1982, and one of her poems, "*Watashi to kotori to suzu to*" (Me, a Bird, and a Bell) is now read in the Japanese national elementary school curriculum. In recent years, her life story has been dramatized in film, drama, and on television. *See also* CHILDREN'S LITERATURE.

KANEKO MITSUHARU (1895–1975). Kaneko Mitsuharu was a poet from Aichi Prefecture. After being educated at the Akeboshi Gakuen private school, he published his first **poetry** magazine, *Kôzu*, at the age of 21. Three years later he published his first anthology of poems, *Akatsuchi no ie* (House of Clay, 1916). At age 62 Kaneko wrote his autobiography, *Shijin* (1957; tr. *Shijin*, 1988). Known for his rebellious spirit embodied in the famous line "to oppose is to live," Kaneko was critical of the **Meiji Restoration** and even kept his son sick during World War II in order to evade conscription.

KARAKI JUNZÔ (1904–1980). Karaki Junzô was a **literary critic** and philosopher from Nagano Prefecture. After graduating from Tokyo University, he took teaching jobs in Nagano, Manchuria, and Hôsei University. Renowned for his research on **Mori Ôgai**, he received the **Yomiuri Prize** in 1955 for his essay "*Chûsei no bungaku*" (Medieval Literature). After World War II, he helped edit the **literary journal** *Tenbô* (Outlook).

KARATANI KÔJIN (1941–). Karatani Kôjin, given name Yoshio, is a **literary critic** and philosopher of global fame. He graduated from Tokyo University, and at the age of 27 he gained attention in literary circles for "*Ishiki to shizen*" (Consciousness and Nature, 1969), his essay on **Natsume Sôseki**. Three years later he published the essay "*Ifu suru ningen*" (Human in Awe, 1972) and was invited to become a visiting professor at Yale University. Karatani has been nicknamed "The Thinking Machine" for the variety and depth of topics he has analyzed. He has also taught at Hosei University in Tokyo, Columbia University, and Kinki University (Osaka). Karatani's *Nihon kindai bungaku no kigen* (1980; tr. *Origins of Modern Japanese Literature*, 1993) has been translated into English, and in 2007 he gave a lecture at Stanford University. He has also written extensively on **Marxism**.

KASAI ZENZÔ (1887–1928). Kasai Zenzô was a novelist born in Aomori Prefecture. When he was two years old his parents died and he moved to his grandparents' home. After finishing elementary school, he became a merchant's apprentice and took many different jobs. Wanting to write, he moved to Tokyo and audited classes at Tôyô and Waseda universities and there became friends with **Hirotsu Kazuo**, with whom he founded the **literary journal** *Kiseki* (Miracle) in 1912. Kasai began his career publishing the story "*Kanashiki chichi*" (1912; tr. *The Sad Father*, 1986) in the first issue of *Kiseki*. Several lean years later he published a collection of writings titled *Ko o tsurete* (With Children in Tow, 1918) in the literary magazine *Shinchô* (New Tide) that established him as an author. Most of Kasai's works were **I-Novels** based on his personal experiences, containing themes of poverty, illness, loneliness, and alcoholism. Scandal over an illegitimate child took its toll, and he died at the age of 41 of tuberculosis.

KATÔ NORIHIRO (1948–). Katô Norihiro is a **literary critic** from Yamagata Prefecture. He graduated from Tokyo University and began his career with the essay "*Amerika no kage*" (The American Shadow, 1985). He has worked for the National **Diet Library** and as a professor at Meiji University and Waseda University. A regular publisher of criticism, he serves as a member of the selection committee for two **literary awards**.

KATÔ SHÛICHI (1919–). Katô Shûichi is a novelist, literary and social critic, medical doctor, and cultural scholar from Tokyo. He graduated in medicine from Tokyo University and while still studying there joined with **Nakamura Shin'ichirô** and **Fukunaga Takehiko** to found the **literary journal** *Matinée Poétique* in which he published

poetry, literary criticism, and novels. After World War II, he became a self-sufficient writer. In 1951, Katô traveled abroad to France to study medicine but continued to contribute to literary journals while there. In 1956, he wrote one of his most famous works, the essay *Zasshu bunka* (Hybrid Culture), which looked at historical materialism from a **Marxist** perspective. In more recent years, he has been a guest professor at many universities and succeeded **Hayashi Tatsuo** as editor-in-chief of the Heibonsha *Sekai Daihyakka jiten* (World Encyclopedia).

KAWABATA YASUNARI (1899–1972). Kawabata Yasunari was a short story writer and novelist who became the first Japanese to win the **Nobel Prize** for Literature in 1968. Orphaned at age two, Kawabata subsequently lost all other close relatives by age 15. After boarding school, Kawabata attended Tokyo Imperial University. During his career, Kawabata wrote numerous well-known novels and short stories, including ***Izu no Odoriko*** (1926; tr. *The Izu Dancer*, 1955), ***Yukiguni*** (1948; tr. *Snow Country*, 1956), ***Senbazuru*** (1949–51; tr. *Thousand Cranes*, 1958), and *Meijin* (1942; tr. *The Master of Go*, 1972). He was part of the **neoperceptionist** school of writing, which he helped define. Kawabata committed **suicide** in 1972, and the **Kawabata Yasunari Prize** was established in 1974 in his honor. *See also* HEARN, LAFCADIO; JAPAN P.E.N. CLUB; MODERNISM; PSYCHOLOGICAL LITERATURE; SHIMAKI KENSAKU; TACHIHARA MASAAKI; WAR LITERATURE; YOKOMITSU RIICHI.

KAWABATA YASUNARI PRIZE FOR LITERATURE. The Kawabata Yasunari Prize for Literature (*Kawabata Yasunari bungaku shô)* was established in 1973 by the **Kawabata Yasunari** Memorial Association to honor Japan's first **Nobel Prize**–winning novelist. The Nobel Prize award money is used to finance the Kawabata Prize, which is presented annually to the year's most accomplished work of short fiction. The winner receives a certificate, a commemorative gift, and a cash award of one million yen. Notable recipients include **Minakami Tsutomu**, **Yasuoka Shôtarô**, and **Sata Ineko**. *See also* LITERARY AWARDS.

KAWAKAMI BIZAN (1869–1908). Kawakami Bizan, given name Akira, was a **Meiji** novelist who attended Tokyo Imperial University but dropped out and joined the **Ken'yûsha** literary circle. Noted for his novels *Shokikan* (The Secretary, 1985–86) and *Kan'on iwa* (The Buddha Crag, 1906), Kawakami committed **suicide** in 1908. *See also* OZAKI KÔYÔ; TRAGIC NOVELS.

KAWAKAMI OTOJIRÔ (1864–1911). Kawakami Otojirô, given name Otokichi, was a Japanese political activist, actor, theater impresario, and comedian. He was born in Hakata, Kyushu, and made his public name as a "hooligan" (*sôshi*) performing ballads and chants for the **Freedom and People's Rights Movement**. His signature song from this period, "*Oppekepe*," satirized the wealthy Meiji oligarchy and underscored the plight of the poor. He studied for a time to be a professional storyteller in the ***yose***, married former geisha Sadayakko, and together formed a theatrical troupe that toured the United States and Europe at the turn of the 20th century and was seen by a number of American and European artists and musicians caught up in the tide of ***japonisme***. Upon returning to Japan, Kawakami staged several Western plays in Tokyo and opened a school for actresses. He collapsed and died in midperformance at age 47. *See also* MODERN THEATER; THEATER REFORM.

KAWAMURA MINATO (1951–). Kawamura Minato is a **literary critic** and professor of international culture at Hosei University. He began his literary career by winning the Gunzô Newcomer Prize in 1980. He started out writing on ancient and modern Japanese literature, but has expanded his focus to include Korean literature and culture. His leftist leanings sometimes put him at odds with major critics. He published the study *Nan'yo Karafuto no Nihon bungaku* (Japanese Literature of the South Sea Islands and Sakhalin, 1994). *See also* MARXISM.

KAWASHIMA CHÛNOSUKE (1853–1938). Kawashima Chûnosuke is best known for his **translation** of Jules Verne's *Around the World in 80 Days*. Kawashima worked as an interpreter for a trading company at the time, and in 1878 published the work, the first of Verne's works to be translated into Japanese, at his own expense. His translation was one of the first correspondent—as opposed to

adaptive—translations of a foreign literary texts. *See also* SCIENCE FICTION.

KAWATAKE MOKUAMI (1816–1893). Kawatake Mokuami, born Yoshimura Yoshisaburô, was a Japanese *kabuki* playwright whose prolific and varied works included short dance pieces, period plays (*jidaimono*), contemporary genre pieces (*sewamono*), tragedies and comedies, as well as **adaptations** of Western stories. He was famous for his *shiranamimono*, plays featuring sympathetic or tragic rogues and thieves. Many of his protagonist roles were written for specific actors. His works, including *Momijigari* (Viewing the Autumn Foliage, 1887), continue to dominate the *kabuki* repertoire today. See *also* KAWATAKE SHINSHICHI III; THEATER REFORM.

KAWATAKE SHINSHICHI III (1842–1901). Kawatake Shinshichi III was born in the Kanda district of Edo (now Tokyo) and became a leading pupil of *kabuki* playwright **Kawatake Mokuami.** Following his mentor's death, he became the foremost Meiji playwright, with roughly 80 plays to his name. He **adapted** many of his stories from the oral storytelling stage (***yose***), including works, such as *Kaidan botandôrô* (The Ghost Tale of the Peony Lantern, 1892), by the famous ***rakugo*** storyteller **San'yûtei Enchô.** Many of his plays are still performed on the *kabuki* stage today. *See also KÔDAN*; THEATER REFORM.

KAZUO ISHIGURO. *See* ISHIGURO KAZUO.

KEIKOKU BIDAN. *Keikoku Bidan* (Inspiring Tales of Statesmanship, 1883) is an adaptive **political novel** by Yano Ryûkei published during the height of the **Freedom and People's Rights Movement.** In the tradition of **Tokugawa literature,** the novel addresses many contemporary political concerns but is reset in a different time and place in order to evade possible **censorship.** The work, written in a mixture of styles, contains a number of tales from Greek history, including the rise and fall of Thebes, which resonated with the contemporary world of Japanese politics. Despite its unevenness, it was very popular and inspired many young readers, including **Tsubouchi Shôyô,**

to try their hand at writing novels. *See also* ADAPTIVE TRANSLATIONS; TRANSLATION.

KEITAI SHÔSETSU. *See* CELL-PHONE NOVELS.

KEN'YÛSHA. The Ken'yûsha (Friends of the Ink Stone), the first modern Japanese writers' society, was founded in 1885 by **Ozaki Kôyô**. Other members included **Kawakami Bizan**, **Yamada Bimyô**, Ishibashi Shian (1867–1927), and Maruoka Kyuka (1865–1927). Ozaki's classicism heavily influenced the works of member **Izumi Kyôka** and was widely published in the *Yomiuri* newspaper. While championing **naturalism** and **realism**, the group introduced Western styles and themes in a venue outside the traditional publishing firms. Famous works by Ozaki that represent the spirit of the Ken'yûsha include *Konjiki yasha* (1897–1903; tr. *The Gold Demon*, 2005) and *Tajô takon* (Passions and Regrets, 1896). The group disbanded shortly after Ozaki's death in 1903.

KIKUCHI KAN (1888–1948). Kikuchi Kan, given name Hiroshi, was a short story writer and publisher born in Takamatsu, Kagawa Prefecture. A colleague of **Akutagawa Ryûnosuke** and **Kume Masao**, Kikuchi helped found the magazine *Shinshichô* (New Trends of Thought) in 1917. Besides pursuing his own writing career, Kikuchi also helped to establish the Japan Writer's Association and the **Akutagawa** and **Naoki prizes** along with the publishing company Bungei Shunjû, which publishes the literary magazines ***Bungei shunjû*** (Literary Chronicle) and ***Bungakkai*** (Literary World). He also founded the **Kikuchi Kan Prize** in 1938. *See also BUNDAN*; YAMAMOTO YÛZÔ.

KIKUCHI KAN PRIZE. The Kikuchi Kan Prize (*Kikuchi Kan shô*) is a **literary award** first proposed by **Kikuchi Kan** that recognizes achievement among senior authors and is sponsored by the **Association for the Promotion of Japanese Literature**. It was first established in 1938 for authors older than age 45. Discontinued six years later, it was revived in 1952 at the death of Kikuchi Kan. The current prize now recognizes achievements in arts and literature as well as film and other genres. The winner receives a table clock and one million yen. Notable recipients include **Masamune Hakuchô**, **Inoue Hisashi**, **Inoue Yasushi**, **Kaikô Takeshi**, and **Uno Chiyo**.

KINOSHITA JUNJI (1914–2006). Kinoshita Junji, playwright and **translator** from Tokyo, graduated from Tokyo University where he studied Shakespeare. After World War II, he taught at Meiji University and wrote folk plays on the side. His most famous play, ***Yûzuru*** (1949; tr. *Twilight Crane*, 1952), was performed in 1949, followed shortly after by *Fûrô* (Wind and Waves). He was able to create a new style that fused together components of **modern theater**, *kabuki*, *nô*, and *kyôgen* and received the **Yomiuri Prize** for *Shigosen no matsuri* (1978; tr. *Requiem on the Great Meridian*, 2000). *See also* THEATER REFORM.

KINOSHITA NAOE (1869–1937). Kinoshita Naoe, socialist, activist, and author, graduated from Waseda University, worked as a newspaper reporter and lawyer, and was baptized a Christian a few years later. Shortly thereafter, he began to take a firm stand on issues of mine pollution, women's rights, and universal suffrage. A pacifist prior to and during the Russo-Japanese War, he published the antiwar novel ***Hi no hashira*** (1903–4; tr. *Pillar of Fire*, 1972), writing for the masses in the ***genbun itchi*** style. *See also* FEMINISM; MILITARISM; NOGAMI YAEKO; WAR LITERATURE.

KISHIDA KUNIO (1890–1954). Kishida Kunio was an author, playwright, **translator**, and director widely recognized as one of the founders of **modern theater** in Japan. He studied French literature and modern drama at Tokyo University and later traveled to France in the early 1920s to study the history of French drama. Upon returning to Japan, he published many plays in **literary journals**, such as *Furui omocha* (Old Toys, 1924) and *Chiroru no aki* (1924; tr. *Autumn in the Tyrol*, 1967). In 1937, he founded the *Bungaku-za* (Literary Theater Company), which produced many famous actors and actresses. The *Kishida Kunio gikyoku shô* (Kishida Kunio Prize for Drama) is named in his honor and is the most prestigious drama award. Kishida died of a stroke suffered during a dress rehearsal in a Tokyo theater. *See also* THEATER REFORM.

KITA MORIO (1927–). Kita Morio is the pen name of Saitô Sôkichi, Tokyo-born novelist, essayist and psychiatrist. He is the second son of the poet **Saitô Mokichi**. Kita was relatively uninterested in literature in his youth but became attached to the works of Thomas Mann in high school. While working as a psychiatrist in a hospital run by his older brother, Kita wrote *Yoru to kiri no sumi de* (In the Corner of Night and Fog, 1960), which garnered him an **Akutagawa Ryûnosuke Prize**. Kita wrote the bestseller *Dokutoru Manbô kôkaiki* (1960; tr. *Doctor Manbo at the Sea*, 1987) while working on a fishing boat as the crew doctor. The novel incorporated American-style absurdist humor. He is a popular writer and essayist, particularly among youth. *See also* TSUJI KUNIO.

KITAHARA HAKUSHÛ (1885–1942). Kitahara Hakushû, given name Ryûkichi, was a popular ***tanka*** poet. Born in Fukuoka Prefecture, he attended Waseda University but dropped out to write **poetry**. Much of his early poetry was published in ***Myôjô*** (Venus) until he formed his own literary group, the *Pan no kai* (The Society of Pan). In 1918, he joined the ***Akai Tori*** (Red Bird) **literary journal**, for which he began collecting children's songs. He published several volumes of Japanese children's song lyrics as well as translations of English nursery rhymes. Kitahara died in 1942 of complications from diabetes. *See also* CHILDREN'S LITERATURE.

KITAMURA TÔKOKU (1868–1894). Kitamura Tôkoku, given name Montarô, was a **Romantic** poet and essayist. Kitamura held extreme political views that led to his expulsion from Waseda University, but he abandoned his political activities before becoming a writer. Many of Kitamura's poems and essays broke from traditional Japanese Buddhist/Shinto thought in favor of Western philosophy, and his writing sometimes reflects his wife's Christian views. Kitamura helped to launch the **literary journal *Bungakkai*** (Literary World) a year before he committed **suicide**. *See also* BUDDHIST LITERATURE; POETRY.

KOBAYASHI HIDEO (1902–1983). Kobayashi Hideo, author and scholar, was one of the foremost Japanese **literary critics** of the 20th century. Kobayashi initially studied French literature at Tokyo

Imperial University. Many of his works were published in the journal ***Bungakkai*** (Literary World). As a critic he praised **Kikuchi Kan** and **Shiga Naoya** and greatly criticized **Akutagawa Ryûnosuke**, as well as the genre of the **I-Novel**. He was a strongly outspoken proponent of the **war** in China. After the war, he continued as a bestselling author, made radio broadcasts, and took part in roundtable discussions with scientists and other artists. He was awarded the **Order of Cultural Merit** in 1967.

KOBAYASHI TAKIJI (1903–1933). Kobayashi Takiji was a renowned author of **proletarian literature**. His most famous work, the novel *Kanikôsen* (1929; tr. *The Factory Ship*, 1956), detailed the oppression of Hokkaido fishermen and the inner working of unions. He joined the Japanese Communist Party in 1931 and two years later, at age 29, was beaten to death by police during an interrogation. *See also* MARXISM; THOUGHT POLICE.

KÔDA AYA (1904–1990). Kôda Aya was a novelist and essayist and the second daughter of author **Kôda Rohan**. Following her father's death shortly after World War II, she began writing her memories of him in essays that were published and well received. She started writing novels and published *Nagareru* (Flowing, 1955), which established her status as an author and was later adapted into a **film**. She also published the novel *Kuroi suso* (1955; tr. *The Black Kimono*, 1970), which won the **Yomiuri Prize**. *See also* FEMINISM; WOMEN IN LITERATURE.

KÔDA ROHAN (1867–1947). Kôda Rohan, given name Shigeyuki, was the author of two **Meiji** stories, *Fûryûbutsu* (The Elegant Buddha, 1889) and *Gojû no tô* (1891–92; tr. *Pagoda*, 1959). His **Romantic**, gothic style paired well with that of his contemporary, **Ozaki Kôyô**. Kôda was one of the first persons to be awarded the **Order of Cultural Merit** when it was established in 1937. He was the father of novelist **Kôda Aya**. *See also* PSEUDOCLASSICISM; TAMURA TOSHIKO.

KÔDAN. *Kôdan* is a style of traditional oral storytelling dating from the 17th century. Similar to the style of storytelling performed by *biwa* (lute) players in feudal Japan, this form of drama involves a solitary performer, called a *kôdanshi*, who kneels at a small table, called a *shakudai*, upon which is an open literary text, and taps out a rhythm with a small folded fan while he or she alternately reads from and comments on the text. The *kôdanshi*'s repertoire contains tales of **war** and martial valor and the occasional ghost story, and the storyteller uses a unique chanted tone when reading and imitates colloquial speech when commenting to enhance the audience's reception of the tale.

The art form, which is performed rhythmically but lacks musical accompaniment, flourished through the beginning of the 20th century, and, along with ***rakugo*** (its comic counterpart), contributed to the development of modern Japanese narrative through *sokkibon*, or **shorthand** transcriptions of oral stories, that were published in the late 19th century. Hundreds of these transcribed tales appeared during the **Meiji** period, training a new market of readers and helping establish vernacular narrative style for literary writing. With the advent of **film** and the demise of ***yose*** performance halls, *kôdan* declined and is performed today in only a handful of theaters in Japan's urban centers. *See also* ADAPTATION; ADAPTIVE TRANSLATIONS; *BENSHI*; *GENBUN ITCHI*; KAWATAKE SHINSHICHI III; TAKUSARI KÔKI.

KOGEKIJÔ ENGEKI. *See* MODERN THEATER.

KOIZUMI YAKUMO. *See* HEARN, LAFCADIO.

KOJIMA NOBUO (1915–2006). Kojima Nobuo was a novelist, playwright, essayist, **translator**, and **literary critic** from Gifu Prefecture who graduated from Tokyo University. After completing a military tour of northeastern China, he started writing while teaching English at a high school in Tokyo and later at Meiji University. Kojima published *Amerikan sukûru* (1954; tr. *The American School*, 1977), which won the **Akutagawa Ryûnosuke Prize**, and his *Hôyô kazoku* (1965; tr. *Embracing Family*, 2005) was awarded the **Tanizaki Jun'ichirô Prize**. Kojima is considered to be a member of the **Third Generation** of **postwar** writers, and also won the **Noma Prize** and the **Yomiuri Prize**, among many other awards. *See also* MODERN THEATER.

KOKKAI TOSHOKAN. *See* DIET LIBRARY.

KOKORO. *Kokoro* (1914; tr. *Kokoro: A Novel*, 1957) is a semi-epistolary novel by **Natsume Sôseki**. First published in serial form in the *Asahi* newspaper, *Kokoro* deals with the tensions of modernity and its concomitant isolation. It is divided into three sections. The first, narrated by a character known only as "I," discusses his friendship with an older man he calls "Sensei" (teacher or master). In the second section, the narrator travels home to the countryside due to his father's failing health, where he receives a letter from Sensei. The entire third section, comprising nearly half the novel, is that singular letter, in which Sensei finally tells the narrator the story of the love triangle that led to the death of his childhood friend, K. Sensei then, out of loyalty and in the spirit of tradition, commits **suicide** in conjunction with the death of the Meiji emperor. *See also BUNGEI EIGA*; FILM AND LITERATURE; I-NOVELS.

KOKUBUNGAKU KENKYÛ SHIRYÔKAN. *See* NATIONAL INSTITUTE OF JAPANESE LITERATURE.

KÔNO TAEKO (1926–). Kôno Taeko is a novelist and **literary critic** from Osaka. During World War II, she attended Osaka University and, after graduating and upon reading Emily Brontë's *Wuthering Heights*, decided to become a professional author. She worked with **Niwa Fumio** on his **literary journal** and won the **Akutagawa Ryûnosuke Prize** for her novel *Kani* (1963; tr. *Crabs*, 1982). She wrote *Fui no koe* (A Sudden Voice, 1968) and won the **Yomiuri Prize.** Kôno champions the style of **Tanizaki Jun'ichirô** and has served on the selection committee of the prize named in his honor. *See also* FEMINISM; WOMEN IN LITERATURE.

KOREAN LITERATURE. *See ZAINICHI* LITERATURE.

KÔYA HIJIRI. "*Kôya hijiri*" (1900; tr. *The Kôya Priest*, 1959–60) is **Izumi Kyôka**'s most famous story, combining strong **Romanticist** elements of **Tokugawa** period fiction with colloquial folklore. The gothic narrative features an itinerant young priest who takes a wrong turn at a crossroads on his journey over the mountains in the Japan

Alps. As evening settles in, he finds himself seeking shelter at an isolated home that proves to be inhabited by a mysterious woman who appears to be able to talk with animals. The priest, though tempted by her beauty, does not yield and endures a raucous, haunted night. On his arrival back in civilization, he determines to abandon the priesthood and return to live with her, but then learns that she is a sorceress who turns humans into animals after they succumb to her charms. *See also* WOMEN IN LITERATURE.

KÔYA PRIEST, THE. *See KÔYA HIJIRI.*

KUBO SAKAE (1900–1958). Kubo Sakae was a poet and playwright from Hokkaido. He graduated from Tokyo Imperial University in German literature. His most famous work is the critically acclaimed **Marxist** play *Kazanbaichi* (1937; tr. *Land of Volcanic Ash*, 1986), which won a theater prize. He also won a **poetry** prize named after **Kitamura Tôkoku** for *Sannin no bokushô no hanashi* (The Story of the Three Lumberjacks). *See also* MODERN THEATER.

KUME MASAO (1891–1952). Kume Masao was a novelist, playwright, **literary critic**, and ***haiku*** poet (under the pseudonym Santei). He had a natural talent for *haiku* and attended Tokyo Imperial University, studying under **Natsume Sôseki** with **Akutagawa Ryûnosuke** and **Kikuchi Kan** as notable classmates. He made his debut as a playwright with *Gyûnyûya no kyôdai* (The Milkman's Brother, 1914), which was well received. Two years later he published his first novel, *Chichi no shi* (My Father's Death, 1916) and in 1918 cofounded the *Kokumin bungeikai* (People's Arts Movement) with **Osanai Kaoru** and Kubota Mantarô (1889–1963). In 1925, he coined the term *junbungaku* (pure literature) and argued that the **I-Novel** is *junbungaku*. *See also* LITERARY CRITICISM; MODERN THEATER.

KUNIKIDA DOPPÔ (1871–1908). Kunikida Doppô, given name Tatsuo, was an early author of **Romantic** novels and **poetry** but went on to become one of the founders of Japanese **naturalism**. Kunikida attended Waseda University, but his politically defiant attitude led to his expulsion before he graduated. He became a Christian at age 21, and reflections of his religion can be seen in his later writings. Kunikida's works include *Musashino* (1901; tr. *Musashino*, 1983) *Azamaukazaru no ki* (An Honest Diary, 1893), and "*Haru no tori*" (1904; tr. *Spring Birds*, 1954). Kunikida died of tuberculosis at age 36.

KUNSHÔ. *See* ORDER OF CULTURAL MERIT.

KURAHASHI YUMIKO (1935–2005). Kurahashi Yumiko, née Kumagai, was a novelist and author born in Kôchi Prefecture. She graduated from a dental hygiene school and was accepted into Meiji University where she also attended graduate school. While in graduate school she published the novel *Parutai* (1960; tr. *Partei*, 1961) in the Meiji University newspaper. *Parutai* was reprinted in the **literary journal *Bungakkai*** (Literary World) and was nominated for the **Akutagawa Ryûnosuke Prize**. The following year it was published as a novel and received the **Women's Literature Prize**, and in 1963 she was awarded the **Tamura Toshiko** Prize. After marrying a television producer, she devoted her time to raising their two daughters, but came back into the literary world in the late 1970s and received the Izumi Kyôka Literary Prize in 1983. Toward the end of her life, she turned her attention to **translating children's literature**. She died of heart disease.

KURATA HYAKUZÔ (1891–1943). Kurata Hyakuzô was an essayist and playwright who dealt with the topic of religion. Though raised in Tokyo, he spent most of his adult life in the Inland Sea region. His major literary works include the best-selling *Shukke to sono deshi* (1917; tr. *The Priest and the Disciples*, 1955), which was a play based on the story of the Japanese **Buddhist** priest Shinran (1173–1263). His other most popular work was a collection of essays titled *Ai to ninshiki to no shuppatsu* (The Beginning of Love and Understanding, 1921) that touched on topics of love, sex, and religion. *See also* MODERN THEATER.

KUROI AME. When author **Ibuse Masuji** was asked about how he created his **atomic bomb** novel *Kuroi ame* (1965; tr. *Black Rain*, 1968), he replied that he took actual documentation, such as letters, journals, and reports, and then raked them together into a fictional story. *Kuroi ame* is a novel about the physical struggles and later social discrimination suffered by atomic bomb survivors. Written in journal form, the novel details the conditions in Hiroshima immediately after the bombing and a number of years later using the characters of Shigematsu Shizuma, his wife, and his niece Yasuko. The niece, orphaned and of marriageable age, finds herself unable to conclude an arranged marriage even several years later owing to rumors of her having been in Hiroshima when the bomb was dropped and the fear of radiation sickness affecting possible offspring. Shigematsu and his wife begin copying their journals from the days surrounding the bombing in an attempt to prove that Yasuko was not exposed to radiation. Another suitor's prospect falls through just as Yasuko reveals that she does, indeed, have radiation sickness. Though somber in plot, the story is filled with Ibuse's characteristic humor and hope for humanity.

KUROI SENJI (1932–). Kuroi Senji is the pen name of Osabe Shunjirô, a novelist from Tokyo who graduated in economics from Tokyo University. He worked as a salaryman while writing novels and was an **Akutagawa Ryûnosuke Prize** candidate in 1968. The following year he published *Jikan* (Time, 1969) and won the **Tanizaki Jun'ichirô Prize** for *Gunsei* (1984; tr. *Life in the Cul-de-Sac*, 2001). He also has won the **Yomiuri Prize** and the **Noma Prize** and currently serves as president of the Japan Writer's Association as well as a member of the selection committee for the Akutagawa Prize.

KUROSHIMA DENJI (1898–1943). Kuroshima Denji was born on an island in Japan's Inland Sea. Conscripted into the army in 1919, he returned to Japan and joined the **proletarian literature** movement and wrote of his experiences in Siberia. Kuroshima's works include numerous short stories and a novel, *Busôseru shigai* (Militarized Streets, 1930), which describes Japanese aggression against China. *See also* MILITARISM; WAR LITERATURE.

KUROTOKAGE. *Kurotokage* (Black Lizard, 1895) was **Hirotsu Ryûrô**'s second novel. Following the lead of his first **serious novel**, ***Hemeden*** (Cross-Eyed Den, 1895), the story follows the life of Otsuga, a woman with tragically repulsive black blotches on her face. She marries a man named Yotarô, becoming his seventh successive wife, and has a child with him. Yotarô's lustful father makes advances on Otsuga, which had driven away Yotarô's previous wives. Otsuga lashes back, poisoning him in order to protect her child. Otsuga then commits **suicide**, throwing herself into a well. *See also* WOMEN IN LITERATURE.

KUWABARA TAKEO (1904–1988). Kuwabara Takeo, born in Fukui Prefecture, was a researcher of French literature and culture. He graduated from Kyoto University in 1926 and was hired as a professor at Tohoku University in 1943. Five years later he took a position at Kyoto University and spent the rest of his life bringing French literature and **literary criticism** to Japan and **translating** many works into Japanese. In 1987, he was awarded the **Order of Cultural Merit** for his lifetime contribution to cultural research.

– L –

LIGHT AND DARKNESS. *See MEIAN.*

LIGHT NOVELS. "Light novels" (*raito noberu*) comprise a new genre of young adult novels with *anime-* or ***manga***-style illustrations. The term light novel, often shortened to *ranobe* or *rainobe*, was coined in the 1990s on a **science fiction** Internet forum. These prose (as opposed to graphic) novels are written with the young adult reader in mind, containing a large percentage of dialogue and the occasional reading gloss. They are often serialized in magazines, and many have been adapted for television. Popular light novel genres include romance, science fiction, fantasy, mystery, and horror. Their enormous popularity among Japanese youth and young adults has led to greater numbers appearing in translation, such as Achi Tarô's (1978–) *Kage kara mamoru!* (Next Door Ninja). *See also* CELLPHONE NOVELS.

LITERARY AWARDS. Japanese literary awards (*bungaku shô*) honor exceptional authors and their works in various categories. Some, including the **Bungakkai** Newcomer Award, target fledgling writers, and among these awards the **Edogawa Rampô** Prize offers an annuity along with publishing contracts. Other prizes target up-and-coming authors and, along with prize monies, are meant to help the winner's career. Three prizes—the **Akutagawa Ryûnosuke Prize**, the **Mishima Yukio** Prize, and the **Noma Prize**—are known as the "triple crown" of newcomer prizes, but to date only one author, **Shôno Yoriko**, has been awarded all three. Newspaper publishing companies also award prizes, including the **Yomiuri Prize for Literature**, the Mainichi Publishing Cultural Prize, and the Osaragi Jirô Prize given by the *Asahi* newspaper. Some of the newspaper prizes are given exclusively for novels, and others have more open criteria; other literary prizes are open to any author. Some focus on genres other than the novel, such as the **Tanizaki Jun'ichirô Prize**, which can include dramas, the Kobayashi Hideo Prize for criticism and essays, the Ôya Prize for nonfiction, and the H-Shi (Mr. H) Prize, named after sponsor Hirasawa Teijirô (1904–91), for anthologies of modern poetry. *See also* DAZAI OSAMU PRIZE; ITÔ SEI PRIZE FOR LITERATURE; KAWABATA YASUNARI PRIZE FOR LITERATURE; KIKUCHI KAN PRIZE; LITERARY CRITICISM; NOBEL PRIZE FOR LITERATURE; ODA SAKUNOSUKE PRIZE; ORDER OF CULTURAL MERIT; WOMEN'S LITERATURE PRIZE; YOSHIKAWA EIJI PRIZE FOR LITERATURE.

LITERARY CRITICISM. Japan has a rich heritage of literary criticism dating from early classical times, with the preface to the *Kokinshû* (ca. 920) addressing the meaning and function of **poetry**. During the **Tokugawa** period, Motoori Norinaga (1730–1801) wrote so forcefully on *The Tale of Genji* (ca. 1008) and the nature of literature that his influence was still strongly felt among writers and critics of the **Meiji** period. Modern literary criticism first appeared as long essays and prefaces written by Meiji writers, especially ***Shôsetsu shinzui*** (1885; tr. *The Essence of the Novel*, 1956), a critique of dogmatism and call for narrative reform published by **Tsubouchi Shôyô**. Behind the essay were several contemporary catalysts: the ***genbun itchi*** debates from the 1870s surrounding how to bring the written language into greater correlation with spoken Japanese; **adaptations** and **translations** of Western literature and poetry that challenged assumptions about styles and the role of literature; Western philosophy and theories, such as **realism** and **naturalism**, that were reflected in both the literature and translations of Western criticism; and a polarizing tension between traditionalists and modernizers that existed among writers and intellectuals.

The tendency to polarize arguments in literary criticism was first demonstrated in a heated exchange of published articles launched by **Mori Ôgai** and Shôyô in 1891–92, wherein they argued the finer points of categorizing Japanese literature. Other critics and writers followed suit, establishing this kind of formal, published debate, called *ronsô*, as a staple of the Japanese critical world. Writers often formed groups that shared similar theoretical enthusiasms, including the *Seitô* (Bluestockings; feminist) and ***Shirakaba*** (White Birch; humanist) schools. Three prominent critic/novelists of the first half of the 20th century were **Masamune Hakuchô**, **Hirotsu Kazuo**, and **Satô Haruo**. By the 1920s critics were less confrontational about the fundamentals of literature, focusing instead on specific authors or works. By the 1930s, **Marxism** had become the dominant ideology of literary criticism, which reflects the contemporary emergence of **proletarian literature**. One critic in particular, **Kobayashi Hideo**, exerted a strong and long-lasting influence on Japanese criticism from the 1930s until his death in 1983.

Though the Marxist mode dominated Japanese criticism well into the latter half of the century, dozens of schools of critical practice have emerged, including comparative approaches. Japanese critics and scholars are quick to assimilate new ideas; critic and philosopher **Karatani Kôjin**, in particular, has risen to prominence with his fusion of Japanese and French critical theory. In addition to formal books, essays, and published *ronsô* debates, criticism in Japan also appears as individual *zuihitsu* (contemplative, informal essays) and *zadankai* (informal roundtable discussions) that are transcribed and published in **literary journals**. *See also* ABE AKIRA; AGAWA HIROYUKI; AKIYAMA SHUN; ARIYOSHI SAWAKO; EDOGAWA RAMPÔ; FUTABATEI SHIMEI; HAGIWARA SAKUTARÔ; HAYASHI TATSUO; ISHIKAWA JUN; ISODA KÔICHI; ITÔ SACHIO; ITÔ SEI; KAIKÔ TAKESHI; KARAKI JUNZÔ; KATÔ NORIHIRO; KATÔ SHÛICHI; KAWAMURA MINATO; KOJIMA NOBUOI; KÔNO TAEKO; KUME MASAO; KUWABARA TAKEO; MAEDA AI; MARUYA SAIICHI; MARUYAMA KAORU; MASAOKA SHIKI; MIYOSHI TATSUJI; MIZUMURA MINAE;

NAGAYO YOSHIRÔ; NAKAGAMI KENJI; NAKAMURA MITSUO; NAKANO SHIGEHARU; NAOKI SANJÛGO; NISHIWAKI JUNZABURÔ; NOMA HIROSHI; ÔBA MINAKO; OGUMA HIDEO; OSANAI KAORU; SHIBUSAWA TATSUHIKO; SHIMAMURA HÔGETSU; TACHIHARA MASAAKI; TANAKA YASUO; TSUJI KUNIO; UEDA BIN; YAMAZAKI MASAKAZU; YASUDA YOJÛRÔ.

LITERARY FILMS. *See BUNGEI EIGA*; FILM AND LITERATURE.

LITERARY JOURNALS. Japan is replete with a variety of literary journals (*bungei zasshi*), both scholarly and popular, that publish **poetry**, essays, lyrics, book reviews, and **literary criticism**. The earliest literary journals emerged in the **Meiji** period from coterie magazines shared among writers. Other journals emerged from the early newspapers, which printed installments of new serialized fiction. During the early decades of the 20th century, specialty journals, such as *Kôdan kurabu* (Kôdan Club) for the masses and ***Akai Tori*** (Red Bird) for children, were produced by major **publishing houses** and achieved long runs and financial success. Some current Japanese literary journals include ***Bungei shunjû*** (Literary Chronicle), ***Bungakkai*** (Literary World), and ***Waseda bungaku*** (Waseda Literature). Articles in literary journals range widely in topic and include the fine arts, music, philosophy, ***manga***, travel, cuisine, and ideology. Journal sales have dropped in recent years, so some journals are often sold as specialty books. *See also AOZORA*; *CHÛÔ KÔRON*; *HAIKU*; HAKUBUNKAN; *MYÔJÔ*; *SHIGARAMI ZÔSHI*; *SHIRAKABA*; *TANKA*.

LITERARY WORLD. *See BUNGAKKAI.*

– M –

MAEDA AI (1931–1987). Maeda Ai, given name Yoshimi, was a literary critic and Japanese literary scholar. He completed his education at Tokyo University and taught at Rikkyô University. He published his groundbreaking critical study *Toshi kûkan no naka no bungaku* (1982; tr. *The Spirits of Abandoned Gardens*, 1997) and wrote criticism on other themes, such as literary theory and semiotics. *See also* LITERARY CRITICISM.

MAIHIME. The story of "*Maihime*" (1890; tr. *The Dancing Girl*, 1948) is based on author **Mori Ôgai**'s own experiences studying medicine in Germany. His first published story, it describes a Japanese exchange student and a German dancing girl who fall in love in Berlin. When he is called back to Japan and ultimately chooses his career over the relationship, the dancer has a nervous breakdown and he is left with bitter regrets. The story underscored the tensions of Japan's contemporary foreign relations challenges, and its autobiographical component has led to generations of scholarly speculation on the identity of the girl and the degree of correspondence with Ôgai's life. *See also* I-NOVELS.

MAKIOKA SISTERS, THE. *See SASAMEYUKI.*

MANGA. The term *manga* (whimsical pictures) was used during the **Tokugawa** period to describe cartoons and sketches drawn by artists in preparation for formal paintings and woodblock prints. Today the term is used to describe the internationally popular genre of Japanese illustrated comic books. Although illustrated stories have been a staple of Japanese literature since the mid-Tokugawa period, the rise of modern *manga* can also be attributed to the influx of American and other Western comic books during the postwar **Occupation Period**.

Manga first appeared in their current form shortly after World War II. *Manga*, which are mostly printed in black and white, are usually serialized in telephone book–size monthly anthologies containing many ongoing stories. The artist (*mangaka*) typically works in a small studio with a few assistants and is associated with a creative editor from a commercial **publishing house**. Popular *manga* series are often published as complete works and may even be **translated** into various languages or made into animated **film adaptations** (*anime*). *Manga* target readers of all ages and cover topics that include adventure, romance, sports, historical drama, comedy, **science fiction**, fantasy, mystery, horror, sexuality, and even business. There are even *manga* adaptations of many works from the Japanese literary canon, both classical and modern. Many countries, including China, America, and France, have developed their own versions of the *manga* comic book style. *See also* KANAGAKI ROBUN; LIGHT NOVELS.

MARUKUSU SHUGI*. *See MARXISM.

MARUYA SAIICHI (1925–). Maruya (family name Nemura) Saiichi is a novelist, **literary critic**, and **translator** from Yamagata Prefecture. He was conscripted into military service while still in secondary school and had to complete his high school degree after World War II. Thereafter, he attended Tokyo University and subsequently taught English literature at the university level while writing novels. His most famous work is *Sasamakura* (1966; tr. *Pillows of Grass*, 1970). Maruya also won the **Akutagawa Ryûnosuke Prize** for *Toshi no nokori* (The Rest of the Year, 1968) and the **Tanizaki Jun'ichirô Prize** for *Tatta hitori no hanran* (1972; tr. *Singular Rebellion*, 1986). He also published numerous essays and translations.

MARUYAMA KAORU (1899–1974). Maruyama Kaoru was a poet, novelist, essayist, and social critic from Oita Prefecture. After graduating from Kyoto University, he attended Tokyo University where he met **Kajii Motojirô**, **Miyoshi Tatsuji**, and **Kuwabara Takeo** and contributed to a magazine focusing on new trends of thought. After getting married in 1928, he turned his attention mainly to **poetry** and, having aspired to be a sailor earlier in his youth, wrote about ships journeying to foreign lands. His anthology *Yônen* (Childhood, 1934) garnered a **literary award**. Having spent his adolescence in Toyohashi, Aichi Prefecture, Maruyama returned there in his later years. In 1994, the city of Toyohashi established the Maruyama Kaoru Prize in his honor.

MARXISM. Marxism (*marukusu shugi*), with its three main items of focus—a philosophical view of man, a theory of history, and a social/economic program—has impacted both Japanese society and literature. **Kobayashi Takiji** and other **proletarian** authors wrote from a perspective that saw class struggle and capitalist oppression of the workers as the great evils of modernization. **Literary critics** and historians in Japan have often used the framework of Marxism for their analyses. Also, though less prominent, several Japanese intellectuals and writers emerged from communal experiments based on Marxist tenets. Marxism took center stage in Taishô Japan when capitalism and economic development were instrumental in Japan's industrialization. The sudden changes in the economy caused the lower classes to be more open to radical ideas in order to help their plight, which in turn spawned the generation of proletarian writers. *See also* CENSORSHIP; CHRISTIAN LITERATURE; DAZAI OSAMU; HANIYA YUTAKA; HAYAMA YOSHIKI; HIJIKATA YOSHI; HIRABAYASHI TAIKO; HIROTSU KAZUO; HORI TATSUO; KARATANI KÔJIN; KAWAMURA MINATO; KUBO SAKAE; MIKI KIYOSHI; MIYAMOTO YURIKO; NAKANO SHIGEHARU; NOMA HIROSHI; SATA INEKO; THOUGHT POLICE.

MASAMUNE HAKUCHÔ (1879–1962). Masamune Hakuchô, given name Tadao, was a novelist, playwright, and **literary critic** from Okayama Prefecture. He graduated from Waseda University in history and English and then worked for the *Yomiuri* newspaper writing about literature, fine arts, and theater. He penned his first work, *Sekibaku* (Loneliness, 1904), and in 1907 left the newspaper to become a full-time author. One year later he released another novel, *Doko e* (Where to?, 1908), which depicted the Russo-Japanese **War** from a young man's perspective. During the 1920s, Masamune focused on **literary criticism** and gained respect in the public eye for his opinions. In 1935, the government asked Masamune, along with **Shimazaki Tôson** and **Tokuda Shûsei**, to establish the **Japan P.E.N. Club**, and he served as its president twice, more recently from 1943–1947. Masamune was awarded the **Order of Cultural Merit** in 1950 and died of pancreatic disease at 83.

MASAOKA SHIKI (1867–1902). Masaoka Shiki, given name Tsunenori, was an author, poet, **literary critic**, essayist, and journalist from Ehime Prefecture. He briefly attended Tokyo Imperial University in 1890 but dropped out that same year and became a newspaper reporter. He worked as a **war** correspondent during the

Sino-Japanese War of 1894–95, which aggravated his tuberculosis and eventually killed him. Masaoka is most renowned for his work in reforming ***haiku*** and ***tanka***. During his short life, he set forth the structure and style of modern *haiku* and founded the *haiku* magazine *Hototogisu* (The Cuckoo). He composed many *haiku* and *tanka* and wrote criticism as well and is considered to be one of the four great masters of *haiku*. His illness influenced his poetry; such works as his essay *Byōshō rokushaku* (1902; tr. *My Six Foot World*, 1971) deal with his convalescence. Masaoka also played baseball in his youth and was posthumously inducted into the Japanese Baseball Hall of Fame in 2002. *See also* ANTINATURALISM; ITÔ SACHIO; NAGATSUKA TAKASHI; NATSUME SÔSEKI.

MASUDA MIZUKO (1948–). Masuda Mizuko is a novelist and scientist from Tokyo who graduated from Tokyo University of Agriculture and Technology, worked in a lab at the Nippon Medical School, and then started writing novels about the after life. Her first, *Koshitsu no kagi* (The Private Key, 1978), was followed by five more novels over the next five years. She won a **Noma Prize** for her novel *Jiyû jikan* (Free Time, 1985) and her novel *Shinguru seru* (1986; tr. *Single Cell*, 1988) won the **Izumi Kyôka** Prize. Her novel *Tsukiyomi no mikoto* (Moon-Viewing God, 2001) won the **Itô Sei Prize**. *See also* WOMEN IN LITERATURE.

MATSUMOTO SEICHÔ (1909–1992). Popular novelist Matsumoto Seichô, given name Kiyoharu, was born in Fukuoka Prefecture. Due to his family's impoverished situation, he spent time after graduation from high school working in menial jobs. In 1950, his first novel was chosen as a winner of the *Asahi Weekly*'s "One Million Novels" competition. His novel *Aru 'Kokura Nikki' Den* (A Story of 'Kokura Diary,' 1953) was awarded the **Akutagawa Ryûnosuke Prize**. Thereafter, Matsumoto became famous for his **detective novels**, many of which were bestsellers, including *Ten to sen* (1958; tr. *Points and Lines*, 1970) and *Suna no utsuwa* (1961; tr. *Inspector Imanishi Investigates*, 1989). An unusually large number of Matsumoto novels have been made into **films**. A **literary award** was founded in his honor. *See also BUNGEI SHUNJÛ*; MINAKAMI TSUTOMU.

MEIAN. Hailed by many critics as **Natsume Sôseki**'s masterpiece, his final, unfinished novel *Meian* (1916; tr. *Light and Darkness*, 1971) was published posthumously. It is the story of a wife who suspects that her husband loves another woman, the husband who still yearns for the former lover, and the complexity of family and social bonds that surround their tangled web of relationships and emotions. Psychologically rich and subtle, the work was "completed" in 1990 by author **Mizumura Minae**. *See also* WOMEN IN LITERATURE.

MEIJI ISHIN. *See* MEIJI RESTORATION.

MEIJI RESTORATION. The Meiji Restoration refers to a series of events between 1854 and 1868, beginning with Japan's opening to the West and culminating in the restoration of Japan's hereditary ruling family to a central place in government. During the **Tokugawa** period, power was in the hands of the Tokugawa clan, whose title *shôgun* included a mandate to protect the Imperial family. In reality, the Imperial family lived under a privileged house arrest in Kyoto while the Tokugawa clan ran the country. The deteriorating Tokugawa government's vulnerability was revealed when Commodore Matthew Perry sailed a fleet of American warships into Edo Bay in 1854–55 and disgruntled fief leaders around Japan, particularly those from Satsuma and Chôshû, seized the opportunity to unite and stage a coup in the name of restoring the Imperial family to rule. By 1867, these forces had succeeded in ousting the Tokugawa shogunate, and, on January 3, 1868, Emperor Meiji regained full power, with pro-Tokugawa troops finally subdued in 1869.

The Meiji Restoration led to many changes in Japan, including rapid industrialization, open borders and trade with the West, the abolition of traditional societal divisions, land reforms, and a new government, essentially an oligarchy consisting of the emperor and leaders from the victorious fiefs. The impact of the Restoration on literature, though not immediate, was profound; social changes in particular led to rapid urban growth and the expansion of literary markets, while trade with the West brought a flood of literary **adaptations** and **translations** that triggered major literary developments. *See also* FUKUZAWA YUKICHI; KANAGAKI ROBUN; *KEIKOKU BIDAN*;

MINISTRY OF EDUCATION; NAGASAKI; NAKAE CHÔMIN; NAKAMURA MASANAO; POLITICAL NARRATIVES.

MIKAN. "*Mikan*" (1919; tr. *Tangerines*, 1949) is one of many beloved short stories written by **Akutagawa Ryûnosuke**. The male narrator, boards the second-class car of a train. After a short while, a young woman holding a third-class ticket takes a seat across from him. Her lack of decorum and repulsive appearance annoy the man, but, when the train passes through a small town, the young woman pulls a handful of mandarin oranges out of a sack and throws them toward a group of young boys waving at the train. This moment of kindness causes the man to have an epiphany that changes his view of both the young woman and life in general. *See also* WOMEN IN LITERATURE.

MIKI KIYOSHI (1897–1945). Miki Kiyoshi was a philosopher who graduated from Kyoto University and studied under Nishida Kitarô (1870–1945) as a member of the Kyoto School. After finishing college, he studied abroad in Germany, focusing on the works of Martin Heidegger and Blaise Pascal, among others. He became a **Marxist** in 1925 and was one of the first to advocate combining Marxism and existentialism. Due to some unfortunate misunderstanding, he was widely ostracized from formal academia owing to perceived connections with the Communist Party. In 1937, he headed up a think tank called the *Shôwa kenkyû kai* (Showa Research Association) that collapsed at the end of the war. Miki was imprisoned for illegally helping a friend run from the government, and he died while in prison. *See also* LITERARY CRITICISM.

MIKI ROFÛ (1889–1964). Miki Rofû, given name Misao, was a **poet** famous for **children's** songs and **symbolist** verse. At an early age he contributed ***tanka*** and ***haiku*** to magazines and newspapers and published his first anthology at 17. He published his most famous work, *Haien* (Abandoned Garden, 1909), at age 20 and is widely considered a genius of the same level as **Kitahara Hakushû**. He attended both Waseda and Keiô universities and joined Suzuki Miekichi (1882–1936) in the ***Akai Tori*** (Red Bird) movement where he became involved in children's song writing. He taught literature in Hokkaido from 1916 to

1924 and was baptized there into the Catholic church. Thereafter, he wrote religious poems and published an essay titled "*Nihon katorikku kyôshi*" (A History of the Catholic Church in Japan, 1929) and was later declared a saint by the Vatican. He died after complications from being hit by a car. *See also* CHRISTIAN LITERATURE.

MILITARISM. Despite the isolation and relative peace of the **Tokugawa** period, Japan's emergence as a modern nation, beginning with the **Meiji Restoration**, was born of conflict and military struggle. Leaders of the Meiji government from the Satsuma and Chôshû fiefs played a central role in Japan's military as well, and through the end of World War II the military was a separate entity in government, with the right to appeal directly to the emperor. During the Meiji period, Japan entered into two major conflicts with other nations, the Sino-Japanese War of 1894–95 and the Russo-Japanese War of 1904–5. Both of these victories brought great pride and a sense of national unity to Japan, and several writers, including **Masaoka Shiki** and **Mori Ôgai**, were involved in the war efforts, while other writers, such as **Yosano Akiko** and **Kinoshita Naoe**, expressed antiwar sentiments and concern in their writings over the rising militarism of the time.

Although military power waned somewhat during the 1910s and 1920s, the Great Depression and Western trade barriers encouraged the Japanese to embrace militarization as a safeguard against foreign threats, and Japan witnessed increasing military control and interference in political and social arenas. By the late 1920s, many writers had either chosen to join the propaganda campaign or remain silent for fear of military and police reprisal. The military-initiated conflict with China that led to World War II began a dark period for Japanese writers, of whom many were conscripted into military service.

Immediately following the war, with pacifism as the new national doctrine, literature saw a flowering of output as such writers as **Ôoka Shôhei** sought to come to grips with the horrors of war, defeat, and the **Occupation**. In recent years, increasing Japan Self Defense Forces involvement in foreign military operations has led to widespread national and international debate on Japan's global military role. *See also* CENSORSHIP; THOUGHT POLICE; WAR LITERATURE.

MINAKAMI TSUTOMU (1919–2004). Minakami (or Mizukami) Tsutomu was a novelist from Fukui Prefecture. When he was nine, Minakami went to Kyoto to study in a Zen temple, but soon ran away, finding it too harsh. He was later brought back and moved to the Tôjiin temple, and his experiences there became the basis of two novels. After leaving the temple in his teens, Minakami unsuccessfully tried writing while working various side jobs. In 1937, he enrolled at Ritsumeikan University in Kyoto but dropped out midway through for financial and health reasons. Throughout his life he married and divorced many times, and the oldest son from his first marriage disowned him. After World War II, he studied under **Uno Kôji** and wrote the autobiographical *Furaipan no uta* (Song of the Frying Pan, 1947). He did not publish for the next decade, but, after reading a **detective novel** by **Matsumoto Seichô**, wrote his own detective novel called *Umi no kiba* (Fangs of the Sea, 1960). Minakami won the **Naoki Prize** for *Gan no tera* (1961; tr. *The Temple of the Wild Geese*, 2008) and the **Tanizaki Jun'ichirô Prize** in 1975 for his biography of the Zen monk Ikkyû. Minakami's writings often deal with **Buddhist** themes, such as his novel *Kinkaku enjô* (The Burning of the Golden Pavilion, 1977), which gives a different spin to the famous arson incident about which **Mishima Yukio** also wrote.

MINISTRY OF EDUCATION. In 1871, the **Meiji** government created the Ministry of Education (*Monbushô*) to oversee science, education, and language matters. Following World War II, the ministry was instrumental in reforming the writing system and simplifying the use of *kanji*, and since 1954 it has sponsored foreign fellowships to assist foreign students studying in Japan. The ministry controls many aspects of education and is charged with providing citizens an abundant life through education and lifelong study. Its broad mandate includes promoting culture and the arts of Japan, and in this capacity it provides funding to new writers and supports **film** as well as traditional and modern drama. It has also recently established a division to promote the **translation** and publication of Japanese literature into foreign languages. Currently the ministry also seeks to develop a copyright system to respond to the Internet age. In 2001, it was merged with another ministry to form the Ministry of Education, Culture, Sports, Science and Technology—abbreviated MEXT (*Monbukagakushô*). *See also* DIET LIBRARY.

MINORITY LITERATURE. *See* AINU LITERATURE; *BURAKUMIN* LITERATURE; RYÛKYÛ LITERATURE; *ZAINICHI* LITERATURE.

MISHIMA YUKIO (1925–1970). Mishima Yukio, given name Hiraoka Kimitake, was an author and playwright famous for his nihilistic post–World War II writings. Mishima's first major work was a prose short story written for his school's literary magazine. He later worked in the Finance Ministry, but exhausted himself writing at night, and so resigned during his first year. The popular success of his first novel, *Kamen no kokuhaku* (1948; tr. *Confessions of a Mask*, 1958), led to an intensive period of prolific writing. Later in life Mishima formed a private army to incarnate his extreme **nationalistic** views. He committed ritualistic **suicide** during an attempt by this army to convince the Japan Self Defense Forces to stage a coup to restore the emperor's status. A **literary award** was named in his honor. *See also* AESTHETICISM; HEARN, LAFCADIO; ISHIHARA SHINTARÔ; ISODA KÔICHI; MINAKAMI TSUTOMU; MODERN THEATER; POSTWAR LITERATURE; THIRD GENERATION; UTOPIAN LITERATURE.

MIURA AYAKO (1922–1999). Miura, née Hotta, Ayako was a female novelist made famous by her work *Hyôten* (1964; tr. *Freezing Point*, 1986). Miura was born in Hokkaido, and, despite pressure to move to Tokyo, she remained there permanently, teaching elementary school for many years and setting many of her novels there, including *Shiokari tôge* (1968; tr. *Shiokari Pass*, 1976). Much of her writing also displays a marked Christian influence. Her conversion to Christianity in 1952 greatly changed the nihilist views she had adopted after World War II and during the 13 years confined to bed by illness. Many of Miura's subsequent works became bestsellers and were remade as **films** or television dramas. *See also* CHRISTIAN LITERATURE.

MIURA TETSUO (1931–). Miura Tetsuo is a novelist from Aomori Prefecture. He attended Waseda University with the intent to study politics and economics, but took a three-year break upon the disappearance and presumed death of his older brother and taught at his hometown high school while starting to write novels. Upon reenrollment, he studied French literature and became a novelist after graduating. He made his authorial debut with the novel *Shinobukawa* (1960, tr. *Shame in the Blood*, 2007), which won the **Akutagawa Ryûnosuke Prize**. He has continued his career focusing on **I-Novels**, and has won the **Noma Prize** (1976) and the **Kawabata Yasunari Prize** (1990).

MIYAMOTO MUSASHI. A fictionalized biography of the famous samurai, the novel *Miyamoto Musashi* (1935; tr. *Musashi*, 1981) by **Yoshikawa Eiji** was originally serialized in the *Asahi* newspaper then published as a single volume. A samurai *bildungsroman*, the work is divided into seven sections that dramatically portray Musashi's development as a warrior (including his signature fighting style, using both a long and short sword simultaneously), his interactions with friend and foe, and the conflicts he surmounts through learning the importance of personal discipline. Wildly popular, the novel was **adapted** for radio and television drama and has been made into a number of **films**, with sequels.

MIYAMOTO TERU (1947–). Miyamoto Teru, given name Masahito, is an author from Kobe. He graduated from Ôtemon Gakuin University and worked as a copywriter for Sankei Advertising Agency. However, he had a nervous breakdown in his mid-20s from the rigor of the salaryman lifestyle and, having read an engaging short story at a bookstore one evening, he decided to become a writer. He won the **Dazai Osamu Prize** for *Doro no kawa* (Muddy River, 1977) and the **Akutagawa Ryûnosuke Prize** for *Hotarugawa* (1978, tr. *River of Fireflies*, 1991). He was also awarded the **Yoshikawa Eiji Prize for Literature** for the novel *Yu-Shun* (The Prize Horse, 1987). All three of these prize-winning stories were subsequently made into **films**.

MIYAMOTO YURIKO (1899–1951). Miyamoto, née Chûjô, Yuriko was a socialist and **feminist** novelist. Miyamoto's first major work was a short story published during her teens, which won a prize sponsored by the ***Shirakaba*** literary circle. During her career, she traveled to the United States, where she met (and divorced) her first husband, and to Russia, where she studied Russian literature and met filmmaker Sergei Eisenstein. Upon her return, she became a leader in the **proletarian literature** movement, joined the Japan Communist Party, and married its secretary general. They were both arrested multiple times for their involvement with the party. Miyamoto's best-known postwar works are two companion novels, *Banshû Heiya* (1946; tr. *Banshu Plain*, 1963) and *Fûchisô* (The Weathervane Plant, 1946), which together won her the Mainichi Cultural Prize in 1947. She died of meningitis at the age of 51. *See also* MARXISM.

MIYAZAWA KENJI (1896–1933). Miyazawa Kenji was a **poet** and author of **children's literature**. While growing up, he temporarily left his home in Iwate Prefecture over disagreements with his family but eventually returned. Miyazawa taught at the local agricultural high school and began to write and publish children's stories, including *Ginga tetsudô no yoru* (ca. 1927; tr. *Night of the Milky Way Railroad*, 1984), as well as free verse poems. Miyazawa's works were influenced by **Romanticism** and the **proletarian literature** movement, but most importantly by his devout **Buddhist** beliefs. He worked throughout his life to educate local farming families and improve the life of peasants. Miyazawa died of pneumonia.

MIYOSHI TATSUJI (1900–1964). Miyoshi Tatsuji was a poet, literary critic, and editor known for his lengthy **free verse poetry**. Born in Osaka, Miyoshi attended Tokyo University and studied French literature, subsequently translating the complete works of Baudelaire. Miyoshi also joined with **Kajii Motojirô** and others to publish the **literary journal** ***Aozora*** (Blue Sky) in 1930. This allowed him a forum in which to publish his poems, many of which were critically acclaimed. Miyoshi also published his first free verse anthology, *Sokuryô sen* (The Surveying Ship, 1930), which established his reputation for incorporating classical themes into his free verse poems. In all, Miyoshi published over 16 poetry anthologies, eight free form essays, and four works of **literary criticism**. In 2004, the city of Osaka established the Miyoshi Tasuji Award for the best nationally published poetry anthology.

MIZUKAMI TSUTOMU. *See MINAKAMI TSUTOMU.*

MIZUMURA MINAE (1951–). Mizumura Minae is a novelist and critic based in Tokyo. Mizumura moved with her family to Long Island, New York, when she was 12 and completed her education through graduate school in America and Europe. She subsequently returned to Japan to devote herself to writing Japanese fiction. Her first novel, *Zoku Meian* (Light and Darkness Continued, 1990), "completed" author **Natsume Sôseki**'s unfinished novel ***Meian*** using his same idiosyncratic style. It won the Minister of Education Award for New Artists in 1991. She has since published a pseudo-**I-Novel** titled *Watakushi shôsetsu from left to right* (An I-Novel from Left to Right, 1995) that innovated literary typography by printing the text horizontally instead of vertically, and *Honkaku shôsetsu* (A Real Novel, 2002), an **adaptation** of Emily Brontë's *Wuthering Heights* reset in postwar Japan, which won the **Yomiuri Prize** in 2003. *See also* LITERARY CRITICISM.

MODANIZUMU. *See* MODERNISM.

MODERN THEATER. Nontraditional or modern theater in Japan embraces a variety of new genres that have emerged since the **Meiji Restoration**. *Shingeki* (new theater) appeared in the early 20th century through the staging of translated Western dramas with high art as their aim, as opposed to the commercialism of contemporary *kabuki* and the political propaganda of ***shinpa***. **Tsubouchi Shôyô, Shimamura Hôgetsu, Osanai Kaoru,** and Ichikawa Sadanji II (1880–1940) were its early proponents. *Shinpa-geki* (also known as *shinpa*) originated in the "hooligan shows" of the early **Freedom and People's Rights Movement**. The foremost playwright from this *kabuki*-esque genre was **Kawakami Otojirô**. The *Asakusa Opera* variety show, beloved of writers, such as **Nagai Kafû**, appeared in the Asakusa district of Tokyo in 1917. Its promoters helped popularize opera and Western music in the prosperous conditions of post–World War I Japan.

Taishû engeki (popular theater) is usually divided into the three subgenres: *kei engeki* (light comedy), *kengeki* (samurai plays), and *rebyû* (reviews). The exact elements of the plays are left up to the theatrical companies, but most perform plays that are accessible to broad audiences, easy to understand, intimate in terms of space, and inexpensive. *Taishû engeki* is currently performed in more than 25 theaters across Japan. Large movie and entertainment companies (such as Shôchiku and Tôhô) sponsor *shôgyô engeki* (commercial theater), so movie stars typically fill the lead roles, and their success is measured by their ability to make audiences respond emotionally. Plays run for a month at a time and are priced for the wealthy. *Kogekijô engeki* (small theater drama) started as a reaction to *shingeki* and originally referred to plays performed in small, intimate theaters. The term was revived in the 1960s to describe underground theater (also called *angura engeki*) and continues to evolve, with over 60 *kogekijô engeki* theaters across Japan. *Jidô engeki* (children's theater) is geared toward middle and elementary school children. Founded by students who had experienced World War II, pledging to prevent future use of child soldiers, its rapid popularity led to the category of "theatrical appreciation" being added to school curricula. *See also* ABE KÔBÔ; ARIYOSHI SAWAKO; BETSUYAKU MINORU; FUJIMORI SEIKICHI; HIJIKATA YOSHI; INOUE HISASHI; KINOSHITA JUNJI; KISHIDA KUNIO; KOJIMA NOBUO; KUBO SAKAE; KUME MASAO; KURATA HYAKUZÔ; MASAMUNE HAKUCHÔ; MISHIMA YUKIO; MORIMOTO KAORU; MUSHANOKÔJI SANEATSU; NAGAYO YOSHIRÔ; NAKAMURA MITSUO; OKAMOTO KIDÔ; SHIMAMURA HÔGETSU; TERAYAMA SHÛJI; THEATER REFORM; TSUJI KUNIO; YAMAMOTO YÛZÔ; YAMAZAKI MASAKAZU; YOSHII ISAMU.

MODERNISM. Modernism (*modanizumu*) manifested itself first in Europe, with notable modernist writers, such as James Joyce and T. S. Eliot. Its influence was quickly felt in Japan by such writers as **Yokomitsu Riichi, Kawabata Yasunari, Hori Tatsuo, Itô Sei**, and **Ishikawa Jun.** Seminal Japanese modernist works include Yokomitsu's *Kikai* (1930; tr. *Machine*, 1961), Ishikawa's *Fugen* (1936, tr. *The Bodhisattva, or, Samantabhadra*, 1990), and Kawabata's *Suishô gensô* (Crystal Fantasies, 1934). The modernist movement in Japan is also associated with the **proletarian literature** movement and the **neoperceptionist school.** *See also* AESTHETICISM; MURANO SHIRÔ; POSTMODERNISM.

MONBUKAGAKUSHÔ. *See* MINISTRY OF EDUCATION.

MONBUSHÔ. *See* MINISTRY OF EDUCATION.

MORI ÔGAI (1862–1922). Mori Ôgai, given name Rintarô, was a **translator**, novelist, and **poet**. He is often paired with **Natsume Sôseki** as the two founding fathers of modern Japanese literature. A **Romanticist** writer, he trained as a physician and graduated with his medical license at 19, whereupon he enlisted in the army as a doctor and spent from 1884 to 1888 in Germany studying medicine. During this time, he took an interest in Japanese and European literature, and upon returning from Germany published a **literary journal**, ***Shigarami Zôshi*** (The Weir). His best-known works include "***Maihime***" (1890; tr. *The Dancing Girl*, 1948), based on his experiences in Berlin, and ***Gan*** (1911–13; tr. *The Wild Geese*, 1951). In his later years, he focused his writing on historical narratives. *See also* AESTHETICISM; KARAKI JUNZÔ; LITERARY CRITICISM; MILITARISM; OSANAI KAORU; THEATER REFORM; WAR LITERATURE; *WASEDA BUNGAKU*; YAMAZAKI MASAKAZU; YOSHII ISAMU.

MORIMOTO KAORU (1912–1946). Morimoto Kaoru was a playwright, actor, director, and **translator**. He was born in Osaka and graduated in English literature from Tokyo University. While still in high school, he wrote his first one-act play, *Damu nite* (At the Dam, ca. 1925). His most well-known play was *Onna no isshô* (1945; tr. *A Woman's Life*, 1961). Morimoto suffered from tuberculosis in high school and had a relapse during World War II. He wrote a second version of *Onna no isshô* just before dying. *See also* MODERN THEATER.

MURAKAMI HARUKI (1949–). Murakami Haruki is a popular contemporary writer and **translator**, known for his fluid, Westernized style, which breaks from the traditional Japanese emphasis on beautiful language. He tends to write his fiction while living abroad, having spent time in Greece, Spain, and the United States. Many of Murakami's novels have been translated into English, including the fantasy *Sekai no owari to hâdoboirudo wandârando* (1985; tr. *Hard-Boiled Wonderland and the End of the World*, 1991), his breakthrough novel *Noruwei no mori* (1987; tr. *Norwegian Wood*, 1989), and the long novel ***Nejimaki-dori kuronikuru*** (1995; tr. *The Wind-Up Bird Chronicle*, 1998) for which he won the **Yomiuri Prize**. Several of Murakami's works have been adapted for **film** and theater. He has also translated works by F. Scott Fitzgerald, Raymond Carver, Truman Capote, John Irving, and Paul Theroux, among others, into Japanese. *See also BUNDAN*; PSYCHOLOGICAL LITERATURE; SUICIDE; UTOPIAN LITERATURE.

MURAKAMI RYÛ (1952–). Murakami Ryû, given name Ryûnosuke, is a novelist born in **Nagasaki**. His first work, published while he was a student in Tokyo, was *Kagirinaku tômei ni chikai burû* (1976; tr. *Almost Transparent Blue*, 1977), for which he won the **Akutagawa Ryûnosuke Prize**. **Film** versions of several of Murakami's novels exist or are in production, including *Kagirinaku tômei ni chikai burû* and *Koinrokkâ Beibîzu* (1980; tr. *Coin Locker Babies*, 1995). In addition to writing and directing films, Murakami has played drums in a rock band and hosted a television show. *See also* OCCUPATION PERIOD; POSTWAR LITERATURE.

MURANO SHIRÔ (1901–1975). Murano Shirô was a poet and accomplished gymnast from Tokyo. After graduation from Keiô University with a degree in economics, he worked for a scientific research company. His **poetry**, inspired by German **modernism**, contains an objective aesthetic sensibility that depicts its subjects calmly and without sentimentality. He made his debut as a poet with the anthology *Wana* (Snares, 1926), and his *Taisho shishû* (Gymnastics Anthology, 1939) received much attention for its novel use of photographs. His anthology *Bôyôki* (Chronicles of the Lost Sheep, 1959) won the **Yomiuri Prize**.

MURÔ SAISEI (1889–1962). Murô Saisei, given name Terumichi, was a novelist and poet. Born an illegitimate child in Kanazawa Prefecture, Murô was adopted and raised by Murô Shinjô, a Buddhist priest. He dropped out of elementary school in 1902 and got a job at the local district court in Kanazawa as an office boy. Noticed by his superiors for his skill in writing, he then took a job at a newspaper and began to write ***tanka*** and other poems. He published his first novel, *Yônen jidai* (1919; tr. *Childhood*, 1985), in 1919 in the magazine ***Chûô Kôron***

(Central Review). He was friends with **Akutagawa Ryûnosuke**, published over eight **poetry** anthologies, and won the **Yomiuri Prize** and the **Noma Prize**. In his later years, he served on the selection committees for the **Akutagawa Ryûnosuke Prize** and the **Kikuchi Kan Prize**. He died of lung cancer. *See also* HAGIWARA SAKUTARÔ.

MUSEUM OF MODERN JAPANESE LITERATURE. The Museum of Modern Japanese Literature (*Nihon kindai bungakukan*) was established in 1967 in order to compile and preserve numerous modern literary documents. Originally proposed in 1962, the leaders of literary circles, academia, and the media collaborated in its formation. The museum has rare periodicals, first-edition printings of masterpiece works, and complete sets of periodicals. The museum also has a reading room and reference materials for the use of students, librarians, and researchers. It is located in Komaba Park, Tokyo. *See also* AOZORA BUNKO; DIET LIBRARY; NATIONAL INSTITUTE OF JAPANESE LITERATURE.

MUSHANOKÔJI SANEATSU (1885–1976). Mushanokôji Saneatsu, a novelist, playwright, poet, artist, and philosopher, attended Tokyo Imperial University, but left before graduation to form a literary circle with others, including **Shiga Naoya** and **Arishima Takeo** (which became the ***Shirakaba*** School). Mushanokôji's writing is known for its humanist style. In 1918, Mushanokôji put his humanitarian philosophies into action by establishing a quasi-socialist arts commune in Kyushu named Atarashiki-mura. Although Mushanokôji left the community shortly after founding it, the village still exists. Purged following World War II, he made a literary comeback and was awarded the **Order of Cultural Merit** in 1951. *See also* MARXISM; MODERN THEATER; NAGAYO YOSHIRÔ; SATOMI TON.

MYÔJÔ. *Myôjô* (Venus) was a **poetry** journal established by **Yosano Tekkan** in 1900 that ran until 1908 (100 issues). Yosano brought together the talents of **Kitahara Hakushû**, **Yoshii Isamu**, **Ishikawa Takuboku**, and future wife **Yosano Akiko** in hopes of revitalizing Japanese poetry through revolutionizing ***tanka***. The magazine was popular among young poets, but was largely rejected in literary circles. *See also* *KAICHÔON*; LITERARY JOURNALS; OKAMOTO KANOKO.

– N –

NAGAI KAFÛ (1879–1959). Nagai Kafû, given name Sôkichi, was the half-brother of **Takami Jun**. He attended a foreign-language college studying Chinese but dropped out to pursue the writing career he had begun to develop while studying with **Hirotsu Ryûrô**. Nagai is best known for his depiction of early 20th-century Tokyo entertainment districts. His works include *Amerika monogatari* (1908; tr. *American Stories*, 1999) and *Ude kurabe* (1916–17; tr. *Geisha in Rivalry*, 1963). *See also* MODERN THEATER; NATURALISM; SATÔ HARUO; THEATER REFORM.

NAGASAKI. Prior to the **Tokugawa** period, Nagasaki, a port city on the extreme western coast of Kyushu, became a center of European trade owing to the conversion of its feudal lord to the newly introduced Christianity. After Christianity and the Portuguese were banished by the Tokugawa family, the Dutch East India Company was allowed a small trading space in Nagasaki. As Dutch books filtered into Japan, Nagasaki became a center of *rangaku* (Dutch learning) studies, and many of the **translators** and diplomats of the **Meiji** period learned their skills through materials imported by way of Nagasaki. The town has historically been associated with Christianity, adding a tragic irony to its site as a nuclear bomb target during World War II. Both Nagasaki's Christian and **atomic bomb** victim conflicts appear often in works by such Japanese writers as **Endô Shûsaku**, Hayashi Kyôko (1930–), and **Sata Ineko**. *See also* HIROTSU RYÛRÔ; ISHIGURO KAZUO; ITÔ SHIZUO; *KAKURE KIRISHITAN*; MURAKAMI RYÛ.

NAGATSUKA TAKASHI (1879–1915). Nagatsuka Takashi was a poet from Ibaraki Prefecture. At the age of 19 he became interested in **Masaoka Shiki**'s lyrical portrayal of nature, and two years later helped Masaoka launch the **poetry** journal *Araragi* (The Yew). Nagatsuka is mainly known for his writing of ***tanka***, and his 1914 collection *Hari no gotoku* (Like a Needle) is his most noteworthy lyrical publication. Nagatsuka also wrote novels, most notably *Tsuchi* (1910; tr. *The Soil*, 1981), a depiction of agrarian poverty written in dialect, which was serialized in the *Asahi* newspaper.

He died of tuberculosis at the young age of 37. *See also GENBUN ITCHI.*

NAGAYO YOSHIRÔ (1888–1961). Nagayo Yoshirô was a novelist, **literary critic**, and playwright. In college, he became acquainted with **Shiga Naoya** and **Mushanokôji Saneatsu** and joined them in publishing the **literary journal *Shirakaba*** (White Birch). Following the 1923 Kantô Earthquake, he and Mushanokôji jointly published *Fuji* (Unique), a new literary magazine. In it, Nagayo's criticism argued against the **proletarian literature** movement. Some of Nagayo's notable works include the play *Indara no ko* (Child of Indra, 1921), the historical novel *Takezawa sensei to iu hito* (Mr. Takezawa, 1924–25), and the screenplay for the **film** *Seidô no Kirisuto* (1956; tr. *The Bronze Christ*, 1959). *See also* MODERN THEATER.

NAKA KANSUKE (1885–1965). Naka Kansuke was an author and poet from Tokyo. He studied Japanese literature at Tokyo University under **Natsume Sôseki**, who recommended that Naka publish his memoir-like novel *Gin no saji* (1913–14; tr. *The Silver Spoon*, 1956) in the *Asahi* newspaper. He distanced himself from the politics of the ***bundan*** (writers' guilds), and was known for keeping aloof from literary cliques or factions. *See also* POETRY.

NAKAE CHÔMIN (1847–1901). Nakae Chômin, given name Tokusuke, was an influential philosopher and **translator** during the **Meiji** period. Nakae translated a number of French works into Japanese after studying in France in the 1870s as a member of the Iwakura Mission. A radical supporter of the **Freedom and People's Rights Movement**, he authored works discussing democracy and criticizing the Meiji government.

NAKAGAMI KENJI (1946–1992). Nakagami Kenji was a writer, critic, and poet of ***burakumin*** ancestry who wrote his first novels while working manual labor at Tokyo's Haneda Airport. Nakagami won the **Akutagawa Ryûnosuke Prize** for *Misaki* (1975; tr. *The Cape*, 1999), but died early from kidney cancer at the age of 46. *See also* POETRY.

NAKAHARA CHÛYA (1907–1937). Nakahara Chûya was a poet from Yamaguchi Prefecture. When Nakahara was just eight years old, his younger brother died and Nakahara sought solace for his mourning in **poetry**. He originally composed ***tanka***, but in his teens became more interested in **free verse** poetry, particularly that of the European Dadaists. He graduated from Tokyo University, and while there rubbed shoulders with many of the leading men of letters of the day, including **Ôoka Shôhei** and **Kobayashi Hideo**, who introduced him to the works of French **symbolist** poets. Mainstream publishers rejected Nakahara's works throughout his life, so he published in small **literary journals**. The death of his only child in infancy was a great source of anxiety and pain depicted in his later writings. Nakahara died of cerebral meningitis. Although only one of Nakahara's anthologies, *Yagi no uta* (1934; tr. *Poems of the Goat*, 2002), was published during his lifetime, Kobayashi and Ôoka promoted his poetry posthumously, and his poems are now studied in Japanese schools. The city of Yamaguchi established the annual Nakahara Chûya Prize in 1996, awarded to a poetry anthology characterized by a "fresh sensibility." *See also* LITERARY AWARDS.

NAKAJIMA ATSUSHI (1909–1942). Nakajima Atsushi wrote poetic short stories set in Micronesia. His one major novel, *Hikari to kaze to yume* (1942; tr. *Light, Wind and Dreams*, 1962), is based on the life of Robert Louis Stevenson. He died at a young age of pneumonia contracted as a teacher in Palau. *See also* COLONIAL LITERATURE; POETRY.

NAKAMURA MASANAO (1832–1891). Nakamura Masanao was a samurai philosopher who was chosen by the **Tokugawa** shogunate to study abroad in Great Britain, where he learned English. Upon returning to Japan, he published loose **translations** of Samuel Smiles' *Self Help* (*Saikoku risshi hen* or Success Stories from Western Countries, 1870) and John Stuart Mill's *On Liberty* (*Jiyû no ri* or The Logic of Liberty, 1871). Both became bestsellers and had a profound impact on the **Meiji Restoration**. Nakamura later taught at Tokyo University and helped found two other universities in Tokyo. He is one of a handful of Japanese philosophers to convert to Christianity, as he considered it the Western powers' source of success. *See also* ADAPTATIONS.

NAKAMURA MITSUO (1911–1988). Nakamura Mitsuo was the pen name of Koba Ichirô, **literary critic**, playwright, and biographer. He attended Tokyo University and there published criticism in the journal ***Bungakkai*** (Literary World). The success of his essay on novelist **Futabatei Shimei** launched his critical career. In 1938, Nakamura studied in France but returned to Japan at the outbreak of World War II. His controversial **postwar** essay "*Fûzoku shôsetsu ron*" (On the Manner of Novels, 1950) attacked the **I-Novel** as little more than a thinly disguised autobiography. He also wrote stage plays and novels. *See also* MODERN THEATER; THEATER REFORM.

NAKAMURA SHIN'ICHIRÔ (1918–1997). Nakamura Shin'ichirô was a novelist born in Tokyo and raised by his maternal grandparents in Shizuoka Prefecture. Nakamura graduated from Tokyo University, where he made the acquaintance of literary figures **Fukunaga Takehiko, Hori Tatsuo,** and **Katô Shûichi.** His works crossed multiple genres, including **translating** works from French and Chinese. He won the **Tanizaki Jun'ichirô Prize** for *Natsu* (Summer, 1978) and the **Yomiuri Prize** for *Kakizaki Hakyô no shôgai* (Life of Kakizaki Hakyô, 1989).

NAKAMURA TEIJO (1900–1988). Nakamura Teijo, given name Hamako, was a ***haiku*** poetess from Kumamoto Prefecture. She published her first set of verses, *Haruyuki* (Spring Snow, 1934), in the journal *Hototogisu* (The Cuckoo). She published a *haiku* collection, *Teijo kushû* (Teijo's Verse Anthology, 1944), and in 1947 founded the *haiku* magazine *Kazabana* (Snow Petals). *See also* POETRY; WOMEN IN LITERATURE.

NAKANO SHIGEHARU (1902–1979). Nakano Shigeharu was a novelist, **literary critic**, and poet from Fukui. While in high school, he met Kubokawa Tsurujirô (1903–74) and began writing ***tanka*** **poetry** and novels. In college, he studied **Marxism**, joined Kubokawa and **Hori Tatsuo** to found the **literary journal** *Roba* (Donkey), and became involved in the **proletarian literature** movement. In 1931, he joined the Communist Party and was later arrested. After World War II, he rejoined the Communist Party and served as a member of the Diet from 1947 to 1950. He is known for his novels, such as *Kôotsu heitei* (A, B, C, D, 1969), and an anthology of poetry. In 1978, Nakano was awarded the Mainichi Prize for his lifetime literary accomplishments. He died of gallbladder cancer the following year.

NAOKI PRIZE. The Naoki Prize (*Naoki Sanjûgo shô*), a semiannual **literary award** given to up-and-coming authors for popular fiction, was founded in 1935 in honor of author **Naoki Sanjûgo. Kikuchi Kan**, editor of ***Bungei shunjû*** (Literary Chronicle) magazine, created the award concurrently with the **Akutagawa Ryûnosuke Prize.** The award is sponsored by the **Association for the Promotion of Japanese Literature** and is given twice per year. The winner receives a watch and one million yen. Notable recipients include **Yamada Eimi** and **Inoue Hisashi.**

NAOKI SANJÛGO (1891–1934). Naoki Sanjûgo was the pen name of Uemura Shûichi, a writer of popular fiction. Born in Osaka, Naoki attended Waseda University but never graduated, instead moving between Tokyo and Osaka, trying his hand at **film** writing before settling as a critic for the **literary journal *Bungei shunjû*** (Literary Chronicle). He made a name for himself writing popular novels, and over 40 of his works were made into films, most notably the historical novel *Kômon kaikokuki* (History of a Roving Aristocrat, 1929). An eccentric, Naoki selected his pen name to match his age (*sanjûgo* mean 35). Following his premature death of encephalitis, his friend and former employer **Kikuchi Kan** established a **literary award** in his name to honor new writers of popular fiction.

NATIONAL DIET LIBRARY. *See* DIET LIBRARY.

NATIONAL INSTITUTE OF JAPANESE LITERATURE. The National Institute of Japanese Literature (*Kokubungaku kenkyû shiryôkan*) is a research institute created in 1972 for the purpose of conducting and publishing research on Japanese literature. It also preserves manuscripts and books pertaining to Japanese literature. Along with housing a large number of classical writings and special collections, it contains over 180,000 microfilm and digital collections of manuscripts and other materials owned by libraries, shrines, and temples. Many of these materials are made available to the public through online databases, which are constantly being expanded. Originally located in the Gotanda area of Tokyo, the institute recently relocated to new facilities in the Tokyo suburb of Tachikawa. *See also* AOZORA BUNKO; DIET LIBRARY; MUSEUM OF MODERN JAPANESE LITERATURE.

NATIONALISM. Nationalism has several manifestations in modern Japan. Politically, it aligns with imperialist movements that emerged in the **Meiji** period and fostered the **militarism** that led to World War II. Japanese cultural nationalism (*nihonjinron*) lacks the imperialist agenda, but, akin to other ethnic chauvinisms, privileges Japanese culture, language, or race above all others. Many modern Japanese authors, particularly during the **war** years, found themselves caught up in nationalist sentiments, for a variety of reasons. Some, such as **Tanizaki Jun'ichirô**, began as proponents of modernization but subsequently became advocates of a return to traditional Japanese ways. During the postbubble recession of the late 20th century, the nationalist writer **Ishihara Shintarô** became the governor of Tokyo. *See also* ATOMIC BOMB LITERATURE; CHRISTIAN LITERATURE; COLONIAL LITERATURE; THOUGHT POLICE.

NATSUME SÔSEKI (1867–1916). Natsume Sôseki, given name Kinnosuke, was a pioneering and influential **Meiji** novelist seen, along with **Mori Ôgai**, as one of the two founding fathers of modern Japanese literature. He took an early interest in literature during middle school but was discouraged by his parents and began writing only in college after meeting **Masaoka Shiki**, who encouraged him to try his hand at **poetry**. He studied abroad in London and worked as a journalist with the fledgling newspaper industry. His style is influenced by both English and Chinese classical literature. His best-known works include the novels ***Wagahai wa neko de aru*** (1905–6; tr. *I Am A Cat*, 1961), ***Botchan*** (1906; tr. *Botchan: Master Darling*, 1947), and ***Kokoro*** (1914; tr. *Kokoro: A Novel*, 1957). Many of his works have been translated into English, and his face has appeared on the one thousand yen note. *See also HAIKU*; I-NOVEL; KARATANI

KÔJIN; KUBO SAKAE; *MEIAN*; MIZUMURA MINAE; NAKA KANSUKE; NOGAMI YAEKO; OSANAI KAORU; PSYCHOLOGICAL LITERATURE; *SANSHIRÔ*; SUICIDE.

NATURALISM. Naturalism (*shizen shugi*) is a 19th-century European literary movement echoed in **Meiji** Japan. Related to **realism**, naturalism attempted to explain characters' actions through scientific means. French author Émile Zola's works spurred such Japanese authors as **Tsubouchi Shôyô**, **Nagai Kafû**, **Shimazaki Tôson**, and **Tayama Katai** to use detailed, realistic description and rationalism in their works of social criticism. *See also* ANTINATURALISM; *BUNDAN*; CHRISTIAN LITERATURE; I-NOVEL; KEN'YÛSHA; KUNIKIDA DOPPÔ; LITERARY CRITICISM; *SHIGARAMI ZÔSHI*; SHIMAMURA HÔGETSU; *SHUGI*; TOKUDA SHÛSEI.

NEJIMAKI-DORI KURONIKURU. *Nejimaki-dori kuronikuru* (1995; tr. *The Wind-Up Bird Chronicle*, 1998) is a novel by **Murakami Haruki** for which he received the **Yomiuri Prize**. The story revolves around Okada Toru, a lawyer unemployed by choice, and the people he meets while trying to find his wife's cat, and later his wife, who both have inexplicably disappeared. Through Toru's interactions with these characters, Murakami explores contemporary themes, such as the effect of the **war** on veterans, youth functioning outside the normal school system, spirituality, and mysticism. Set in a very Westernized Japan, the novel is accessible to non-Japanese readers, although its lack of plot and low-key protagonist disappointed some critics. Individual chapters appeared in English in the *New York Times* and other venues before the first full English translation was published in 1997. *See also* POSTMODERNISM.

NEOPERCEPTIONIST SCHOOL. The term *Shinkankaku-ha* (Neoperceptionist School) was coined by author Chiba Kameo (1878–1935) to describe a literary movement of the 1920s and 1930s centered among rising novelists who published in the **literary journal** *Bungei jidai* (Literary Times). Trademarks of the neoperceptionsts include the rejection of traditional **I-Novel realism**, an emphasis on creating an intellectual reality grounded in modes of perception (hearing, sight, taste, etc.), and a subjective approach to understanding modern consciousness, sensation, and circumstance. The school's popularity rivaled that of the contemporary **proletarian literature** movement. Authors prominently involved in the movement include **Yokomitsu Riichi, Kawabata Yasunari**, Nakagawa Yoichi (1897–1994), and Kataoka Teppei (1894–1944). *See also* MODERNISM.

NIHON BUNGAKU HÔKOKUKAI. See PATRIOTIC ASSOCIATION FOR JAPANESE LITERATURE.

NIHON BUNGAKU SHINKÔKAI. See ASSOCIATION FOR THE PROMOTION OF JAPANESE LITERATURE.

NIHON KINDAI BUNGAKUKAN. See MUSEUM OF MODERN JAPANESE LITERATURE.

NIHON PEN KURABU. See JAPAN P.E.N. CLUB.

NISHIWAKI JUNZABURÔ (1894–1982). Nishiwaki Junzaburô was a poet and **literary critic** from Niigata Prefecture. He attended Keiô University to study economics and foreign languages and there became interested in writing English **poetry** and published a few poems in **literary journals**. After graduating, he studied abroad at Oxford, where he was exposed to **modernist** literature and French surrealism. Upon returning to Japan, Nishiwaki took a teaching post at Keiô and continued writing on the side, composing poetry in Japanese for the first time. He published the first Japanese surrealist poetry magazine in 1927 and founded a poetry journal, *Shi to shiron* (Poetry and Poetics). After World War II, Nishiwaki published another large poetry collection and **translated** T. S. Eliot's *The Waste Land* into Japanese.

NIWA FUMIO (1904–2005). Niwa Fumio, born the son of a **Buddhist** priest, was a novelist and essayist from Mie Prefecture. After graduating from Waseda University, he entered the Buddhist priesthood reluctantly, but gave it up two years later in order to become a writer. His most popular novel *Bodaiju* (tr. *The Buddha Tree*, 1966) tells of a young boy growing up in a Buddhist temple whose mother runs off with an actor. He worked as a **war** correspondent during World War II and wrote many novels with military themes. His *Hebi to hato* (Snakes and Doves, 1953) won the **Noma Prize**, and *Ichiro* (One Road, 1966) won the **Yomiuri Prize**. In 1977, he was awarded the **Order of Cultural Merit**. *See also* KÔNO TAEKO.

NIWA JUN'ICHIRÔ (1851–1919). Niwa, family name Oda, Jun'ichirô studied abroad in Great Britain immediately following the **Meiji Restoration** and, upon returning to Japan, published *Karyû shun'wa* (A Spring Tale of Blossoms and Willows, 1878). This work, an **adaptation** of Edward Bulwer-Lytton's rambling *Ernest Maltravers*, was one of the earliest Western novels redone into Japanese and exercised a strong impact on subsequent **translations**. *See also* ADAPTIVE TRANSLATIONS.

NOBEL PRIZE FOR LITERATURE. The Nobel Prize for Literature is an international literary prize established in the will of Alfred Nobel to be awarded to an author who has produced "the most outstanding work of an idealistic tendency." In 1968, **Kawabata Yasunari** became the first Japanese writer to win the prize "for his narrative mastery, which with great sensibility expresses the essence of the Japanese mind." In 1994, a second Japanese author, **Ôe Kenzaburô**, was awarded the prize for creating "an imagined world where life and myth condense to form a disconcerting picture of the human predicament today." Each year a number of Japanese **literary critics** speculate on when the next Japanese Nobel laureate will be chosen, and who that might be. *See also* LITERARY AWARDS.

NOGAMI YAEKO (1885–1985). Nogami Yaeko, née Kotegawa Yae, was born in Usuki, Ôita Prefecture, to a wealthy *sake* brewer. At the urging of **Kinoshita Naoe**, she enrolled in Meiji Jogakkô, a girls' school in Tokyo, and studied under **Natsume Sôseki**. She later married and made her debut as an author with the short story "*Enshi*" (Ties of Fate, 1907) in the magazine *Hototogisu* (The Cuckoo) and was an active writer from then on. She served as honorary president of Hôsei University and made famous the saying, "*Josei de aru mae ni mazu ningen de are*" ("Before being a woman, you must first be a human being"). Nogami was an active member of the **proletarian**

literature movement and focused her writings on troubled youth and mankind's inhumanity. She also wrote works critical of the **war**. Nogami received many literary awards, including the **Yomiuri Prize** for *Meiro* (Maze, 1957) the Women's Literature Prize for *Hidekichi to Rikyû* (Hidekichi and Rikyû, 1964), and the Asahi Prize in 1981. In 1971, Nogami was awarded the **Order of Cultural Merit**. She died at age 99. *See also* FEMINISM; MARXISM; WOMEN IN LITERATURE.

NOMA HIROSHI (1915–1991). Noma Hiroshi was a novelist, critic, and poet born in Kobe to devout **Buddhist** parents. In 1935, Noma graduated from Kyoto University, where he was interested in French **symbolist** poetry and took part in antiwar movements. He was drafted in 1941 and fought in China and the Philippines before being sent home after contracting malaria. In 1944, he joined the Communist Party (from which he was later expelled) and began his literary career with the novel *Kurai e* (1946; tr. *Dark Pictures*, 2000). His greatest literary accomplishment is the antiwar novel *Shinkû chitai* (1952; tr. *Zone of Emptiness*, 1956), which garnered him the Mainichi Prize and was quickly translated into both English and French. He was also awarded the **Tanizaki Jun'ichirô Prize** in 1971. *See also* MARXISM; NATIONALISM; WAR LITERATURE.

NOMA PRIZE FOR LITERATURE. The Noma Prize for Literature (*Noma bungei shô*), for new works in a wide variety of genres, including nonfiction, was formed by the Noma Service Association in 1941 after the death of Noma Seiji (1878–1938), founder of the Kôdansha **publishing house**. In 1989, the outstanding **translation** of modern Japanese literature into foreign languages was added to the genres covered by the prize. Winners receive a medal, three million yen, considerable media attention, and often go on to fill the ranks of the ***bundan*** (writers' guilds). Notable recipients include **Kawabata Yasunari**, **Hirotsu Kazuo**, and **Sata Ineko**. *See also* LITERARY AWARDS.

NORUWEI NO MORI. Named for a famous Beatles' tune, *Noruwei no mori* (1987; tr. *Norwegian Wood*, 1989), by **Murakami Haruki**, is a novel set in 1960s Tokyo at a time of worldwide student protests.

The novel focuses on a low-key university student Watanabe Toru, who wanders through a number of relationships as he experiences love and loss. The protagonist's general ambivalence about life and the events he experiences mirror the contemporary lack of student resolve and passion during Japan's version of campus unrest. The novel has been translated into English twice, in 1989 and 2000. *See also* POSTMODERNISM.

NORWEGIAN WOOD. *See NORUWEI NO MORI.*

NOSAKA AKIYUKI (1930–). Nosaka Akiyuki is a novelist, singer, lyricist, and politician from Kamakura. Nosaka was adopted and grew up in Kobe, but lost his adoptive father in the fire raids of World War II and his younger sister to malnutrition. These experiences became the basis of his award-winning *Hotaru no Haka* (1967; tr. *Grave of the Fireflies*, 1978), which was awarded the **Naoki Prize**, along with his *Amerika Hijiki* (1967; tr. *American Hijiki*, 1978); the former was later made into an animated **film**. In 1950, Nosaka enrolled in Waseda University's French Department, aspiring to become a chanson singer. While in college he worked as a songwriter and broadcast novelist. He also published the novel *Erogotoshi-tachi* (1963; tr. *The Pornographers*, 1968). Nosaka has been awarded the **Yoshikawa Eiji Prize**, the Kôdansha Essay Prize, and the Izumi Kyôka Literary Prize, among others. In 1983, Nosaka was elected to the Diet and served for eight months. He suffered a stroke in 2003, from which he is still recovering. *See also* WAR LITERATURE.

– O –

ÔBA MINAKO (1930–2007). Ôba Minako was an author and social critic from Tokyo. Her father served as a rescue worker in Hiroshima after the **atomic bombing**, and Ôba's experiences there generated her interest in literature. Ôba graduated from Tsudajuku University and followed her husband's job to Alaska, where she wrote her first novel, *Sanbiki no kani* (1968; tr. *The Three Crabs*, 1978), which depicted American life and was awarded the **Akutagawa Ryûnosuke Prize**. Along with novels, Ôba also wrote essays, **literary criticism**,

poetry, anthologies, and **translated children's literature** from English into Japanese. Ôba served on many committees, including the Akutagawa Prize selection committee and as vice president of the **Japan P.E.N. Club**. She was awarded eight literary prizes in all, including the **Kawabata Yasunari Prize** twice (1989, 1996), the **Tanizaki Jun'ichirô Prize** (1982), the **Women's Literature Prize** (1975), the **Noma Prize** (1986), the Murasaki Shikibu Literary Prize (2003), and the **Yomiuri Prize** (1991). *See also* FEMINISM; WOMEN IN LITERATURE.

OCCUPATION PERIOD (1945–1952). After Japan's surrender at the end of World War II, U.S. General Douglas MacArthur was appointed to oversee the Allied occupation of Japan. Initially, the occupation of Japan's central archipelago was to be divided among the United States, Great Britain, Russia, and China, but mistrust of the Soviets led to a division of former Japan-held territories instead. The terms of surrender called for Japan to scale down its industrial assets, as well as sell land to farmers and eliminate the landlord hierarchy that had existed for centuries. A new constitution was also drafted by the Occupation forces that gave women the right to vote, guaranteed personal and civil rights, disenfranchised the nobility, established the emperor as the symbol of a constitutional monarchy system, abolished Shintô as the state religion, and included a "peace clause" that disallowed Japan to have any standing military. Educational reforms included the simplification of the *kanji* writing system and a more colloquial orthography, universal school lunch, and health reforms.

Although the Occupation forces exercised **censorship** of some literature, the concomitant presence of thousands of foreign military and civilian workers served to bring Western, particularly American, popular culture to Japan following a period of **nationalism**. Although the occupation officially ended in 1952, there is still a U.S. military presence in Japan that has found its way into works by such contemporary writers as **Yamada Eimi** and **Murakami Ryû**. *See also* HAKUBUNKAN; *MANGA*; POSTWAR LITERATURE; TOKUTOMI SOHÔ; WOMEN IN LITERATURE; *ZAINICHI* LITERATURE.

ODA SAKUNOSUKE (1913–1947). Oda Sakunosuke, nicknamed Saku, was an Osaka-born novelist. While at Kyoto University he suffered a lung hemorrhage and had to recuperate in the country for two years. When he returned to school he was unable to concentrate and dropped out and began writing plays and novels, the latter influenced by Stendhal. His first two novels, *Ame* (Rain, 1938) and *Zokushû* (Vulgarity, 1939), brought him a nomination for the **Akutagawa Ryûnosuke Prize**. His *Meoto zenzai* (1940; tr. *Stories of Osaka Life*, 1990) followed the life of a married couple whose relationship survives, despite the husband's neglect, and was the catalyst to his becoming a full-time writer. During the war, some of his very realistic novels were banned. Critics sometimes group him with **Dazai Osamu** and **Sakaguchi Ango** as the *Buraiha* (hoodlums clique). Oda died in 1947 of tuberculosis in Tokyo and is currently memorialized through the **Oda Sakunosuke Prize**. *See also* CENSORSHIP.

ODA SAKUNOSUKE PRIZE. Oda Sakunosuke Prize (*Oda Sakunosuke shô*) is a **literary award** established in memory of **Oda Sakunosuke** to promote literature of the Kansai (Kobe–Osaka–Kyoto) region. It was founded in 1983 by the Osaka Association for the Promotion of Literature and is awarded annually to new authors for original fiction. The winning work is published in the **literary journal *Bungakkai*** (Literary World). The winner receives a certificate, a commemorative gift, and a cash award of 500,000 yen.

ÔE KENZABURÔ (1935–). Ôe Kenzaburô is the second Japanese to win the **Nobel Prize for Literature**. His works reflect the angst of his time, addressing the issues of nuclear weapons, social nonconformism, and existentialism. Among his most well-known novels are *Kojinteki na taiken* (1964; tr. *A Personal Matter*, 1968), *Man'en gannen no futtobôru* (1967; tr. *The Silent Cry*, 1974), and *Pinchi rannâ chôsho* (1976; tr. *The Pinch Runner Memorandum*, 1993), all strongly influenced by Western literary theory. These works contain several recurring themes, including the American **Occupation** of Japan as well as physical disability, reflecting his own experiences with his brain-damaged eldest son, Hikari. He was awarded the

Akutagawa Ryûnosuke Prize in 1958, the **Tanizaki Jun'ichirô Prize** in 1967, and the Nobel Prize in 1994. He was also awarded the **Order of Cultural Merit** in 1994, but refused it. *See also* POST-WAR LITERATURE; SUICIDE; UTOPIAN LITERATURE.

OGUMA HIDEO (1901–1940). Oguma Hideo was an author from Hokkaido. He wrote **poetry** for the **proletarian literature** movement, was a member of the Proletarian Writers League, and wrote fairy tales, **literary criticism**, and comic books before dying of tuberculosis at age 39. *See also* CHILDREN'S LITERATURE; *MANGA*; MARXISM.

OKAMOTO KANOKO (1889–1939). Okamoto Kanoko was an author and scholar of **Buddhism**. She took an interest in literature at a young age and, after a visit with **Yosano Akiko**, began writing ***tanka*** poetry for magazines, such as ***Myôjô*** (Venus). Okamoto turned to Jôdo Shinshû Buddhism when trouble arose in her personal and family life, and many of her novels reflect Buddhist themes, such as ancestral karma. Okamoto died early of a brain hemorrhage, and many of her works were published posthumously. *See also* WOMEN IN LITERATURE.

OKAMOTO KIDÔ (1872–1939). Okamoto Kidô was a novelist, journalist, playwright, and **theater reformer**. After finishing his secondary education, Okamoto worked as a reporter for the next 24 years at various newspapers and information agencies. During that time, he published his first novel, *Takamatsu jô* (Takamatsu Castle, 1891) and his first play, *Shishinden* (The Shishinden, 1896). The success of his subsequent plays galvanized the *shin kabuki* (new *kabuki*) genre, and their positive reception strengthened his resolve to write his long-running hit *Shûzenji monogatari* (Tale of Shûzen Temple, 1911). After 1913, he published a host of serialized narratives, including **detective novels** and thrillers. He studied Western theater on a trip abroad in 1918 and incorporated psychological insight and realism into his *shin kabuki* works. See *also* MODERN THEATER.

OKINAWAN LITERATURE. *See* RYÛKYÛ LITERATURE.

OMOIDE NO KI. *Omoide no ki* (1901; tr. *Footprints in the Snow*, 1970), by Meiji writer **Tokutomi Roka**, is a semiautobiographical story of boyhood experiences during the **Meiji** era. After the loss of his father and family fortune, the hero Kikuchi Shintarô and his mother move in with Shintarô's accomplished uncle. Shintarô is there refined through formalized education until he is asked to become his uncle's heir through adoption and marriage into his uncle's family. Shintarô runs away, overwhelmed with the situation presented to him. Following a trail of adventures Shintarô transfers from Dôshisha University to Tokyo University, where he eventually becomes a writer. The story finishes with his marriage to his sweetheart, showing romance triumphant amid adversity. *See also* I-NOVEL.

ONO TÔSABURÔ (1903–1996). Ono Tôsaburô was a poet, novelist, and children's author from Osaka. He dropped out of Tôyô University in the early 1920s to write **poetry** and became acquainted with **Tsuboi Shigeji** and other anarchist poets, helping to found the poetry journals *Aka to Kuro* (Red and Black) and *Dandô* (Ballistic). In 1933, he returned to Osaka and later published the anthology *Ôsaka*, which focused on the industrial area of the city. After World War II, Ono founded a school of literary studies, of which he served as principal until 1991. He also wrote and published novels and children's stories along with poetry. His anthology *Kyozetsu no ki* (Tree of Rejection, 1975) won the **Yomiuri Prize**. *See also* CHILDREN'S LITERATURE.

ÔOKA SHÔHEI (1909–1988). Ôoka Shôhei was born in Tokyo, studied French at Kyoto University, and was a literary student of **Kobayashi Hideo**. He translated Stendhal into Japanese and, as World War II progressed, was drafted into the army, where he was posted to the Philippines and was captured and became a prisoner of **war**. After the war, he began writing, and much of his work reflects his experiences during the war, including his autobiographical short story *Furyoki* (1948; tr. *Taken Captive: A Japanese POW's Story*, 1967). His best-known novel, *Nobi* (1951; tr. *Fires on the Plain*, 1957), was awarded the **Yomiuri Prize** and was made into an award-winning **film**. *See also* MILITARISM; POSTWAR LITERATURE.

ORDER OF CULTURAL MERIT. The Order of Cultural Merit (*Bunka kunshô*) is a national honor conferred upon a recipient by the emperor. On November 3 of each year (Culture Day), the prime minister awards certificates to recipients at a ceremony in the Imperial Palace. The Order of Cultural Merit is awarded to select Persons of Cultural Merit (another related national award). The Order is given to artists, including writers and **poets**, who have demonstrated highly valuable achievements, and encourages creative activities. Notable author recipients include **Kawabata Yasunari**, **Tanizaki Jun'ichirô**, **Shiga Naoya**, and **Yoshikawa Eiji**.

OSANAI KAORU (1881–1928). Osanai Kaoru was a playwright, director, and **literary critic** known for his innovations in **modern theater**. He edited a literary magazine in high school and at Tokyo University was an English student of **Natsume Sôseki**, met **Mori Ôgai**, worked in stage production, and wrote **poetry** and fiction. After graduation, along with **Tanizaki Jun'ichirô**, he helped launch the **literary journal** *Shinshichô* (New Trends of Thought). His autobiographical novel *Ôkawabata* (By the Banks of the Great River, 1909) was serialized in the *Yomiuri* newspaper. Teaming up with *kabuki* actor Ichikawa Sadanji, who had recently returned from living in Europe, he formed a new theater named the *Jiyû gekijô* (Free Theater), modeled on the **naturalist** theaters of Paris (Théâtre Libre) and Berlin (Freie Bühne). The first play performed there was Henrik Ibsen's *John Gabriel Borkman*, a work that was instrumental in Japanese **theater reform**. Osanai later traveled to Europe to observe Western theater firsthand, and in 1924 was instrumental in establishing the *Tsukiji shôgekijô* (Tsukiji Little Theater) following the Kantô Earthquake. A **modern theater** with state-of-the-art lighting and technical capabilities, the Tsukiji Little Theater, which Osanai limited to performances of Western dramas in **translation**, polarized Japanese *shingeki* playwrights and the rifts continued well after his untimely death. *See also* I-NOVELS.

OUTCAST LITERATURE. *See BURAKUMIN* LITERATURE.

OZAKI KAZUO (1899–1983). Ozaki Kazuo was an author from Kanagawa Prefecture who graduated from Waseda University. He studied under **Shiga Naoya** and published his first work, *Nigatsu no mitsubachi* (February Bees, 1925) in the **literary journal** *Shuchô* (Modern Trends). He published the autobiographical novel *Nonki megane* (1933; tr. *Rosy Glasses*, 1988) and won the **Akutagawa Ryûnosuke Prize** for it in 1937. Ozaki was an **I-Novelist**, and several of his novels were made into **films**. He won the **Order of Cultural Merit** in 1978.

OZAKI KÔYÔ (1868–1903). Ozaki Kôyô was the son of a famous *netsuke* carver. In 1885, while studying at Tokyo Imperial University, he formed the **Ken'yûsha** literary society with friends, and many of his early works were published in its journal and in the *Yomiuri*, Japan's largest newspaper. Among his most renowned works are *Konjiki yasha* (1897–1903; tr. *The Gold Demon*, 1905) and *Tajô takon* (Passions and Regrets, 1896). Ozaki served as a mentor to **Izumi Kyôka**, who continued to write in Ozaki's style after his mentor's death. *See also* KAWAKAMI BIZAN; KÔDA ROHAN; PSEUDOCLASSICISM; THEATER REFORM; WOMEN IN LITERATURE.

– P –

PATRIOTIC ASSOCIATION FOR JAPANESE LITERATURE. The Patriotic Association for Japanese Literature (*Nihon Bungaku Hôkokukai*), established in 1942 with **Tokutomi Sohô** as president, was essentially a selective reorganization of the Japan Writers' Association aimed to assist with Imperial rule. Many authors who were members of the **proletarian literature** movement were denied access to the association. In the summer of 1942, the organization conducted a "Patriotic Literature Movement Lecture Series" across the nation, and at the end of World War II it was dissolved as part of the reformation of the Japan Writers' Association. *See also* NATIONALISM; WAR LITERATURE.

PILLAR OF FIRE. *See HI NO HASHIRA.*

PLUM BLOSSOMS IN THE SNOW. *See SETCHÛBAI.*

POETRY. Poetry has always played an integral role in Japanese literature. From the earliest introduction of the Chinese writing system, Japanese language poetry was being collected and written in such works as the eighth-century *Man'yôshû* (Collection of Myriad Leaves, ca. 760) and the 10th-century *Kokin wakashû* (Collected Japanese Poems of Ancient and Modern Times, ca. 920). Lyric verse was written in both Chinese and Japanese, but over time the native *waka* form of 5–7–5–7–7 syllables came to predominate. From the 12th century onward, a new form of poetry called *renga* (linked verse) appeared, involving *waka* chains composed by multiple poets. During the **Tokugawa** period, a 5–7–5 syllable form called *haikai*, an offshoot of *renga,* emerged as well, and both *waka* and *haikai* continued to dominate the lyric tradition into the **Meiji** period.

During the late 19th century, writers such as **Mori Ôgai** and **Ueda Bin** published anthologies of **translated** Western poetry that had a profound effect on new poets. Some experimented with **free verse**, others sought to breathe new life into the *waka* and *haikai* forms. *Waka* underwent a transformation and became known as ***tanka***, and *haikai* was transformed into the now-familiar ***haiku***. Poets in the 1920s and 1930s experimented with other **modernist** forms, including expressionism, **symbolism**, and Dadaism. All three genres have flourished during the modern period, and poetry circles and contests are ubiquitous in Japan today. *See also* AIDA MITSUO; FUKUNAGA TAKEHIKO; HORIGUICHI DAIGAKU; INOUE YASUSHI; SATÔ HARUO; SHIMAZAKI TÔSON; TACHIHARA MICHIZÔ; TAKAMI JUN; TAKAMURA KÔTARÔ; TAWARA MACHI; TOMIOKA TAEKO; TSUBOI SAKAE; TSUBOI SHIGEJI; YAMADA BIMYÔ; YAMAMOTO MICHIKO; YOSANO AKIKO; YOSANO TEKKAN; YOSHII ISAMU.

POLITICAL NARRATIVES. The short-lived genre of Japanese political narratives (*seiji shôsetsu*) appeared during the 1870s, fed by a contemporary popular interest in politics in the wake of the **Meiji Restoration**. The stories, whose flat characterizations and simple, propagandistic plots lacked serious literary quality, nevertheless helped shape readers' thoughts on Meiji politics. Author Yano Ryûkei (1851–1931) helped establish the genre with his ***Keikoku bidan*** (Inspiring Tales of Statesmanship, 1883). Other key authors include

Tokutomi Sohô, who edited *Kokumin no tomo* (The People's Friend) from 1887 to 1898, **Suehiro Tetchô**, whose **science fiction** work ***Setchûbai*** (Plum Blossoms in the Snow, 1886) envisaged a futuristic Japan, and **Tôkai Sanshi**, whose ***Kajin no Kigû*** (1885–97; tr. *Strange Encounters with Beautiful Women*, 1948) included a bevy of foreign protagonists. Flagging popular interest in politics following the establishment of the Diet, as well as the rise of newspapers as a vehicle for political discourse, led to the rapid decline of political narratives by the end of the 19th century. *See also* MODERN THEATER.

POSTMODERNISM. Postmodernism (*posuto modan shugi*) is a post–World War II literary movement that both continued and reacted against the ideas of **modernism**. In Japan, the movement began with **Tanaka Yasuo**'s novel *Nantonaku Kuristaru* (Somewhat Like Crystal, 1980). The novel, depicting a female college student's life and her intricate web of tastes, consumer products, and restaurants, was an original, self-aware twist on its mundane and pessimistic subject matter. Modern writers Takahashi Gen'ichirô's (1951–) *Sayônara Gyangutachi* (Goodbye, Gangsters, 1981), Shimada Masahiko's (1961–) *Yasashii sayoku no tame no kiyûkyoku* (A Divertimento for the Kind Left Wing, 1983), and Kobayashi Kyôji's *Denwa otoko* (Telephone Man, 1985) represent pioneering postmodernist works, for which they have been dubbed the "Big Three" of Japanese postmodernism. *See also* MURAKAMI HARUKI.

POSTWAR LITERATURE. Postwar literature is a term used for fiction written immediately following World War II that arose out of the disaffection and loss of purpose caused by Japan's defeat. Themes often include the **Occupation**, soldiers' experiences, and the terrors of nuclear war. Beyond the direct influences on authors' choices of topics, the end of the war caused a shift in Japanese religious and social attitudes that permeates the literature of the time. As Western, particularly American, cultural influences began to enter the country, Japanese literature also began to take on some of its aspects. Examples of postwar authors include **Dazai Osamu**, **Mishima Yukio**, and **Ôe Kenzaburô**. *See also* ATOMIC BOMB LITERATURE; LITERARY CRITICISM; THIRD GENERATION; WAR LITERATURE.

POSUTO MODAN SHUGI. *See* POSTMODERNISM.

PROLETARIAN LITERATURE. The proletarian literature movement in Japan (1920s to 1930s) followed similar political and artistic movements in Europe and Russia. Japan's isolationist period ended with the **Meiji Restoration**, when a rapid push toward industrialization caused Japan to rely on its **colonized** Chinese and Korean workers to fuel industrial growth in an effort to keep stride with its Western rivals. Japanese proletarian writers were heavily influenced by the 1920 Baku Conference, which transferred European ideals of communism and anticolonialism to movements in Asia and Africa. The proletarian movement in Japan began in 1921 when Komaki Ômi (1894–1978) published the workers' journal *Tanemaku hito* (The Sowers). In 1928, the Nippona Artista Proleta Federacio was formed, eschewing "arts" and embracing "culture" as their key focus. The expansion of international proletarian arts groups grew to include a new variety of writers who fought government criticism and dealt with the social trials of the working class.

Notable Japanese proletarian works include **Kobayashi Takiji**'s *Kanikôsen* (1929; tr. *The Factory Ship*, 1956), an illustration of the early unionization of fishing workers; **Hirotsu Kazuo**'s *Izumi e no michi* (Road to the Spring, 1953–54); and *Matsukawa Saiban* (The Matsukawa Trial, 1954–58), a responsive defense of supposed Japanese Communist saboteurs after the Matsukawa railway accident in 1949; and **Hayama Yoshiki**'s *Umi ni ikiru hitobito* (Men Who Live on the Sea, 1926), a novel about the appalling labor conditions on work boats. Other notable writers include **Miyamoto Yuriko** and Nogawa Takashi (1901–44). Proletarian literature is occasionally partnered with **modernism** or descriptive **neoperceptionism**. *See also* CENSORSHIP; ENCHI FUMIKO; FUJIMORI SEIKICHI; HIJIKATA YOSHI; HIRABAYASHI TAIKO; HORI TATSUO; I-NOVELS; KOBAYASHI HIDEO; KUROSHIMA DENJI; LITERARY CRITICISM; MARXISM; MIYAZAWA KENJI; MODERN THEATER; NAGAYO YOSHIRÔ; NAKANO SHIGEHARU; NATIONALISM; NOGAMI YAEKO; OGUMA HIDEO; PATRIOTIC ASSOCIATION FOR JAPANESE LITERATURE; *SHUGI*; THOUGHT POLICE; TOKUNAGA SUNAO; TSUBOI SHIGEJI; WAR LITERATURE.

PSEUDOCLASSICISM. Pseudoclassicism (*gikoten shugi*), the imitation of classical literature in modern works, is an offshoot of the classicist emphasis on past art styles and forms. In Japan, the tradition of pseudoclassicism, seen in the overt classical allusions of Heian works by such authors as Ihara Saikaku (1642–93), were resurrected during the **Meiji** period by **Ozaki Kôyô**, **Kôda Rohan**, and **Higuchi Ichiyô**. *See also* AESTHETICISM; *GENBUN ITCHI*.

PSYCHOLOGICAL LITERATURE. As early as the *Tale of Genji* (ca. 1008), Japanese literature has explored the inner workings of the human psyche. During the **Meiji** period, when Western **translations** and **adaptations** made their way to Japan, writers and intellectuals were struck by the psychological **realism** found therein, and early narrative experiments, such as those in the writing of **Futabatei Shimei** and **Natsume Sôseki**, focus heavily on point of view and employ self-conscious narration. Indeed, the **I-Novel** can be read as a type of psychological literature. Plot development has long been secondary to the inner emotions of Japanese protagonists, so it is unsurprising that many of the best-known modern Japanese authors are considered to have written psychological stories, including **Kawabata Yasunari**, **Akutagawa Ryûnosuke**, and **Murakami Haruki**. *See also* FUTABATEI SHIMEI; *MEIAN*.

PUBLISHING HOUSES. The modern Japanese publishing industry began during the **Meiji** period with the widespread use of moveable type. Prior to that time, Japanese publishers favored wood block printing, owing to its facility for including illustrations. As newspapers began to appear in the late 19th century, they sought to expand readership by adding serialized tales written by avant-garde writers or transcribed from the performances of professional storytellers (*see KÔDAN; RAKUGO*). Book publishers also emerged as the market grew for reprints of **Tokugawa**-period fiction, **translations** of Western literature, and contemporary experimental fiction. Many modern publishing houses, such as Kôdansha and **Hakubunkan**, made their initial capital off the success of publishing *taishû bungaku* (popular literature) written in a colloquial (***genbun itchi***) style. In postwar Japan, such **literary journals** as ***Bungei shunjû*** (Literary Chronicle) bolstered publishers' reputations and coffers. In recent years, publishing houses have faced growing pressures owing to the postbubble recession and advances in Internet publishing. *See also AKAI TORI*; *BUNDAN*; CENSORSHIP; *CHÛÔ KÔRON*; KIKUCHI KAN; LITERARY AWARDS; LITERARY JOURNALS; *MANGA*; TOKUGAWA LITERATURE; TOKUTOMI SOHÔ; *YOSE*.

– Q –

QUILT, THE. *See FUTON.*

– R –

RAINOBE or RAITO NOBERU. *See* LIGHT NOVELS.

RAKUGO. *Rakugo* (punch line talk) is a form of comic oral storytelling. During the **Tokugawa** period, itinerant oral storytellers would gather crowds and recite **war** narratives, romances, humorous stories, and other tales for profit. By the **Meiji** period, oral performance theaters (***yose***) were found in nearly every urban neighborhood, and professional storytellers would make their nightly rounds reciting the latest installment of a long human drama or delivering a brief comic monologue with a punch line at the end. **San'yûtei Enchô**, one of the most famous storytellers of the 19th century, incorporated **adaptations** of Western stories into his repertoire and became the model for stenographers employing the newly invented Japanese **shorthand** system who published his oral stories as printed texts.

Writers used these examples of written colloquial style in their experiments to unite spoken and written Japanese (*see GENBUN ITCHI*). By the turn of the 19th century, *yose* were losing customers to the cinema, and some professional storytellers became ***benshi*** (silent **film** narrators). The remaining storytellers focused primarily on humorous tales, or *rakugo*, and today professional storytellers are almost exclusively raconteurs of these comic monologues.

Storytellers limit their use of props to a hand towel and a fan and dress in formal kimono as they tell their stories, sitting on a cushion before the audience. Each story is concluded with a pun (*ochi*). In the later part of the 20th century, *rakugo* witnessed something of a revival in popularity, and Katsura Shijaku (1939–99) performed many *rakugo* shows abroad, using English. *See also* ADAPTIVE TRANSLATIONS; FUTABATEI SHIMEI; KAWATAKE SHINSHICHI III; *KÔDAN*; PUBLISHING HOUSES.

RANOBE. *See* LIGHT NOVELS.

RASHÔMON. "*Rashômon*" (1915; tr. *Rashomon*, 1952), a short story by **Akutagawa Ryûnosuke**, is based on an old Japanese tale and deals with moral ambiguities in a life-or-death situation. The story tells of a man, recently fired from his job, who encounters a poor, elderly woman stealing hair from corpses on the second floor of the Rashô Gate in Kyoto. She meets his disgust with the explanation that the hair will allow her to make wigs to sell to survive, upon which he, in turn, steals her kimono and runs off. The story was adapted for a **film** of the same title by Kurosawa Akira (1910–98), which blends "*Rashômon*" with another of Akutagawa's stories, "*Yabu no naka*" (1921; tr. *In a Grove*, 1952).

REALISM. *Shajitsu shugi* (realism) is the Japanese literary and artistic term used to describe the depiction of reality without interpretation or exaggeration, in contrast to **Romanticism**. The term *shajitsu* implies the sketching or copying of reality, and it appeared during the late 19th century as a **translation** of the realism and **naturalism** of European artists and writers. **Tsubôchi Shôyô**'s critical essay ***Shôsetsu Shinzui*** (1885; tr. *The Essence of the Novel*, 1956) helped establish the realist movement by criticizing earlier forms of comic narrative (*gesaku*) and morality dramas (*kanzen chôaku*). *See also* KEN'YÛSHA; LITERARY CRITICISM; OKAMOTO KIDÔ; SERIOUS NOVELS; TRAGIC NOVELS.

RED BIRD. *See AKAI TORI.*

RELIGIOUS LITERATURE. *See* BUDDHIST LITERATURE; CHRISTIAN LITERATURE.

RÔMAN SHUGI. *See* ROMANTICISM.

ROMANTICISM. Romanticism (*roman shugi*), a late 18th-century European philosophical and literary movement, privileged emotion as the supreme manifestation of individual will. Romanticism came to Japan through **translations** and **adaptations** in the **Meiji** period, and resonated with such writers as **Kitamura Tôkoku**, **Shimazaki Tôson**, and **Yosano Akiko**. Although Romanticism was eclipsed by **naturalism** and **realism**, it saw resurgence during the war years in 1935 when **Yasuda Yojûrô** created the *Nihon Rôman-ha*, or Japan Romanticism School, calling for a return to Japanese tradition and criticizing modernization. *See also* HIGUCHI ICHIYÔ; IZUMI KYÔKA; KUNIKIDA DOPPÔ; MIYAZAWA KENJI; MORI ÔGAI; TOKUTOMI ROKA.

RYÛKYÛ LITERATURE. What is called Okinawa today has historically been called the Ryûkyû (or Loo-Choo) Kingdom. Situated between China and Japan, the people of the Ryûkyû islands have mediated between the two larger countries, and their culture represents a fusion of both with its own unique religion and language. Historically Ryûkyû literature was an oral tradition containing several genres, including epic **poetry**, ballads, ritual prayers, and short lyric poetry called *ryûka* that is similar to ***tanka***. The Japanese government formally annexed the Ryûkyûs following the **Meiji Restoration** and, as Japanese language education became the norm, Ryûkyûan writers, such as Oshiro Tatsuhiro (1925–) and Higashi Mineo (1938–), began publishing stories in Japanese. *See also* AINU LITERATURE; COLONIAL LITERATURE.

– S –

SAITÔ MOKICHI (1882–1953). Saitô, born Moriya, Mokichi was a bright son of a Yamagata Prefecture farmer who was raised by a relative in Tokyo to be a doctor. He studied medicine in Vienna and Munich for four years and was a practicing psychiatrist. He was a founding member of the **poetry** journal *Araragi* (The Yew). Saitô's works comprise 17 anthologies of poems, including his renowned first collection *Shakkô* (1913; tr. *Red Lights*, 1989). As **Akutagawa Ryûnosuke**'s family doctor, he is also known for having assisted in Akutagawa's **suicide**. He won both the **Yomiuri Prize** and the **Order of Cultural Merit**. Author **Kita Morio** is Saitô's second son. *See also* ITÔ SACHIO; *MYÔJÔ*; *TANKA*; YOSANO AKIKO; YOSANO TEKKAN.

SAKAGUCHI ANGO (1906–1955). Sakaguchi Ango, given name Heigo, was a novelist and essayist from Niigata Prefecture. An aspiring writer in his teenage years, Sakaguchi made a name for himself only after World War II when he published his popular essay, "*Darakuron*" (On Decadence, 1946). He attended college at Tôyô University and graduated in ethics and Indian philosophy. He wrote historical and **detective novels** and **literary criticism**, including the essay "*Nihon bunka shikan*" (1942; tr. *A Personal View of Japanese Culture*, 2005) and the novel *Hakuchi* (1946; tr. *The Idiot*, 1961), but is most renowned for *Darakuron*. Sakaguchi died of a brain aneurism at the age of 50. In 2005, the city of Niigata established the Sakaguchi Ango Award in his honor. *See also* POSTWAR LITERATURE.

SANBORIZUMU. *See* SYMBOLISM.

SANSHIRÔ. *Sanshirô* (1908; tr. *Sanshiro*, 1977), written by **Natsume Sôseki**, is a coming-of-age novel about the social consequences of rapid industrialization in **Meiji**-era Tokyo. The main character, Sanshirô, transplanted from his rural village into the intellectual fray of urban university life, makes friends and struggles with a confusing, changing world. As Sanshirô's relationship with the Westernized Mineko undergoes ups and downs, their struggle parallels Japan's own contemporary turmoil.

SAN'YÛTEI ENCHÔ (1839–1900). San'yûtei Enchô, born Izubuchi Jirokichi to **Tokugawa**-period storyteller Tachibanaya Entarô (?–1872), was a renowned professional storyteller. Enchô (as he is usually called) excelled as a raconteur, mastering all the genres of comedy (***rakugo***), human drama (*ninjôbanashi*), ghost stories (*kaidan*), and **adaptive translations** of foreign tales (*hon'anmono*). Enchô collaborated with **Takusari Kôki** to establish the speech of working-class Edo as a model for ***genbun itchi*** colloquial written language. While Enchô recited his tales, students from Takusari's stenography school would sit backstage and use the new system of **shorthand** to transcribe and publish the stories. Some of his stories were remade as *kabuki* plays. Authors **Futabatei Shimei** and **Yamada Bimyô** also modeled their new style of narrative on Enchô's storytelling patois. *See also* KAWATAKE SHINSHICHI III.

SASAMEYUKI. When novelist **Tanizaki Jun'ichirô** first began publishing his long novel *Sasameyuki* (1943–48; tr. *The Makioka Sisters*, 1957) in serialized form, the wartime **censors** took issue with its portrayal of the affluence of a wealthy family and suspended its publication. Once the war was over, it was finally completed and became Tanizaki's most famous work. The Jane Austen–like novel portrays the Makioka sisters, four daughters of a once-wealthy family in decline. The plot focuses on the family's attempts to marry off the third daughter, and the fourth daughter's unseemly behavior as she impatiently waits to be the next in line for marriage. Less overtly sensual than many of Tanizaki's works, this novel contains elaborate character development and a nostalgic, melancholy description of the fading glories of Japanese tradition as it is increasingly eclipsed by Westernization. The Makioka family, despite the crumbling of their fortunes in the face of social change, clings tightly to Japanese values and **aesthetics**, typifying traditional aristocratic culture. The popular novel has been made into a **film** three times. *See also* WOMEN IN LITERATURE.

SATA INEKO (1904–1998). Sata Ineko, given name Ine, was a novelist from **Nagasaki**. Before completing elementary school, Sata moved to Tokyo with her parents and worked in a caramel factory. After her first marriage failed, she worked for the **literary journal** *Roba* (Donkey), where she met contributors **Hori Tatsuo, Nakano Shigeharu**, and her future husband Kubokawa Tsurujirô. Her earlier factory experiences formed the basis of her first short story, "*Kyarameru kôjô kara*" (From a Caramel Factory, 1928), which linked her to the **proletarian literature** movement. After World War II, Sata divorced Kubokawa and joined the Japanese-Soviet Communist Party, from which she was later expelled. She also wrote of the **atomic bomb** victims. Sata's career was laden with awards, including the **Women's Literature Prize** (1962), the **Noma Prize**

(1972), the **Kawabata Yasunari Prize** (1976), the Mainichi Art Prize (1983), and the **Yomiuri Prize** (1985). *See also* FEMINISM; MARXISM; WOMEN IN LITERATURE.

SATÔ HARUO (1892–1964). Satô Haruo was a **poet** and novelist from Wakayama Prefecture. After graduating from middle school, he moved to Tokyo and eventually dropped out of Keiô University. However, while at Keiô he was a student of **Nagai Kafû**. In 1909, he published poems in the **literary journals** *Subaru* (Pleiades) and *Mita bungaku* (Mita Literature) and gained the attention of intellectuals. He published many other poems and in 1948 became a member of the Japan Art Academy. In 1960, he received the **Order of Cultural Merit** and died of a heart attack in 1964.

SATOMI TON (1888–1983). Satomi Ton is the pen name of Yamanouchi Hideo, author and younger brother of authors Arishima Ikuma (1882–1974) and **Arishima Takeo**. Born into the Arishima family, he was legally adopted by his mother whose surname was Yamanouchi. He attended the Gakushûin Peers School in Tokyo where he first became interested in literature, and also attended Tokyo University before dropping out in 1910. Thereafter, he became acquainted with other Gakushûin alumni authors, such as **Shiga Naoya** and **Mushanokôji Saneatsu**, through his brother, Ikuma. Satomi also became a disciple of **Izumi Kyôka**. His major works include *Zenshin akushin* (Good Heart, Evil Heart, 1916) and *Tajô Busshin* (The Compassion of Buddha, 1922–23). He also collaborated on a number of **film** scripts. He was awarded the **Order of Cultural Merit**.

SCIENCE FICTION. Science fiction as a genre came early to **Meiji** Japan, with the Dutch futurist novel *Anno 2065: een Blik in de Toekomst* (*2065: A Glimpse of the Future*) appearing in Japanese **translation** in 1868. Jules Verne was a popular author during this era as well, and many of his works were either **adapted** or translated into Japanese. Japanese science fiction did not witness great development until after World War II, when copies of English-language science fiction novels made their way into Japan with the **Occupation** forces. Some **postwar** writers, seeing that this genre was growing in popularity in the West, experimented with science fiction and even started a magazine, which quickly folded, as did many others, creating a publishing commonplace at the time that science fiction would never sell.

The genre broke through, however, in the 1960s when a combination of science fiction movies, such as *Godzilla*, and the success of the first science fiction novel, *Hikari no tô* (Tower of Light, 1962) by Aran Kyôdomari (1910–2008), signaled a change in reader tastes. Science fiction ***manga*** and animated cartoons (*anime*), such as Tezuka Osamu's (1928–89) *Tetsuwan Atomu* (Astro Boy), fed the popular interest in science fiction as well, and mainstream writers, such as **Abe Kôbô**, also began to write science fiction. By the end of the 20th century, science fiction **films**, television shows, *anime*, and plays had become staples of Japanese popular culture, and science fiction continues as a thriving genre. *See also* ARAI MOTOKO; FUKUNAGA TAKEHIKO; HOSHI SHIN'ICHI; KAWASHIMA CHÛNOSUKE; LIGHT NOVELS; *SETCHÛBAI*; SUEHIRO TETCHÔ; UTOPIAN LITERATURE.

SEIJI SHÔSETSU. *See* POLITICAL NARRATIVES.

SEITÔ. *See* FEMINISM.

SENBAZURU. *Senbazuru* (1949–51; tr. *Thousand Cranes*, 1958) was one of the three representative novels cited by the **Nobel Prize** Committee when author **Kawabata Yasunari** was announced as the winner of the 1968 literary prize. The story centers on a young man who finds himself attracted to his late father's mistress. Following the death of the mistress, the young man's affections transfer to her daughter, who runs away from his advances. The tea ceremony, with its timeless rituals and traditional implements, is used throughout the novel to highlight the theme of death and the impermanence of human life. *See also* WOMEN IN LITERATURE.

SERIOUS NOVELS. Closely related to **tragic novels**, the term *shinkoku shôsetsu* denotes a genre of fiction that emerged from narrative experiments with social **realism** written by authors in the early 1900s. These novels deal realistically with the state of society and tragic or difficult human situations. One prominent author of serious novels was **Hirotsu Ryûrô**, who published two serious novels, ***Hemeden*** (Cross-Eyed Den, 1895) and ***Kurotokage*** (Black Lizard, 1895).

SETCHÛBAI. *Setchûbai* (Plum Blossoms in the Snow, 1886), written by **Suehiro Tetchô**, is a quintessential example of the **Meiji political** novel. The story opens in the future, AD 2040, when Japan has become a dominant world power. A landslide reveals an artifact that leads to the discovery of a story written in 1890, four years in the future for contemporary readers of the novel. The story describes the young patriot Kunino Motoi and his fiancée, Tominaga Oharu, as they struggle to establish the principles of the **Freedom and People's Rights Movement**. Suehiro draws upon his own experience in prison to add **realism** to the story, which critics have noted transcended the typical romances of the day by being useful and instructive as well. *See also* SCIENCE FICTION.

SETOUCHI JAKUCHÔ (1922–). Setouchi Jakuchô was born Setouchi Harumi in Tokushima, attended Tokyo Women's Christian University, and graduated in Japanese literature. After a love affair with one of her husband's students led to divorce, she moved to Tokyo to pursue a writing career. In 1973, she took vows and became a **Buddhist** nun at Chûsonji Temple in Hiraizumi, Iwate Prefecture, and received her name Jakuchô. She is noted for her 1997–98 modern translation of the *Tale of Genji* (ca. 1008). Her accolades include the **Women's Literature Prize** for *Natsu no owari* (End of Summer, 1962), the **Tanizaki Jun'ichirô Prize** for her novel *Hana ni toe* (Ask the Flowers, 1992), and the **Noma Prize** for her novel *Basho* (Place, 2001). She was awarded the **Order of Cultural Merit** in 2006. *See also* FEMINISM; WOMEN IN LITERATURE.

SETTING SUN, THE. *See SHAYÔ.*

SHAJITSU SHUGI. *See* REALISM.

SHAYÔ. *Shayô* (1947; tr. *The Setting Sun*, 1956), a best-selling novel by **Dazai Osamu**, is set in **postwar** Japan. Mirroring Dazai's riotous lifestyle and deep interest in **suicide**, the tragic narrative is told by

Kazuko, a young woman from a once-noble lineage. Her impoverished life after the war is further complicated by the loss of both her mother and drug-addicted brother. Kazuko's loss of identity and emptiness deepen as she tries to adopt new Western fashions, despite her fundamentally traditionalist soul. Ultimately, after taking up with Uehara, a self-indulgent writer, she willfully becomes pregnant in an attempt to bring hope to her dismal life. *See also* WOMEN IN LITERATURE.

SHIBA RYÔTARÔ (1923–1996). Shiba Ryôtarô is the pen name of Fukuda Tei'ichi, a novelist and essayist from Osaka. He studied Mongolian at Osaka University of Foreign Studies. After graduating, he worked for a newspaper and published his novel *Fukurô no shiro* (Castle of the Owls, 1958), for which he was awarded the **Naoki Prize**. He published *Hitobito no ashioto* (People's Footsteps, 1981) that won the **Yomiuri Prize** and also won the **Kikuchi Kan Prize**. In 1993, he was awarded the **Order of Cultural Merit**. He is best known for his historical novels and essays. He was one of the most widely read authors in Japan.

SHIBATA SHÔ (1935–). Shibata Shô is a novelist and scholar from Tokyo. He originally enrolled at Tokyo University to study engineering but switched to German literature. After completing his doctorate, he traveled to Germany to study. Upon his return to Japan, he published *Saredo warera ga hibi* (Anyway, That Was Our Time, 1964), which won the **Akutagawa Ryûnosuke Prize**. He wrote novels for the next decade while serving as a German literature professor at Tokyo University. From 1970 to 1972, Shibata formed the **literary journal** *Ningen Toshite* (As Humans) with the help of **Takahashi Kazumi**, Oda Makoto (1932–2007), **Kaikô Takeshi**, and Matsugi Nobuhiko (1932–). Takahashi's sudden death led the journal to fold, and Shibata left his novel *Non-chan no bôken* (Little Non's Adventure) unfinished. Although his focus is on teaching, he has published two subsequent novels. He currently serves on the review board for the **Dazai Osamu Prize**.

SHIBUSAWA TATSUHIKO (1928–1987). Shibusawa Tatsuhiko, given name Tatsuo, was an art critic, novelist, and **translator** of

French literature. Born in a wealthy district of Tokyo, he attended the University of Tokyo, graduating in French literature in 1953. Unable to find work after graduation, Shibusawa continued in a master's program but fell ill to tuberculosis and began a freelance writing career. His first publication was a translation of Jean Cocteau's *Le Grand Ecart* in 1954. He worked for the magazine *Janru* (Genre) and wrote his first novel, ***Bokumetsu no fu*** (Poem of Extermination, 1955). Several years later, Shibusawa published *Akutoku no sakae* (Glory of Vice, translation of Marquis de Sade's *L'Histoire de Juliette; ou, Les Prospérités du vice*, 1959). The work was controversial, and Shibusawa and the publisher were prosecuted for public obscenity. The so-called Sade trial finally ended after nine years, and Shibusawa was penalized a minimal amount. He continued thereafter to write on eroticism as well as essays critiquing art, became an expert in medieval demonology, and published fantasy novels. Shibusawa died of larynx cancer. *See also* CENSORSHIP.

SHIGA NAOYA (1883–1971). Shiga Naoya, an author from Miyagi Prefecture, was converted to Christianity through the influence of Uchimura Kanzô (1861–1930) while studying at the Gakushuin Peer's School. He also became friends and formed the literary group Shirakaba at the school with other authors, such as **Mushanokôji Saneatsu**. Shiga is famous for his **I-Novels** and earned the sobriquet "the god of novels." His works include such short stories as "*Kamisori*" (1910; tr. *The Razor*, 1957) and "*Seibei to Hyôtan*" (1913; tr. *Seibei and His Gourds*, 1956), as well as such novels as *Wakai* (Reconciliation, 1917) and ***An'ya Kôro*** (1921–37; tr. *A Dark Night's Passing*, 1976). Shiga was awarded the 1949 **Order of Cultural Merit** and produced very little new work in the last decades of his life, dying of pneumonia at 88. *See also* AGAWA HIROYUKI; ARISHIMA TAKEO; BUDDHIST LITERATURE; CHRISTIAN LITERATURE; OZAKI KAZUO.

SHIGARAMI ZÔSHI. *Shigarami Zôshi* (The Weir), a **literary journal** founded by such intellectuals, as **Mori Ôgai** in 1889, saw wide distribution until Mori's departure to the Sino-Japanese front in 1894. The journal, with its large distribution, sought to revitalize Japanese literature with particular emphasis on **naturalism** and **Romanticism**. *See also* WAR LITERATURE.

SHIINA RINZÔ (1911–1973). Shiina Rinzô was a novelist and screenplay writer from Hyôgo Prefecture. He dropped out of middle school, worked odd jobs, and joined the Communist Party, which led to his being arrested and imprisoned by the **thought police**. While in prison he read Friedrich Nietzsche's *Ecce Homo*, which piqued his interest in literature. Shiina made his literary debut with *Shin'ya no shuen* (1947; tr. *Midnight Banquet*, 1970). He was introduced to Christianity through reading Fyodor Dostoevsky, and his subsequent works dealt with **Christian** themes. Shiina's *Utsukushii onna* (Beautiful Woman, 1955–56) was based on his experiences while working as a train conductor. *See also* FILM AND LITERATURE; MARXISM.

SHIMAKI KENSAKU (1903–1945). Shimaki Kensaku was the pen name of novelist Asakura Kikuo, born in Sapporo. He attended Tôhoku University but contracted tuberculosis and was forced to drop out. Living in poverty, he became attracted to the labor movement and moved to a farm in Shikoku. He later joined the Communist Party and spent years in prison as a result, but was finally released because of his worsening tuberculosis. Shimaki's novel *Rai* (Leprosy, 1934), based on his prison experiences, was serialized in the **literary journal** *Bungaku Hyôron* (Literary Review) to critical acclaim. In 1937, Shimaki moved to Kamakura where he joined the literary circle of **Kawabata Yasunari**, **Kobayashi Hideo**, and **Takami Jun**. He lost his battle with tuberculosis shortly thereafter. *See also* MARXISM; PROLETARIAN LITERATURE; THOUGHT POLICE.

SHIMAMURA HÔGETSU (1871–1918). Shimamura Hôgetsu, born Sasayama Takitarô, was a **literary critic**, playwright, and pioneer of the *shingeki* (new theater) movement. After graduating from college, he worked as a reporter for ***Waseda Bungaku*** (Waseda Literature) and also for the *Yomiuri* newspaper before being hired as a college lecturer. From 1902 to 1905, he lived abroad in Germany and England, and upon his return was hired as a professor at Waseda University. He also was appointed chairman of *Waseda* and was active in the **naturalism** movement. Together with **Tsubouchi Shôyô**, he formed the *Bungei kyôkai* (Society of Arts and Literature) in 1906 and went on to perform theatrical **translations** of plays by Henrik Ibsen and William

Shakespeare. He withdrew from the Society in 1913 after a scandal over his relationship with actress Matsui Sumako (1886–1919). In that same year, he and Matsui formed the *Geijutsuza* (Arts Theater) and performed his **adaptation** of Leo Tolstoy's novel *Resurrection* to wide critical acclaim. Shimamura died in the influenza epidemic of 1918. *See also* MODERN THEATER; THEATER REFORM.

SHIMAO TOSHIO (1917–1986). Shimao Toshio was an author from Yokohama. He graduated from Kyushu University, where he met **Shôno Junzô**, and during the war moved to nearby Amami Oshima island where he met and married his wife, a schoolteacher on the island. They moved to Kobe, then to Tokyo, where he started a **literary journal** called *Gendai Hyôron* (Modern Criticism), but ultimately moved back to Amami Oshima where he taught high school. Shimao's most famous literary works were based on his wartime experiences, and he also wrote of women and madness. His collection *Shi no toge* (1960; tr. *The Sting of Death*, 1985) was awarded the **Yomiuri Prize** in 1977, and in that same year he was awarded the **Tanizaki Jun'ichirô Prize** for *Hi no utsuroi* (Movement of the Sun). Shimao also won the **Noma Prize** in 1982. He died of a brain hemorrhage. *See also* CHRISTIAN LITERATURE; WAR LITERATURE.

SHIMAZAKI TÔSON (1872–1943). Shimazaki Tôson, given name Haruki, was a poet and **naturalist** author. Much of Shimazaki's writing reflects his childhood experiences in Nagano Prefecture and his family's struggles with mental illness, which took the lives of his father and sister. Shimazaki took an interest in literature after his graduation from Meiji Gakuin University, and joined ***Bungakkai*** (Literary World). He taught temporarily in Sendai, where he published a collection of verse titled *Wakanashû* (*Collection of Young Herbs*, 1897), which stands as one of the beacons of **Meiji-era Romanticism**. However, he returned to Tokyo permanently after being discovered in an affair with a female student and losing a close friend, **Kitamura Tôkoku**, to **suicide**. Shimazaki's works include ***Hakai*** (1906; tr. *The Broken Commandment*, 1956), which is often regarded as Japan's first naturalist novel, as well as *Haru* (Spring, 1908), *Ie* (1910–11; tr. *The Family*, 1976), the greatly controversial

Shinsei (New Life, 1918–19), and *Yoake mae* (1929–35; tr. *Before the Dawn*, 1987). *See also BURAKUMIN* LITERATURE.

SHINGEKI. *See* MODERN THEATER.

SHINKANKAKU-HA. *See* NEOPERCEPTIONIST SCHOOL.

SHINKOKU SHÔSETSU. *See* SERIOUS NOVELS.

SHINPA. *Shinpa*, also known as *shinpa geki*, refers to an avant-garde theatrical style originating in the *sôshi shibai* (hooligan shows) that emerged during the **Freedom and People's Rights Movement** in the late 19th century. Though the term itself contains the character *shin* for "new," the form of *shinpa* was quite similar to traditional *kabuki*. *Shinpa* themes focused on contemporary political or social issues. **Kawakami Otojirô**, one of the "hooligans," became one of the foremost *shinpa* playwrights who helped bring legitimacy to the new dramatic form. *See also* MEIJI RESTORATION; MODERN THEATER; THEATER REFORM.

SHIRAKABA. *Shirakaba* (*White Birch*) was a humanistic **literary journal** published from 1910 to 1923. The journal was named after the literary circle founded by **Shiga Naoya**, **Mushanokôji Saneatsu**, **Satomi Ton**, and other Peers School alumni. *Shirakaba* focused on Tolstoyan humanism rather than the **naturalism** that prevailed in other literary journals of the time. Many of the contributing authors were also leaders of the **I-Novel** movement. Functioning as both a literary journal and art magazine, *Shirakaba* helped introduce new Western art styles, including impressionism and postimpressionism. Publication ceased following the 1923 Kantô Earthquake. *See also* ARISHIMA TAKEO; LITERARY CRITICISM; MIYAMOTO YURIKO; NAGAYO YOSHIRÔ.

SHIZEN SHUGI. *See* NATURALISM.

SHIZUOKA INTERNATIONAL TRANSLATION COMPETITION. The Shizuoka International **Translation** Competition (*Shizuoka sekai hon'yaku konkûru*) was created to introduce outstanding works of Japanese literature to foreign audiences and to promote international understanding. Begun in 1995 by Shizuoka Prefecture, the biannual competition has included the target languages English, French, Korean, Chinese, Russian, and German. Prizes are given for translations of contest-selected short stories and critical reviews. Only previously unpublished translators may compete.

SHÔCHÔ SHUGI. *See* SYMBOLISM.

SHÔGYÔ ENGEKI. *See* MODERN THEATER.

SHÔNO JUNZÔ (1921–). Shôno Junzô, an author from Osaka, graduated from Kyushu University, where he met **Shimao Toshio**. His writing, though autobiographical, lacks the self-conscious correspondence of **I-Novels.** He writes of the daily dramas of domestic life in suburban, contemporary Japan. Shôno won the **Akutagawa Ryûnosuke Prize** for *Pûrusaido shôkei* (1954; tr. *Evenings at the Pool*, 1958). He was part of the **Third Generation** of postwar writers and is a member of the Japan Art Academy. Shôno has been awarded the **Noma Prize** (1971) and the **Yomiuri Prize** (1965), among others. He continues writing today, with novels that feature retirement-age protagonists.

SHÔNO YORIKO (1956–). Shôno Yoriko (real name Ishikawa Yoriko) was born in Yokkaichi, Mie Prefecture and studied in Kyoto. She started writing while at Ritsumeikan University and made her publishing debut with the story "*Gokuraku*" (Paradise, 1981). She did not publish again until 10 years later, when her short-story collection *Nani mo shitenai* (Doing Nothing, 1991) won the **Noma Prize for Literature** for New Writers. Her story "*Nihyaku kaiki*" (Bicentennial Death Anniversary, 1994) won the Mishima Yukio Prize, and another story, "*Taimu surippu kombinaato*" (Time Slip Industrial Complex, 1994), won the **Akutagawa Ryûnosuke Prize**, making her the first writer to win the new writers' "triple crown." *See also* WOMEN IN LITERATURE.

SHORTHAND (*SOKKI*). Although various stenographic systems for transcribing written speech had been developed in Japan, an effective version of shorthand that could be used to record in real time was not invented until the 1880s. **Takusari Kôki** saw shorthand used by his employer, a foreign mining engineer, and spent several years adapting Graham shorthand to fit Japanese. Once the technique had proven its utility, a number of stenographic schools and styles appeared, all based on Takusari's original model. By 1910, there was a great demand for stenographers, so the government supported training programs and, as the century progressed, other widely divergent styles appeared. By the end of the 20th century, stenography was largely superseded by electronic recording technology.

Literarily shorthand played a key role in resolving the conflicts of the ***genbun itchi*** debates. One of the first targets for shorthand were oral performances delivered by **San'yûtei Enchô,** a professional oral storyteller. Many colloquial oral stories found their way into printed, serialized form through the placement of stenographers backstage in the urban ***yose*** theaters to record the storyteller's performance. The narrative style of these transcriptions provided written models of spoken language that spurred avant-garde writers, such as **Futabatei Shimei,** to try new modes of written narrative. *See also KÔDAN*; *RAKUGO*.

SHÔSETSU SHINZUI. *Shôsetsu shinzui* (1885; tr. *The Essence of the Novel*, 1956) is a long essay written by **Tsubouchi Shôyô**. He argues that novels are the ideal literary genre, and, citing both Western and traditional Japanese examples, argues for a new kind of novel that avoids didacticism and uses a **realistic** style. He also spells out some of the stylistic rules that should govern novel writing. Although published originally as nine modest fascicles, the work galvanized cotemporary writers searching for a colloquial ***genbun itchi*** narrative style and has come to be seen as a watershed in the development of modern Japanese literature. *See also* LITERARY CRITICISM; MORI ÔGAI.

SHUGI. In the early half of the **Meiji** period, the term *shugi* came into use as a translation of the English word "principle" and quickly began to be used to render the suffix *-ism* into Japanese. As waves of philosophical and literary movements washed ashore in Japan, the suffix was attached to most, and its prevalence today (there are over 500 words in Japanese bearing the *shugi* suffix) bears witness to the passion for categorization characteristic of modern Japanese intellectuals. Literary examples include *hanshizen shugi* (**antinaturalism**), *roman shugi* (**Romanticism**), and *gikoten shugi* (**pseudoclassicism**).

SHUPPANSHA. *See* PUBLISHING HOUSES.

SILENT FILM NARRATORS. *See BENSHI.*

SNOW COUNTRY. *See YUKIGUNI.*

SOKKI. *See* SHORTHAND.

SOME PREFER NETTLES. *See TADE KÛ MUSHI.*

SONO AYAKO (1931–). Sono Ayako is a Catholic author of the **Third Generation** of postwar writers. Her *Enrai no kyakutachi* (Visitors from Afar, 1954) was considered for the **Akutagawa Ryûnosuke Prize**. Her novel *Kami no yogoreta te* (1979; tr. *Watcher from the Sea*, 1989) deals with the themes of abortion and the dignity of life, with a gynecologist as the protagonist. Sono and her husband, Miura Shumon, were both awarded the **Order of Cultural Merit**. In addition to writing narratives and essays, she has served in the leadership of nonprofit foundations. *See also* FEMINISM; WOMEN IN LITERATURE.

SOUND OF THE TIDE, THE. *See KAICHÔON.*

STORYTELLING. *See KÔDAN*; *RAKUGO.*

STORYTELLING THEATERS. *See YOSE.*

SUEHIRO TETCHÔ (1849–1896). Suehiro Tetchô, given name Yûjirô, was a politician, novelist, journalist, and proponent of the **Freedom and People's Rights Movement**. Born of samurai lineage in what is now Ehime Prefecture, he graduated from the local samurai school and became a teacher in 1869. Thereafter, he moved to Tokyo and worked for the Ministry of Finance for six years before going into the newspaper business. He was imprisoned twice for challenging the existing free press laws and was instrumental in forming the first national political party. He wrote a political, proto-**science fiction** novel ***Setchûbai*** (Plum Blossoms in the Snow, 1886), and in 1890 he was elected in the first national election, but was later ousted because he left the Liberal Party. Suehiro died in 1896 of tongue cancer and is buried in Ehime. *See also* MEIJI RESTORATION.

SUICIDE. Japan's suicide rate continues to be one of the highest among industrialized nations (a 1993 manual describing suicide methods sold more than one million copies), and this trend is manifest in both the works and lives of modern writers. During the **Tokugawa** period, suicide played several literary roles. Suicide was sometimes the only option for star-crossed lovers whose social disparity precluded their earthly union, a popular theme in the theater. Suicide was the only path to preserve warrior and family honor, another popular literary context. Suicide was also the last resort for desperate or depressed literary characters. Modern literature inherited all three of these aspects of suicide, and they can be found in a wide range of texts, from **Natsume Sôseki**'s ***Kokoro*** (1914; tr. *Kokoro: A Novel*, 1957) to the contemporary novels of **Murakami Haruki** and **Ôe Kenzaburô**. (*See KUROTOKAGE*; *MIYAMOTO MUSASHI*; *SHAYÔ*.)

Many notable Japanese authors have also taken their own lives, including **Akutagawa Ryûnosuke, Kawakami Bizan, Tamiya Torahiko, Kitamura Tôkoku, Dazai Osamu, Kawabata Yasunari, Mishima Yukio**, and **Arishima Takeo**. Some scholars speculate that the pressures of Japan's conformist society, combined with the peripheral status of writers, may contribute to this phenomenon. Mishima's ritual self-disembowelment following a failed coup attempt in 1970 shocked the nation and is perhaps the most dramatic of author suicides. The motives for suicide among writers range from "a vague sense of anxiety" (Akutagawa) to fear of being discovered in an extramarital affair (Arishima), and many authors who commit suicide give their reasons in a suicide note, which itself constitutes a literary subgenre in Japan. Not all writers, however, provide their motives; Kawabata took his own life just four years after winning the

Nobel Prize for Literature and experiencing supreme success as an author, yet left no note.

SUIRI SHÔSETSU. *See* DETECTIVE NOVELS.

SUNA NO ONNA. An existential novel written by **Abe Kôbô**, *Suna no onna* (1962; tr. *The Woman in the Dunes,* 1964) is the story of an entomologist named Junpei who becomes stranded during a research trip to a coastal sand dunes region. After accepting the hospitality of locals, who have him stay with a widow required to dig sand to prevent the dunes from overtaking the village, he finds himself trapped, forced to work with the widow. Digging sand endlessly, they fall in love and eventually he chooses to willfully remain in the village. Abe wrote the screenplay for an award-winning **film** adaptation of this novel in 1964.

SYMBOLISM. Symbolism (*shôchô shugi* or *sanborizumu*), a late 19th-century French literary movement, is primarily a reaction against **naturalism** and **realism**. Symbolist poets sought an art form that would reflect a deeper experience of existence. The symbolists also reacted against the growth of science as a means to explain reality, using symbols in their writing to evoke and suggest rather than to explain. Japanese writers and poets saw affinities between the symbolists' vagueness and traditional Japanese **aesthetics** that favored ambiguity and indirectness. One of the main vectors of symbolism between East and West was the poet **Ueda Bin** whose translations of Western symbolist poets, found in his anthology ***Kaichôon*** (The Sound of the Tide, 1905), introduced symbolism to Japan. *See also* POETRY.

– T –

TACHIHARA MASAAKI (1926–1980). Tachihara Masaaki was born to Korean parents in Japan-occupied Korea. After his father's death in 1931, he moved with his mother to Japan and subsequently changed his Korean name, Kim Yun Kyu, several times in accordance with

Japanese name laws for Koreans and eventually became a naturalized Japanese citizen (*see ZAINICHI* LITERATURE). As a student at Waseda University, he became interested in the novels of **Kawabata Yasunari** and the literary criticism of **Kobayashi Hideo**. Tachihara's affection for medieval culture, in particular *nô* theater, and his love of gardens are reflected in his writings. His first novel, *Bakushû* (Autumn Wheat, 1945), published in the **literary journal** *Bungei Kenkyûkai* (Literary Studies Association), was well received by critics, and he won the **Naoki Prize** for his novel *Shiroi Kesho* (White Poppy, 1965). One of his books, *Yume wa kareno o* (1979; tr. *Wind and Stone*, 1991), has been translated into English along with other stories. He lived in Kamakura from 1950 until his death of esophageal cancer.

TACHIHARA MICHIZÔ (1914–1939). Tachihara Michizô was a poet and architect from Tokyo. He had a natural affinity toward drawing at a young age and was one of the top architecture students at Tokyo University. He visited acclaimed poet **Kitahara Hakushû** at age 13 and by 16 had published 11 ***tanka*** poems. Prior to enrolling in college, he changed his emphasis from *tanka* to **free verse** and read the works of European poets Rainer Maria Rilke, Paul Valéry, and Charles Baudelaire. He also published two anthologies. He graduated from college in 1937 and took employment at Ishimoto Architects. However, through his **poetry** he communicated his dislike of his job and of urban life. In 1938, Tachihara started showing symptoms of tuberculosis that went undiagnosed until three months before his death. He was awarded the **Nakahara Chûya** Prize in 1939 just prior to his death. The anthologies *Yasashiki uta I* (Kind Verses I) and *Yasashiki uta II* (Kind Verses II) were compiled and published posthumously by various authors.

TADE KÛ MUSHI. *Tade kû mushi* (1929; tr. *Some Prefer Nettles*, 1955), a novel by **Tanizaki Jun'ichirô**, explores the loveless marriage between protagonist Kaname and his wife, Misako. Each is reluctant to initiate divorce, and throughout the novel their relationship finds parallels in the false dichotomy between Japan and the West. As the story unfolds the reader comes to see that Kaname's sense of traditional Japan is more fantasy than real, and that he views women more as dolls or puppets than as human beings.

TAISHÛ ENGEKI. See MODERN THEATER.

TAKAHASHI KAZUMI (1931–1971). Takahashi Kazumi was a novelist and scholar of Chinese literature from Osaka, married to **Takahashi Takako.** He graduated from Kyoto University in 1954, having already contributed to the **literary journal** *Gendai Bungaku* (Modern Literature), and earned his doctorate in Chinese literature there in 1959. He began teaching at Ritsumeikan University and published two renowned novels, *Hi no utsuwa* (Vessel of Sadness, 1962) and *Jashûmon* (Heretical Faith, 1965). He taught at Meiji University and then Kyoto University until 1969, when he resigned to protest a campus dispute.

TAKAHASHI TAKAKO (1932–). Takahashi Takako, née Okamoto, is a novelist from Kyoto who graduated from Kyoto University in 1954 and married **Takahashi Kazumi** six months later. She began writing novels following Kazumi's death from cancer in 1971 and has received many literary awards, including the **Tamura Toshiko** Prize for *Sora no hate made* (To the Edge of the Sky, 1972), the **Women's Literature Prize** for *Ronrî ûman* (Lonely Woman, 1976), the **Yomiuri Prize** for *Ikari no ko* (Angry Child, 1985), and the Mainichi Art Prize for *Kirei na hito* (Beautiful Person, 2004). Takahashi has also **translated** numerous novels from French into Japanese. *See also* FEMINISM; WOMEN IN LITERATURE.

TAKAMI JUN (1907–1965). Takami Jun was the pen name of Takama Yoshio, a novelist and poet from Fukui Prefecture. He was born the illegitimate son of the governor of Fukui; **Nagai Kafû** was his half brother. Takami graduated from Tokyo University and became involved in the **proletarian literature** movement. He was imprisoned in 1932 on suspicion of violating the Peace Preservation Law of 1925, but was released six months later after confessing his disaffiliation with the Communist Party. He was a nominee for the first **Akutagawa Ryûnosuke Prize** in 1935 and was acclaimed during the war for his story *Ikanaru hoshi no shita ni* (Under Any Star, 1939). Takami continued to write **I-Novels** and also wrote **poetry**, publishing the anthology *Shi no fuchi yori* (1964; tr. *By the Abyss of Death*, 1965). *See also* MARXISM; MILITARISM; THOUGHT POLICE; WAR LITERATURE.

TAKAMURA KÔTARÔ (1883–1956). Takamura Kôtarô was a sculptor who was also famous for his **poetry**. He studied in Japan and traveled to the United States and Europe from 1906 to 1908 to study with famous sculptors. His sculptures reflect his admiration for Rodin in particular. As a **free verse** poet he is famous for his anthology of poems titled *Chieko shô* (1941; tr. *Chieko's Sky*, 1978), about his wife, Takamura Chieko, who passed away in 1938 following a long battle with mental illness. *See also* WOMEN IN LITERATURE.

TAKEDA TAIJUN (1912–1976). Takeda Taijun was a Tokyo-born novelist and member of the First Generation of postwar writers. He attended Tokyo University, but abandoned his degree as he became involved in leftist activity, for which he was arrested and imprisoned. In 1937, he was conscripted and sent to the front in central China, but was released two years later. However, he stayed in China through the rest of the war and wrote *Shibasen* (Shiba Sen, 1943), a novel about the Chinese historian Sima Qian. In 1947, he began working at Hokkaido University but quit a year later to give full attention to writing. His most well-known novel, *Hikarigoke* (1954; tr. *Luminous Moss*, 1967), is based on an incident of cannibalism (known as the Hikarigoke Incident) on a naval vessel during World War II in northern Hokkaido. In 1971, Takeda was hospitalized with complications from diabetes and was thereafter forced to dictate novels to his wife. He published the novel *Memai no sanpo* (Vertigo Walk, 1976) and won the **Noma Prize**, but died shortly thereafter. *See also* WAR LITERATURE.

TAKEKURABE. *Takekurabe* (1895–96; tr. *Growing Up*, 1956), a novella written by **Higuchi Ichiyô**, portrays a group of children growing up on the outskirts of the Yoshiwara pleasure quarters in the **Meiji** period. A classic coming-of-age story, it shows how social and gender differences and expectations quickly and permanently alter the loose and open relationships children naturally form. A **film** adaptation was produced in 1953. *See also* WOMEN IN LITERATURE.

TAKUSARI KÔKI (1854–1938). Takusari Kôki is noted for his groundbreaking invention of a Japanese **shorthand** system (*sokki*) in 1884. *Sokki* allowed political debates and oral stories, such as the ghost tales of **San'yûtei Enchô**, to be quickly transcribed from the stage and published in newspapers or as serialized books, making them more widely available. Takusari was born in Iwate Prefecture, attended Tokyo University, and, while staying with an acquaintance at a gold mine in Akita Prefecture, met a foreign mining engineer who used shorthand. Takusari asked about the curious-looking marks and over time came up with a similar system for Japanese, which he began teaching to others after founding Japan's first stenographic school in Tokyo. *See also GENBUN ITCHI.*

TAMIYA TORAHIKO (1911–1988). Tamiya Torahiko was a novelist from Kobe. He graduated in Japanese literature from Tokyo University and, while still a student, published his first story in a **literary journal**. He later taught at an all-girls school and focused on writing **I-Novels**. He garnered attention for his *Kiri no naka* (In the Mist, 1947) and subsequently published the long story *Ashizuri misaki* (1949; tr. *The Promontory*, 1966). After the death of his wife, Tamiya published a collection of letters between the two that became a best-seller, but subsequent criticism caused him to take the collection out of print. Tamiya suffered a stroke in 1988 and, unable to continue writing, he committed **suicide** a few months later.

TAMURA TOSHIKO (1884–1945). Tamura Toshiko was the pen name of Satô Toshi, an early modern **feminist** novelist. Tamura studied writing with **Kôda Rohan** and with **Okamoto Kidô**. After becoming a best-selling writer in Japan with such works as *Akirame* (Resignation, 1911), *Miira no kuchibeni* (Lip Rouge on a Mummy, 1913), and *Onna sakusha* (Woman Writer, 1913), she left her husband and moved to Canada for 18 years with her lover, journalist Suzuki Etsu. She also lived in China for the final years of her life, where she edited a literary magazine until her death of a brain hemorrhage. Her posthumous royalties were used to establish a literary prize for women authors. *See also* WOMEN IN LITERATURE.

TANAKA YASUO (1956–). Tanaka Yasuo is an author, **literary critic**, and politician from Tokyo. After two failed entrance exams for Tokyo University, he ended up attending Hitotsubashi University instead. While a student there, he published *Nantonaku, kurisutaru* (Somewhat Like Crystal, 1980), a **postmodern** novel that won him the Bungei Prize. None of his subsequent novels have been as popular, but he continues to write essays, criticism, and *nikki bungaku* (literature written in diary form). As a politician, Tanaka was elected governor of Nagano Prefecture and served from 2000 to 2006. He has also served in both branches of Japan's Diet and as an executive of a political party.

TANBI SHUGI. *See* AESTHETICISM.

TANGERINES. *See MIKAN.*

TANIZAKI JUN'ICHIRÔ (1886–1965). Tanizaki Jun'ichirô was the immensely popular author of such novels as ***Tade kû mushi*** (1929; tr. *Some Prefer Nettles*, 1955) and ***Sasameyuki*** (1943–48; tr. *The Makioka Sisters*, 1957). Although Tanizaki began writing in college, most of his fame was gained after he moved to Kyoto shortly after the 1923 Kantô Earthquake. Much of Tanizaki's early work reflects the Western-influenced bohemian lifestyle he adopted after dropping out of Tokyo Imperial University due to lack of money, although in later years he favored more traditional **aesthetics**. His works are often characterized by obsessive sensuality. Tanizaki was awarded the **Order of Cultural Merit** by the Japanese government in 1949. The **Tanizaki Jun'ichirô Prize** was established in his honor in 1965 by **Chûô Kôron** publishing house and is one of the most sought-after literary awards in Japan. *See also* ANTINATURALISM; *BUNGEI EIGA*; CENSORSHIP; NATIONALISM; WAR LITERATURE.

TANIZAKI JUN'ICHIRÔ PRIZE. The **Tanizaki Jun'ichirô** Prize (*Tanizaki Jun'ichirô shô*) was established in 1965 to honor novelist Tanizaki Jun'ichirô. The prize, established by the **Chûô Kôron** publishing house, is awarded annually to the author of that year's most exemplary full-length fiction or drama and is one of the highest literary merits for a professional author. The winner receives a commemorative plaque and a cash prize of one million yen. Notable recipients include **Endô Shûsaku**, **Ôe Kenzaburô**, **Ôba Minako**, and **Murakami Haruki**.

TANKA. For more than 1,000 years prior to the **Meiji Restoration**, *waka* (Japanese verse)—also known as *tanka* (short verse)—reigned as the quintessential Japanese lyric form. *Waka* does not employ the concept of rhyme and is not organized into lines. Instead, *waka* employs a system of units and phrases, often turned into lines in English translations, composed of 31 syllables (7–7–5–7–5). By the early Meiji period, *waka* had been thoroughly explored, codified, and canonized. Along with calls for narrative reforms, Meiji critics, such as **Tsubouchi Shôyô**, urged a reassessment of *waka*, and the genre was soon targeted by avant-garde poets who used the term *tanka* for their efforts to distinguish it from earlier, hidebound *waka*. Expanding into topical and expressive realism that had been taboo prior to the Meiji period, *tanka* underwent reform under the influence of such poets as **Yosano Tekkan** and his wife, **Yosano Akiko**, as well as **Masaoka Shiki** and **Saitô Mokichi**. Their works were published to great acclaim in ***Myôjô*** (Venus) and other **literary journals**. A revival of *tanka* began in the 1980s, and, with **poetry** circles common, many **newspapers** run *tanka* contests and publish the winning poems monthly. *See also* ABE TOMOJI; HAGIWARA SAKUTARÔ; *HAIKU*; HORIGUICHI DAIGAKU; ITÔ SACHIO; KITAHARA HAKUSHÛ; MIKI ROFÛ; MURÔ SAISEI; NAGATSUKA TAKASHI; NAKAHARA CHÛYA; NAKANO SHIGEHARU; OKAMOTO KANOKO; TAWARA MACHI; TERAYAMA SHÛJI; YOSHII ISAMU.

TANTEI SHÔSETSU. *See* DETECTIVE NOVELS.

TAWARA MACHI (1962–). Tawara Machi is a poet and **translator** from Osaka who graduated from Waseda University in Japanese literature. She is credited with revitalizing ***tanka*** and is an accomplished translator of classical texts into modern Japanese, including *Man'yôshû* (Collection of 10,000 Leaves, ca. 760) and *Taketori monogatari* (The Tale of the Bamboo Cutter, ca. 950). She worked as a high school teacher in Kanagawa Prefecture from her college graduation until 1989. She has released major **poetry** collections, including her *Sarada kinenbi* (1987; tr. *Salad Anniversary*, 1988), a compilation of *tanka* that sold over two million copies. Her popularity is due, in part, to her ability to **adapt** principles of classical literature in a way that appeals to modern youth. Tawara has also released a collection of *tanka* sent to her by fans in response to *Sarada kinenbi. See also* FEMINISM; WOMEN IN LITERATURE.

TAYAMA KATAI (1872–1930). Tayama Katai, given name Rokuya, was one of the founding writers of Japanese **naturalism**. He began writing following a stint in the Russo-Japanese **war**. The bulk of Katai's novels are autobiographical, and his most famous works include ***Futon*** (1907; tr. *The Quilt*, 1978) and *Inaka kyôshi* (1909; tr. *Country Teacher*, 1984). *See also* I-NOVELS.

TERAYAMA SHÛJI (1935–1983). Terayama Shûji was a poet, novelist, essayist, director, and playwright from Aomori Prefecture. He showed signs of being a **poetry** prodigy, winning the ***Tanka*** Studies Award at the age of 18, and attended Waseda University, but dropped out due to illness. In 1967, Terayama cofounded the controversial, avant-garde *Tenjô sajiki* (Peanut Gallery) theater group and wrote and directed many plays performed there. Terayama is considered one of Japan's most creative and provocative artists, and his oeuvre consists of over 200 literary works and 20 **films** of varying lengths. *See also* MODERN THEATER; THEATER REFORM.

THEATER. *See KÔDAN*; MODERN THEATER; *RAKUGO*; *SHINPA*; THEATER REFORM.

THEATER REFORM. At the beginning of the **Meiji** period, Japanese theater consisted of the traditional dramatic forms *nô*, *kyôgen*, *bunraku*, and *kabuki* and popular vaudeville-like variety acts and oral storytelling found in the ***yose*** theaters. Two prolific playwrights, **Kawatake Mokuami** and **Kawatake Shinshichi III**, helped preserve that classical *kabuki* tradition even as they incorporated new sources (including Western plots and tales from the storytelling theater) into works that continue to be performed today.

New political and social developments, such as the **Freedom and People's Rights Movement** and the establishment of Japanese newspapers, led to theater reforms at both the traditional and popular levels. Political reformers incorporated *kabuki*-like bravado into *sôshi shibai* (hooligan shows) aimed at rallying the masses. These improvisations on political issues developed into the new ***shinpa*** theater reform movement. A major shift occurred when **Kawakami Otojirô** and his wife, Sadayakko, **adapted** Shakespearean works for performance at home and abroad. At the same time, such writers as **Ozaki Kôyô** adapted works of Western drama, and such playwrights as **Osanai Kaoru** rose to the performance challenges these new works presented and created theater troupes to adapt Shakespeare, Moliere, and Henrik Ibsen for the Japanese stage. **Mori Ôgai** and **Tsubouchi Shôyô** updated *kabuki*, *nô*, and *kyôgen* into more modern, colloquial Japanese. Theatrical **realism** also moved to center stage with a shift from verse to colloquial speech and from stylized dance patterns to realistic movements.

By the early 20th century, established playwrights were to be found in production residency at newly built theaters in both Tokyo and Osaka. Throughout the 20th century, Japanese drama witnessed constant change and metamorphosis, including a period of underground theater during the 1960s, and continues to serve as a bellwether for many political and social movements. *See also GENBUN ITCHI*; HIJIKATA YOSHI; KINOSHITA JUNJI; *KÔDAN*; MODERN THEATER; NAGAI KAFÛ; NAKAMURA MITSUO; OKAMOTO KIDÔ; OZAKI KÔYÔ; *RAKUGO*; SHIMAMURA HÔGETSU; TERAYAMA SHÛJI; TOKUDA SHÛSEI; YOSHII ISAMU.

THIRD GENERATION. The Third Generation of postwar writers (*daisan no shinjin*) is a term coined by **literary critic** Yamamoto Kenkichi (1907–88) to refer to a cohort of novelists making their debut on the literary scene between 1953 and 1955. Unlike the post–World War I writers (First Generation) and post–World War II writers (Second Generation) who tended to write full-length novels modeled after the European style, Third Generation writers largely turned back to the prewar mainstream genres of the **I-Novel** and the short story, focusing on depictions of everyday life. Representative members of the group include **Yasuoka Shôtarô**, **Sono Ayako**, **Shôno Junzô**, and **Endô Shûsaku**. *See also* KOJIMA NOBUO; POSTWAR LITERATURE; WAR LITERATURE; YOSHIYUKI JUN'NOSUKE.

THOUGHT POLICE. The thought police, also called the Special Higher Police (*Tokubetsu kôtô keisatsu*, abbreviated *Tokkô*), was a police force established to investigate and punish "dangerous" political groups and ideologies. In 1910, there was a conspiracy plot to assassinate Emperor Meiji, and the thought police was formed in 1911 to stop similar situations from happening in the future. Initially, the *Tokkô* focused on communists, anarchists, socialists, and **feminists**, but in 1925 a law was passed that greatly empowered the organization, allowing it to work overseas in areas with high densities of Japanese (e.g., London, Berlin, Shanghai). In its first 25 years of existence, the organization arrested nearly 60,000 people, 5,000 of whom were brought to trial, with half of those being sentenced to death. **Shiina Rinzô** and other Japanese authors with communist ties were among those arrested, some multiple times. The thought police was disbanded by order of the American **Occupation** authorities in 1945. *See also* CENSORSHIP; MARXISM; MILITARISM; NATIONALISM.

THOUSAND CRANES. *See SENBAZURU.*

TÔDÔ SHIZUKO (1949–). Tôdô Shizuko is the pen name of Sapporo-born novelist Kumagai Masae. Tôdô graduated from Fuji Women's Junior College and continues to live in Sapporo. She published her first **poetry** anthology, *Suna no shôkei* (Longing of the Sand, 1968) at the age of 19, and is a Hokkaido Newspaper Literary Prize winner. After winning the **Naoki Prize** for *Urete Yuku Natsu* (The Ripening Summer, 1989), she became primarily a romance novelist, pioneering and popularizing the genre. She continues to publish romance novels today. *See also* WOMEN IN LITERATURE.

TÔKAI SANSHI (1853–1922). Tôkai Sanshi is the pen name of Shiba Shirô, a politician and novelist from Chiba Prefecture. In the early years of the **Meiji** era, Tôkai studied abroad in the United States, graduating with a business degree from the University of Pennsylvania, and returned to Japan in 1885. Thereafter, he published the exotic novel ***Kajin no kigû*** (1885–97; tr. *Strange Encounters with Beautiful Women*, 1948), which met with popular acclaim. Over the next 12 years, Tôkai extended the series into eight more works, including *Tôyô no kajin* (Beauties of the Orient) and *Ejiputo kinseishi* (Modern Egyptian History). Tôkai's political career began in 1892 when he won election as a Lower House representative for Fukushima Prefecture. He was reelected seven times and went on to hold other esteemed political offices. *See also* POLITICAL NARRATIVES; WOMEN IN LITERATURE.

TOKKÔ. *See* THOUGHT POLICE.

TOKUBETSU KÔTÔ KEISATSU. *See* THOUGHT POLICE.

TOKUDA SHÛSEI (1871–1943). Tokuda Shûsei was a **naturalist** writer from Kanazawa. He is noted for his novel *Kabi* (Mold, 1911) and was praised for his empathetic portrayal of women. Following the decline of naturalism, Tokuda shifted his focus to writing narratives in the **I-Novel** genre. Several of his novels, which sketch particularly fine portraits of life in everyday Japan, were turned into **films**.

TOKUGAWA LITERATURE. Lasting from roughly 1600 through 1868, the Tokugawa period witnessed over two centuries of cultural and literary flowering during a time of relative isolation from the West. Since the political capital shifted from Kyoto to Edo, it is also known as the Edo period, and the shift had cultural ramifications as well. Edo grew rapidly in size and became a melting pot as the warlords from across Japan were required to build and maintain Edo mansions for alternate-year residence. Craftsmen, workers, and merchants filled the capital to support this influx, and a dynamic economy and cultural sphere quickly materialized.

Many unique forms of literature emerged from this milieu, including theater, such as *kabuki* and puppet plays, ***haiku*** poetry and its humorous complement *senryû*, and a broad array of narrative forms loosely categorized as *gesaku* (playful writings). The latter included **adaptations** of Chinese novels, illustrated tales that prefigured later ***manga*** comic books, simple illustrated stories for children, novels of romance and urban manners, and, into the 19th century, serialized narratives based on travelers or warrior families that captured the hearts of readers so well that the authors kept adding sequels, in some cases for decades. A growing readership encouraged new marketing techniques, such as lending libraries, and the burgeoning publishing industry of the Tokugawa period set the scene for the emergence of newspapers and **publishing houses** of the **Meiji** period. Professional storytelling also developed during this period, with the establishment of ***yose*** theaters in many of the urban districts of both Edo and Osaka. *See also AWARE*; CHILDREN'S LITERATURE; CHRISTIAN LITERATURE; FUKUZAWA YUKICHI; *GENBUN ITCHI*; *KAKURE KIRISHITAN*; *KÔDAN*; LITERARY CRITICISM; NAGASAKI; *RAKUGO*; SUICIDE; THEATER REFORM; TRANSLATION.

TOKUNAGA SUNAO (1899–1958). Tokunaga Sunao was a novelist from Kumamoto Prefecture. He was introduced to literature and the labor movement at a young age while working in a tobacco bureau. In 1922, at the age of 13, he moved to Tokyo and worked as a typesetter. While there he started to write novels and released *Musansha no koi* (Proletarian Love, 1925) and *Uma* (Horses, 1925). After being discharged from his job during a labor strike, he wrote and serialized his most revered **proletarian** novel, *Taiyô no nai machi* (The Street without Sunlight, 1929). Although he briefly left the union, he kept writing even in the face of opposition from the government. *Shizuka naru yamayama* (Quiet Mountains, ca. 1956), one of his notable works, is based on a labor dispute within Toshiba and has been translated into many languages. Tokunaga died of stomach cancer at the age of 59. *See also* MARXISM.

TOKUTOMI ROKA (1868–1927). Tokutomi Roka, given name Kenjirô, was a novelist born in Kumamoto Prefecture, younger brother to author **Tokutomi Sohô**. While attending what is now Dôshisha University in Kyoto, he was influenced by Christianity, especially the writings of Leo Tolstoy. Later, on a pilgrimage to Jerusalem, he met Tolstoy at his Russian estate. His traveler's journal, *Junrei kikô* (1906; tr. *Five days at Iasnaya Poliana*, 1986), is a valuable literary work. Tokutomi's most famous work was ***Hototogisu*** (The Cuckoo, 1898), and his prose poem *Shizen to Jinsei* (Nature and Man, 1900) was critically acclaimed. Tokutomi died following an illness. After his death, his widow donated his estate to Tokyo and it is now a park. His legacy is preserved as well by a memorial park in Kumamoto and a literary museum in Gunma Prefecture. *See also* CHRISTIAN LITERATURE; WOMEN IN LITERATURE.

TOKUTOMI SOHÔ (1863–1957). Tokutomi Sohô, given name Ichirô, was a journalist and historian and the older brother of novelist **Tokutomi Roka**. He was born in Kumamoto Prefecture, studied at Dôshisha University in Kyoto, dropped out, moved to Tokyo, and established the Min'yûsha Publishing Company. In the late 1880s, Min'yûsha published Japan's first general news magazine, *Kokumin no tomo* (The People's Friend), and *Kokumin shimbun* (The People's Newspaper), both of which played important roles in **Meiji**-period politics and society. Tokutomi started out as an advocate for the **Freedom and People's Rights Movement** but changed political orientation by the end of the 19th century, moving in favor of the Meiji oligarchy. Tokutomi's life work was his monumental 100-volume *Kinsei Nihon kokumin shi* (A People's History of Early Modern Japan, 1918–52). The government recognized his lifelong efforts and awarded him the **Order of Cultural Merit** in 1943. Tokutomi was deemed a class-A war criminal under the postwar **Occupation** and died under house arrest. *See also* PUBLISHING HOUSES.

TOMIOKA TAEKO (1935–). Tomioka Taeko is a poet and novelist from Osaka Prefecture. She graduated from Osaka Women's University and began writing **poetry**, but subsequently has written novels as well as criticism, essays, and screenplays. Tomioka has received many literary prizes, including the **Women's Literature Prize** (1973), the **Kawabata Yasunari Prize** (1977), the **Yomiuri Prize** (1993), the **Noma Prize** (1997), and the Japan Art Academy Prize (2004). *See also* FEMINISM; LITERARY CRITICISM; WOMEN IN LITERATURE.

TRAGIC NOVELS. Tragic novels (*hisan shôsetsu*) comprise a genre that is closely related to **serious novels**, and the two terms are often used interchangeably. Both emerged from the experiments with social **realism** written by authors in the early 1900s and deal frankly with human hardship, pitiful situations, and flaws in society. Well-known authors of tragic novels include **Hirotsu Ryûro, Kawakami Bizan**, and **Izumi Kyôka**.

TRANSLATION. During the **Tokugawa** period, Chinese fiction was often in vogue and led to the publication of many Japanese **adaptive**

translations of Chinese novels. This penchant for reading literature in translation continued into the **Meiji** period, and Western works of fiction soon found their way into Japanese incarnations. Initially, these were done as **adaptations**, but as language facility improved among Japanese, more and more stories from the Western canon, including Victorian novels, **poetry** by Goethe and Heinrich Heine, and Shakespearean theater, made their way into Japanese. Some of the revolutionary changes in literary style, such as the emergence of the *de aru* copula ending in written Japanese, stem from grammatical challenges faced by early translators of Western prose (*see GENBUN ITCHI*).

Throughout the 20th century, translations of nearly every major Western novel were completed, often within months of the original's publication, and Japan became, in literary terms, one of the most translating nations in the world. Some of Japan's early writers, such as **Futabatei Shimei** and **Mori Ôgai**, began their publishing careers as translators, and that trend continues today with **Murakami Haruki** beginning his career as a translator of F. Scott Fitzgerald, Raymond Carver, John Irving, and Paul Theroux. Murakami's own style is considered a dialect of Japanese that imitates the style of a translation from English. *See also* ABE TOMOJI; FUKUZAWA YUKICHI; FURUI YOSHIKICHI; HIROTSU KAZUO; HORI TATSUO; HORIGUICHI DAIGAKU; KINOSHITA JUNJI; KISHIDA KUNIO; KOJIMA NOBUO; MARUYA SAIICHI; MORIMOTO KAORU; NAGASAKI; NAKAE CHÔMIN; SHIBUSAWA TATSUHIKO; SHIZUOKA INTERNATIONAL TRANSLATION CONTEST; TAWARA MACHI; TSUJI KUNIO; UEDA BIN; WATANABE KAZUO.

TSUBOI SAKAE (1899–1967). Tsuboi Sakae, née Iwai, was a **poet** and novelist, and the wife of poet **Tsuboi Shigeji**. Born in Kagawa Prefecture under poor circumstances, she worked for the postal service and town government after graduating high school. In 1925, she moved to Tokyo and married Shigeji. Her first novel, *Daikon no ha* (Radish Leaf, 1938), launched her literary career and she became an award-winning author in many genres. In 1954, her novel *Nijûshi no hitomi* (1952; tr. *Twenty-Four Eyes*, 1957) was made into a **film**. In 1979, the Tsuboi Sakae Prize was established to honor exceptional children in Kagawa Prefecture. *See also* FEMINISM; WOMEN IN LITERATURE.

TSUBOI SHIGEJI (1897–1975). Tsuboi Shigeji was a poet from Kagawa Prefecture and husband of novelist **Tsuboi Sakae**. After graduating from Waseda University and marrying Sakae, he affiliated with the anarchist movement in the 1920s and published the verse anthology *Aka to Kuro* (Red and Black). Later he joined the Communist movement and was also a key member of the **proletarian literature** movement. After being imprisoned several times in the 1930s, he moved to the countryside during World War II and was inactive except for writing humorous prose with hidden antiwar messages as part of the *Sancho Kurabu* (Sancho Panza Club) with **Oguma Hideo** and Murayama Tomoyoshi (1901–77). After the war, Tsuboi helped found two **literary journals** and published one of his most famous anthologies, *Fûsen* (Balloon, 1957). He also helped establish and promote the *Shin Nihon Bungakkai* (New Japanese Literature Association). His decision to abstain from writing during the war alienated him from the younger generation of poets, which led to his forming a new **poetry** group that focused on democratic poetry. *See also* MARXISM; THOUGHT POLICE; WAR LITERATURE.

TSUBOUCHI SHÔYÔ (1859–1935). Tsubouchi Shôyô, given name Yûzô, was an author and translator famous for both his groundbreaking **literary criticism**, exemplified in his essay ***Shôsetsu shinzui*** (1885; tr. *The Essence of the Novel*, 1956), and for his original plays and novels. A scholar and teacher, he married a former geisha and was instrumental in encouraging his pupil **Futabatei Shimei** to write in a new, colloquial written narrative style. He is noted as the father of Japanese **modern theater** and is renowned for his life work, the first Japanese **translation** of the complete works of Shakespeare. *See also BUNDAN*; *GENBUN ITCHI*; *KEIKOKU BIDAN*; MORI ÔGAI; NATURALISM; *TANKA*; THEATER REFORM; *WASEDA BUNGAKU*.

TSUJI KUNIO (1925–1999). Tsuji Kunio was a novelist, playwright, **literary critic**, essayist, **translator**, and scholar from Tokyo. As a youth he was interested in literature, led ***haiku*** circles, and performed in plays. He became friends with **Kita Morio** at his boarding school and enrolled in Tokyo University where he studied under **Watanabe Kazuo**. After graduation, he wrote a dissertation on Stendhal, then taught at Rikkyô and Gakushûin universities before leaving for Paris in 1957 to study abroad. After returning from France, he made his literary debut with the novel *Kairô nite* (In the Corridor, 1963). He won the **Tanizaki Jun'ichirô Prize** for *Saigyô kaden* (Tales of the Poet Saigyo, 1995).

TSUSHIMA YÛKO (1947–). Tsushima Yûko, given name Satoko, is a novelist and essayist and the daughter of **Dazai Osamu**. She studied English literature at Shirayuri Women's University, began her literary career there as a student, and published her first collection of stories at 24. She was an **Akutagawa Ryûnosuke Prize** finalist in 1972, and in 1979 was awarded the first annual **Noma Prize**. She published *Hi no kawa no hotori de* (By the River of Fire, 1983) and won the **Kawabata Yasunari Prize** in 1983 for a different work, *Damari ichi* (1983; tr. *The Silent Traders*, 1984). She has also won the **Women's Literature Prize**, the **Yomiuri Prize**, and the **Tanizaki Jun'ichirô Prize**. Her works have been translated widely abroad. *See also* FEMINISM; WOMEN IN LITERATURE.

– U –

UEDA BIN (1874–1916). Literary critic, scholar, translator, and **poet**, Ueda Bin was born in Tsukiji, Tokyo, and graduated from Tokyo Imperial University. A student of languages, he was praised as "one in a million" by **Lafcadio Hearn**. He traveled to Europe in 1908, and his major work, ***Kaichôon*** (The Sound of the Tide, 1905), is a collection of **translations** from Western poets. He died of renal failure at age 41. *See also* FREE VERSE; *MYÔJÔ*; SYMBOLISM; YOSHII ISAMU.

UKIGUMO. *Ukigumo* (1887; tr. *The Drifting Clouds*, 1967) was a fledgling novel by **Futabatei Shimei**. Considered by many to be the first modern Japanese novel, in large part because of its use of ***gen-***

bun itchi colloquial narrative language, the story centers on Utsumi Bunzô, a young member of the samurai class who loses his government job by refusing to display the proper subordinate attitude to his boss. He is in love with his cousin and is reluctant to tell his aunt of his misfortune for fear of losing the prospect of marriage. His fellow worker, whose pragmatic approach to workplace deference keeps him employed, has eyes for Utsumi's cousin as well, and this creates a romantic tension that permeates this novel up through its premature conclusion.

UMEZAKI HARUO (1915–1965). Umezaki Haruo was a novelist from Fukuoka. He graduated from Tokyo University and worked in the research department of the Tokyo City Educational Office, where he began his writing career. In 1954, Umezaki won the **Naoki Prize** for *Boroya no shunjû* (1954; tr. *Occurences of an Old Dilapidated House*, 1968). Another novel, *Sunadokei* (The Hourglass, 1955), met with great critical acclaim. Umezaki is considered part of the First Generation of postwar writers along with **Noma Hiroshi**, **Nakamura Shin'ichirô**, and **Takeda Taijun**.

UNEXPECTED ENCOUNTERS WITH BEAUTIES. *See KAJIN NO KIGÛ.*

UNIFICATION OF WRITING AND SPEECH. *See GENBUN ITCHI.*

UNO CHIYO (1897–1996). Uno Chiyo was a novelist and member of the Japan Art Academy. Raised in Yamaguchi Prefecture, she made her literary debut shortly after marrying by winning a novel-writing contest sponsored by a local newspaper. She then left her husband and young child to go to Tokyo to write. She published *Irozange* (tr. *Confessions of Love*, 1986) in 1935 to great acclaim. She finished the novel *Ohan* (1957; tr. *Ohan*, 1961) after 10 years' labor, and it was later made into a **film**. While in Tokyo, she was involved in design, editing, and business, had several failed marriages with famous writers, and stopped writing until the 1960s, when she took up the pen once more. Uno was awarded the **Women's Literature Prize** (1970), the Japan Art Academy Prize (1972), the **Kikuchi Kan Prize** (1982), and the **Order of Cultural Merit** (1990). She died of pneumonia in a Tokyo hospital at the age of 98. *See also* FEMINISM; WOMEN IN LITERATURE.

UNO KÔJI (1891–1961). Uno Kôji, given name Kakujirô, was a novelist from Fukuoka who graduated in English literature from Waseda University. He published a collection of stories, *Seijirô yume o miru ko* (Seijiro, the Child Who Dreams, 1913). He further established himself as a writer with the novel *Kura no naka* (1919; tr. *In the Storehouse*, 1997), and thereafter made friends with **Hirotsu Kazuo** and **Akutagawa Ryûnosuke**. He also wrote **I-Novels** and **children's literature**. He encouraged **Minakami Tsutomu** in his early writing efforts, was on the selection committee for the **Akutagawa Ryûnosuke Prize**, and won the **Yomiuri Prize** for *Omoikawa* (River of Thoughts, 1951).

UTOPIAN LITERATURE. Although utopian themes are present in premodern Japanese literature, a distinctive kind of utopian literature emerged in Japan in the wake of the **Meiji Restoration**. As early as 1868, the Dutch utopian text *Anno 2065: een Blik in de Toekomst* (*2065: A Glimpse of the Future*) appeared in Japanese **translation** and helped spark a short-lived wave of *miraiki* (futurist) fiction that included over 100 stories written during the late 19th century. Western utopian (and dystopian) works, such as Jonathan Swift's *Gulliver's Travels*, the **science fiction** writings of Jules Verne, and even Thomas Moore's *Utopia* itself (1882), combined with the optimism and promise of change that coincided with the **Freedom and People's Rights Movement** and fueled a speculative reconsideration of social structures. Throughout the 20th century writers created imaginative utopias and dystopias, either to underscore the absurdity of life, as in the writings of **Mishima Yukio** and **Abe Kôbô**, or to avoid **censorship**, as in the case of **Akutagawa Ryûnosuke**'s dystopian novel *Kappa* (1927; tr. *Kappa*, 1947). More recently, **Ôe Kenzaburô**'s *Chiryôtô* (The Treatment Tower, 1991) and many of **Murakami Haruki**'s novels contain utopian or dystopian themes.

– V –

VENUS. *See* ***MYÔJÔ.***

– W –

WAGAHAI WA NEKO DE ARU. *Wagahai wa neko de aru* (1905–6; tr. *I Am a Cat*, 1961) is a novel by **Natsume Sôseki** that first appeared in installments in *Hototogisu* (The Cuckoo), a **literary journal**. The satirical novel comically touches on current issues, such as the intermingling of traditional Japanese customs and new, imported Western ideas. The novel documents, from the point of view of a haughty house cat, the lives of several middle-class Japanese, including the cat's master, his family, and a young couple. The cat continually asserts the superiority of the feline race, judging the humans foolish for their mistakes, though, in the end, the drunken cat drowns in a water barrel.

WAKA. *See* ***TANKA.***

WAR LITERATURE. Tales of military valor (*gunki, gundan*) were an important genre prior to the **Meiji** period, with such works as the 14th-century *Heike monogatari* (Tale of the Heike) and *Taiheiki* (Chronicle of the Peace) appearing in both written and oral versions throughout the **Tokugawa** period. **Nationalism** soared following Japan's defeat of Qing China (1894–95), and when Japan fought Russia in 1904–5, many writers and poets participated in this new, modern war, often as correspondents for newspapers. Some wrote of the events using classical allusions to earlier war tales, while others, such as **Yosano Akiko**, took an antiwar stance in her **poetry**.

Japan's **militarism** during the 1920s and 1930s led to greater literary oppression. Writers were subject to heavy **censorship**, and paper was strictly rationed. Many novels published during this time, such as those by **Hino Ashihei**, glorified the war and even served as propaganda. Some authors, such as **Tanizaki Jun'ichirô** and **Kawabata Yasunari**, largely avoided censorship by writing beautiful but politically neutral love stories. Others distinctly opposed the war, including **Ishikawa Tatsuzô**, **Oguma Hideo**, and **Kuroshima Denji**, attempting to publish antiwar literature or disturbing, realistic accounts of attacks. Many of these writings, however, were not published until after the war was over. Some writers spent time working as war correspondents in China and Southeast Asia and later drew on these wartime experiences for their literary and nonfiction works. Military tales remain a staple of popular Japanese fiction, which contains a plethora of samurai stories as well as tales of valor and tragedy from World War II. *See also* ATOMIC BOMB LITERATURE; KINOSHITA NAOE; MISHIMA YUKIO; MORI ÔGAI; NOMA HIROSHI; NOSAKA AKIYUKI; PATRIOTIC ASSOCIATION FOR JAPANESE LITERATURE; POSTWAR LITERATURE; PROLETARIAN LITERATURE; SAKAGUCHI ANGO; SHIMAO TOSHIO; TAKAMI JUN; TAKEDA TAIJUN; THIRD GENERATION; THOUGHT POLICE; TSUBOI SHIGEJI.

WASEDA BUNGAKU**.** *Waseda bungaku* (Waseda Literature) is the journal of Waseda University's literature department. Since **Tsubouchi Shôyô** published the first issue in 1891, the journal has witnessed 10 different "eras," each emphasizing a different style and featuring various authors. The longest hiatus between eras was eight years. The first era featured Tsubouchi's literary criticism, **Mori Ôgai**'s **realist** theory, and the writings of **Shimamura Hôgetsu** and **Hirotsu Ryûrô**. Subsequent eras focused on **naturalist** writing. Tanizaki Seiji (1890–1971), the younger brother of **Tanizaki Jun'ichirô**, was chairman during the third era, and **Tachihara Masaaki** was editor-in-chief during the seventh era. In recent years, the Waseda Bungaku Newcomer Prize was established, and the journal has featured the work of critic Ikeda Yûichi (1969–). The 10th era began in 2008, featuring a novel by Kawakami Mieko (1976–). *See also* LITERARY JOURNALS.

***WASEDA* LITERATURE.** *See WASEDA BUNGAKU.*

WATAKUSHI SHÔSETSU**.** *See* I-NOVEL.

WATANABE KAZUO (1901–1975). Watanabe Kazuo was a Tokyo-born scholar and well-known **translator**. He started learning French in middle school and graduated from Tokyo University in French literature in 1925. Thereafter, he taught high school in Tokyo and then was employed at the **Ministry of Education** as a researcher, which took him to France from 1931 to 1933. In 1940, he was hired at Tokyo University, and during World War II he spent his time translating works by Rabelais and Thomas Mann. He received the **Yomiuri Prize** in 1964 for his translation of Rabelais's *The Life of Gargantua and of Pantagruel* (which was said to be untranslatable), and the Asahi Cultural Prize in 1971.

WEIR, THE. *See SHIGARAMI ZÔSHI.*

WHITE BIRCH SOCIETY. *See SHIRAKABA.*

WILD GEESE, THE. *See GAN.*

WIND-UP BIRD CHRONICLES, THE. *See NEJIMAKI-DORI KURONIKURU.*

WOMAN IN THE DUNES. *See SUNA NO ONNA.*

WOMEN IN LITERATURE. Women play an important role in all forms of Japanese literature. Many classical Japanese authors were women and even the very style of vernacular written Japanese has origins in writing that was used by women in the Heian court. The metamorphosis of female characterization speaks volumes about cultural expectations and changing social roles for women in Japan. In the earliest mythology, Amaterasu, the sun goddess, has great power and gives birth to the Japanese imperial line. Folklore contains a variety of women stereotypes, including the angelic self-sacrificing wife and virtuous maiden, as well as the demonic *yamauba* (mountain hag) and *yukionna* (snow woman). Classical Japanese narratives, such as the *Tale of Genji* (ca. 1008), were often written by women and include memorable female protagonists of complex psychological depth. The lyric tradition includes not only women poets who express their longings openly, but also a variety of female archetypes for, or about whom, **poetry** was written. In drama, the *nô* and *kabuki* traditions contain a full spectrum of both good and evil women characters.

Women's roles in society underwent reevaluation following the **Meiji Restoration.** On the one hand, the government promoted traditional roles and values in such slogans as "*ryôsai kenbo*" (good wives, wise mothers), and didactic fiction tended to empasize this stereotype. Yet other narrative works, such as **Izumi Kyôka**'s "***Kôya hijiri***" (1900; tr. *The Kôya Priest*, 1959–60), underscore the mystical, demonic female character. The ***tanka*** of **Yosano Akiko**, with their overt description of female desire, offered a profound challenge to the Meiji-period stereotypes. By the 20th century, **translations** of Western novels and a swing toward **realist** fiction, along with the influence of Japanese **feminism**, led to more complex and three-dimensional female protagonists, such as the four sisters in **Tanizaki Jun'ichirô**'s wartime novel ***Sasameyuki*** (1943–48; tr. *The Makioka Sisters*, 1957).

After the **war**, the **Occupation** brought new cultural innovations and expectations to Japanese women, which were expanded during the 1960s and 1970s as waves of new women writers published stories that explored the range of changing female stereotypes and the tensions of the Japanese workplace. Many contemporary novels, such as the stories of **Tsushima Yûko**, depict women who are confused by the array of expectations and options available to them, while others, such as works by **Yamada Eimi**, portray aggressive female characters in control of their destinies. *See also* ARAI MOTOKO; ARIYOSHI SAWAKO; CELL-PHONE NOVELS; ENCHI FUMIKO; FEMINISM; *FUTON*; *GAN*; HAYASHI FUMIKO; HAYASHI MARIKO; HIGUCHI ICHIYÔ; HIRABAYASHI TAIKO; *HOTOTOGISU*; *IZU NO ODORIKO*; *KAJIN NO KIGÛ*; KANEKO MISUZU; KÔNO TAEKO; *KUROTOKAGE*; *MAIHIME*; *MEIAN*; MIZUMURA MINAE; ÔBA MINAKO; OKAMOTO KANOKO; OZAKI KÔYÔ; SATA INEKO; SETOUCHI JAKUCHÔ; *SHAYÔ*; SHIMAO TOSHIO; SONO AYAKO; *TADE KÛ MUSHI*; *TAKEKURABE*; TOKUDA SHÛSEI; *UKIGUMO*; WOMEN'S LITERATURE PRIZE; YAMAMOTO MICHIKO; YOSHIMOTO BANANA; *YUKIGUNI*.

WOMEN'S LITERATURE PRIZE. The Women's Literature Prize (*Joryû bungaku shô*) is a **literary award** given annually for the best work of fiction written by a woman. The prize was established in

1961 and sponsored by the **Chûô Kôron** publishing house to encourage literary talent among women and has been awarded to authors including **Enchi Fumiko, Sata Ineko,** and **Uno Chiyo.** The winner receives a commemorative plaque and a cash award of one million yen. In 2001, the name of the award was changed to Fujin Kôron Literary Prize.

WRITERS' GUILDS. *See BUNDAN.*

– Y –

YAMADA BIMYÔ (1868–1910). Yamada Bimyô, given name Taketarô, was an author, poet, and critic credited with helping create colloquial written narrative style and for pioneering new forms of **poetry**. While preparing for college, Yamada and his friends formed a **literary journal** titled *Garakuta bunko* (Rubbish Library), where Yamada published his first short sketch, *Azakai shôsetsu tengu* (Mockery and Reproof for a Braggart Novelist, 1886), written in colloquial language. In an 1888 essay, he codified some of his ideas about ***genbun itchi*** (unifying speech and writing), attributing both Western novels and the storyteller **San'yûtei Enchô** as sources for his style. Although his later historical novels were well received at the time, they were quickly eclipsed by newer experiments. He had a falling out with his former colleagues, and, following his wife's **suicide**, died in poverty at age 42. *See also KÔDAN*; *RAKUGO.*

YAMADA EIMI (1959–). Yamada Eimi, given name Futaba, is a controversial author born in Tokyo. Yamada's novels depict issues generally not discussed openly in Japanese culture, such as sexuality and racism. Having been forced to move frequently in childhood because of her father's job, Yamada was faced with trials of bullying and separation that come out in her novels. She attended Meiji University but dropped out and unsuccessfully tried to become a ***manga*** writer. Her breakthrough as an author came with her novel *Beddo taimu aizu* (1985; tr. *Bedtime Eyes*, 2005), which was awarded the Bungei Prize. She has also won the **Naoki Prize** for *Sôru myûjikku rabâzu onrî* (Soul Music Lovers Only, 1987), the **Women's Literature Prize** for

Torasshu (1991; tr. *Trash*, 1994), the **Yomiuri Prize** for *A2Z* (2000), and the **Tanizaki Jun'ichirô Prize** for *Fûmizekka* (Wonderful Flavor, 2005). *See also* FEMINISM; WOMEN IN LITERATURE.

YAMAMOTO MICHIKO (1936–). Yamamoto Michiko is the pen name of Furuya Michiko, a **poet** and prize-winning author of short stories. She based her first collection of short stories, *Betei-san no niwa* (1973; tr. *Betty-san*, 1983) on her experiences in Australia, where she had traveled with her husband. It won the **Akutagawa Ryûnosuke Prize** in 1973. Yamamoto currently resides in Tokyo. *See also* WOMEN IN LITERATURE.

YAMAMOTO SHÛGORÔ (1903–1967). Yamamoto Shûgorô was the pen name of Shimizu Satomu, a novelist from Yamanashi Prefecture. His pen name is borrowed in homage to the owner of the bookstore where he worked after dropping out of secondary school. The owner, Yamamoto Shûgorô, let Shimizu go to school part-time. The author Yamamoto came onto the literary scene in the mid-1920s with the short story "*Sumadera fukin*" (Sumadera and Its Environs, 1925), which was serialized in the **literary journal** ***Bungei shunjû*** (Literary Chronicle). His early work was aimed toward **children**, but he also wrote popular adult novels, and even ventured into the genres of historical fiction and **detective novels**. His wartime novel *Nihon fudôki* (Lives of Great Japanese Women, 1942) was very popular and was awarded the **Naoki Prize**, but Yamamoto refused to accept it on the premise that his works, which he considered popular stories, should not be confused with true literature. Yamamoto continued writing until the end of his life, publishing the novel *Aobeka monogatari* (This Madding Crowd, 1960). Many of his works have been made into **films**. *See also* WAR LITERATURE.

YAMAMOTO YÛZÔ (1887–1974). Yamamoto Yûzô was a playwright and novelist from Tochigi Prefecture who graduated from Tokyo University. He made his debut as a playwright with *Seimei no kanmuri* (1920; tr. *The Crown of Life*, 1935). He also wrote novels and **children's literature** and helped found the Japanese Writer's Association with **Kikuchi Kan** and **Akutagawa Ryûnosuke**. During World War II, he spoke out against the government's **censorship**

policies, and after the war served in the Diet on Japanese language reform, advocating for limited use of complex ideograms (*kanji*). He was awarded the **Order of Cultural Merit** in 1965. After his death, his European-style home in Mitaka, Tokyo, was converted into a museum. *See also* MODERN THEATER; THEATER REFORM.

YAMAZAKI MASAKAZU (1934–). Yamazaki Masakazu is a playwright, theater scholar, and **literary critic** from Kyoto Prefecture. He studied art history at Kyoto University and eventually received his doctorate there, following which he studied at Yale and taught at Kansai and Osaka universities. He garnered a reputation for solid analysis with his essay on the style of author **Mori Ôgai** titled "*Ôgai: tatakau kachô*" (Ôgai: Combative Patriarch, 1972). Yamazaki has also been involved in politics, advocating for Japan to be more like the Western powers than its Asian neighbors. His works are included in high school textbooks and college entrance exams. Yamazaki has also served as a member of the **Ministry of Education** and Science's Central Education Council. *See also* MODERN THEATER.

YASUDA YOJÛRÔ (1910–1981). Yasuda Yojûrô, pen name of Yuhara Toshimi, was a **literary critic** who graduated in art history from Tokyo University. After gaining exposure to European thought via Karl Marx, Friedrich Hölderlin, and Friedrich Schlegel, he made his critical debut with *Nihon no hashi* (Bridge to Japan, 1936), which was an immediate success, garnering the Iketani Shinzaburô Prize and establishing him as a literary critic. Thereafter, he became a central figure in the Japan **Romantic** school. During World War II, he justified Japan's aggression in the Pacific and was pro-expansion, for which he was ostracized by other critics when the war ended. His reputation recovered, however, when later he published a pacifist manifesto under a pseudonym. *See also* PATRIOTIC ASSOCIATION FOR JAPANESE LITERATURE; WAR LITERATURE.

YASUOKA SHÔTARÔ (1920–). Yasuoka Shôtarô is an author from Kôchi Prefecture. In middle school, he was banished to a Zen **Buddhist** temple for three years, and after multiple unsuccessful attempts was accepted into Keiô University in 1941. In 1944, however, he was drafted into the military and spent a year in Manchuria before being discharged with tuberculosis. In 1948, he finally graduated and his *Garasu no kutsu* (1951; tr. *The Glass Slipper*, 1961) was nominated for an **Akutagawa Ryûnosuke Prize**, giving him exposure in literary circles. In 1953, the Akutagawa Prize committee, at an impasse over two of his works, awarded him the prize for both *Warui nakama* (1953; tr. *Bad Company*, 1984) and *Inki na tanoshimi* (1953; tr. *Gloomy Pleasures*, 1984). In addition, Yasuoka has won the **Noma Prize** twice (1960, 1989), the **Yomiuri Prize** (1973), and the **Kawabata Yasunari Prize** (1991). *See also* COLONIAL LITERATURE.

YOKOMITSU RIICHI (1898–1947). Yokomitsu Riichi was an author and a member of the **neoperceptionist** school. In 1923, he published "*Nichirin*" (The Sun), "*Hae*" (1923; tr. *The Fly*, 1965), and other short pieces of fiction in ***Bungei shunjû*** (Literary Chronicle). He also founded the magazine *Bungei jidai* (Literary Times) with **Kawabata Yasunari**. Yokomitsu, along with his peers, emphasized the multiple senses and imbued his writing with novel and often startlingly fresh images. *See also* MODERNISM.

YOMIURI PRIZE FOR LITERATURE. The Yomiuri Prize for Literature (*Yomiuri bungaku shô*) was first awarded by the *Yomiuri* newspaper in 1948 with the aim of building a "cultural nation." The prizes were initially offered for four categories: novels, **poetry**, scholarly studies, and **literary criticism**. Since then, awards for theater, travel writing, criticism, biography, and **translation** have been added to the prize categories. Winners receive a commemorative ink stone and a cash award of one million yen. Famous recipients for fiction include **Abe Kôbô**, **Murakami Haruki**, and **Ôoka Shôhei**.

YOSANO AKIKO (1878–1942). Yosano Akiko, née Hô Shiyô, was a ***tanka*** poet and **feminist** from Osaka. During high school, she subscribed to the **literary journal** ***Myôjô*** (Venus) and later became one of its major contributors. Through this relationship, she met the founder of the journal, **Yosano Tekkan**, and the two fell in love and eventually married in 1901. That same year she published the feminist *tanka* collection *Midaregami* (1901; tr. *Tangled Hair*, 1948). One of her most popular compositions was the antiwar poem *Kimi shinitamau koto nakare* (1904; tr. *Beloved, You Must Not Die*, 1974), published in *Myôjô* and addressed to her brother who was fighting in the Russo-Japanese War at the time. In 1938, she published a **translation** of the classical *Tale of Genji* (ca. 1008) into modern Japanese, an effort that took three drafts spanning 17 years. A pacifist and feminist throughout her career, she became a social activist and promoted educational reform. Her crowning work was a compilation of over 26,000 poems by more than 6,600 contributors collected over a 60-year period and fittingly titled *Shin man'yôshû* (The New 'Man'yôshû,' 1937–39). *See also* POETRY; WAR LITERATURE; WOMEN IN LITERATURE.

YOSANO TEKKAN (1873–1935). Yosano Tekkan, given name Hiroshi, was an author and **poet** from Kyoto. He graduated from Keiô University and taught Japanese language at a women's school in the provinces. After being fired because of impropriety with a student (with whom he had a child), he went to Tokyo, became interested in Japanese literature, and worked as a staff writer for a newspaper. There he published *Bôkoku no ne* (Sounds Ruinous to the Country, 1894), a critical manifesto calling for ***tanka*** reform. The manifesto catapulted his career, and in 1900 he founded the **literary journal *Myôjô*** (Venus), which drew together a circle of famous poets, such as **Kitahara Hakushû**, **Yoshii Isamu**, and **Ishikawa Takuboku**, who became regular contributors. He met, lived with, and eventually married an early contributor and poet, **Yosano Akiko**, whose career he subsequently supported at the expense of his own writing.

YOSE*.** The *yose* (storytelling theaters) of Japan originated during the **Tokugawa** period as small roadside shacks wherein itinerant professional storytellers would tell their tales to passersby for a small fee. By the **Meiji** period, they had become village and neighborhood theaters with a small stage that featured not only storytelling but also variety acts, such as magicians, comedians, and musicians. As Tokyo grew in the 1870s and 1880s *yose* increased in number and in popularity among the immigrants from the countryside. With the invention of Japanese **shorthand** (*sokki*), fledgling **publishing houses** in the 1880s turned to the *yose* as a source of transcribed narrative to serialize in magazines and newspapers. Storytellers initially benefited from the publicity, but over time were replaced by musicians and ***rakugo performers. As cinema, radio, and eventually television became more available, theaters decreased in popularity. Today *yose* can only be found in large cities and are few in number, with the majority specializing in *rakugo*. *See also* FUTABATEI SHIMEI; *GENBUN ITCHI*; KAWATAKE SHINSHICHI III; *KÔDAN*; SAN'YÛTEI ENCHÔ; TAKUSARI KÔKI.

YOSHII ISAMU (1886–1960). Yoshii Isamu was a ***tanka*** poet and playwright. He dropped out of Waseda University to contribute to ***Myôjô*** (Venus), the **literary journal** of the growing *Tôkyô Shinshisha* (Tokyo New Poetry Society), which he subsequently joined and affiliated with **Mori Ôgai**, **Ueda Bin**, and **Kitahara Hakushû**. He later left the society and joined with **Romanticist** Kitahara to form the *Pan no kai* (Society of Pan). In 1909, Yoshii broke away and, with the help of Mori, founded the literary journal *Subaru* (Pleiades). In the ensuing decade, he published the **poetry** anthologies *Sakehogai* (Revelry, 1910), *Gion kashu* (Gion Verses, 1915), and *Tôkyô kôtô shû* (Collection from the Tokyo Red-Light District, 1916), which helped solidify his status as a major *tanka* poet. Thereafter, he contributed to the *shingeki* (new theater) movement by publishing plays in *Subaru*. He also wrote scripts for programs that were performed on the radio in the 1920s. *See also* MODERN THEATER; THEATER REFORM.

YOSHIKAWA EIJI (1892–1962). Yoshikawa Eiji was one of Japan's preeminent historical novelists. Born in Yokohama, he joined a Tokyo **poetry** society in his youth and won first prize in a novel-writing contest sponsored by Kôdansha with *Enoshima monogatari* (The Tale of Enoshima, 1914). He went on to publish many accessible revisions of Japanese and Chinese classics, including ***Miyamoto musashi*** **(1935;** tr. *Musashi*, 1981). He was awarded the **Order of Cultural Merit** in 1960, the Order of the Sacred Treasure, and the Mainichi Art Award just before his death of cancer in 1962. A **literary award** was named in his honor. *See also* SUICIDE; WAR LITERATURE.

YOSHIKAWA EIJI PRIZE FOR LITERATURE. The **Yoshikawa Eiji** Prize for Literature (*Yoshikawa Eiji shô*) was established in 1967 by the Yoshikawa Eiji Citizens' Cultural Promotion Association to commemorate the work of the famous novelist. The prize is awarded annually to an outstanding work in a variety of literary genres based on initial recommendations submitted by several hundred professionals working in the arts, media, and other fields. The winner receives a commemorative plaque and a cash award of three million yen. Notable recipients include **Shiba Ryôtarô**, **Matsumoto Seichô**, and **Hayashi Mariko**. *See also* LITERARY AWARDS.

YOSHIMOTO BANANA (1964–). Yoshimoto Banana, given name Mahoko, became a best-selling author upon the publication of her debut novel ***Kitchin*** (1987; tr. *Kitchen*, 1991) at the age of 23. Several of her novels, including *Kitchin* and *Tugumi* (1989; tr. *Goodbye Tsugumi*, 2002), have been adapted for television and film. Yoshimoto's writing, including 12 novels and seven essay collections, incorporates traditional Japanese elements in a lighthearted manner, but is sometimes criticized for being superficial and commercial. *See also* FEMINISM; WOMEN IN LITERATURE.

YOSHIYUKI JUN'NOSUKE (1924–1994). Yoshiyuki Jun'nosuke was a novelist and short-story writer from Okayama Prefecture. He attended Tokyo University in 1945 but was displaced that same year due to the fire bombings. Before completing his degree, he was persuaded by his boss at an editing company to drop out of school. Yoshiyuki had already been exposed to some **literary journals** in college, and he continued to contribute to them while editing. His novel *Shû'u* (1954; tr. *Sudden Shower*, 1972) won the **Akutagawa Ryûnosuke Prize**, and, unemployed after becoming infected with tuberculosis and having no other money with which to subsist, he decided to become a professional writer. In 1963, he published the popular novel *Suna no ue no shokubutsu gun* (Vegetable Garden in the Sand) and won the **Tanizaki Jun'ichirô Prize** for *Anshitsu* (1970; tr. *The Dark Room*, 1975). His novel *Yûgure made* (Until Evening, 1978) took 13 years to write, but won the **Noma Prize**. Yoshiyuki is considered to be a member of the **Third Generation** of **postwar** writers.

YUIBI SHUGI. *See* AESTHETICISM.

YUKIGUNI. *Yukiguni* (1948; tr. *Snow Country*, 1956) was author and **Nobel Prize** laureate **Kawabata Yasunari**'s first full-length novel.

Originally published in serial form over 12 years' time and across five **literary journals**, the work is set in the mountain spa resort of Yuzawa, which receives heavy snowfall each winter. The story describes a failing love affair between a man from Tokyo and a geisha who lives in the remote town. The novel portrays the lackluster career of a country geisha and the effects of modernization on traditional Japanese arts. The work has been twice adapted for **film.** *See also* WOMEN IN LITERATURE.

– Z –

***ZAINICHI* LITERATURE.** Many Koreans immigrated to Japan following the annexation of Korea in 1910, which made all Koreans Japanese citizens. Often this was an economic necessity, and throughout the 1920s Korean communities developed across Japan. During the Kantô Earthquake of 1923, rumors quickly spread that Koreans fleeing the damaged areas were saboteurs, with tragic consequences. Wartime lack of manpower led to forced conscription of Koreans who were displaced to Japan to work in factories and on farms, often in oppressive circumstances. By the end of the war, nearly two million Koreans were in Japan and many were quickly repatriated. After the **Occupation** ended, Koreans in Japan were no longer Japanese citizens, so their citizenship reverted back to Korean. More than 500,000 remained in Japan, garnering the *zainichi* (remaining in Japan) epithet. These Korean families have raised children, run businesses, and lived their lives with dual identities. They speak Japanese primarily, but some have divided into factions following the North–South Korean divide and are ambivalent about their Korean identities in the Japanese context.

A number of writers have emerged from the *zainichi* community in Japan, and their work deals with the issues of prejudice, deprivation, and identity struggles they face living as outsiders in what, to many of the younger generation, is their homeland. Notable among the *zainichi* authors are Kim Yun Kyu (1926–80; Japanese: **Tachihara Masaaki**), Lee Hoesung (1935–; Japanese: Ri Kaisei), Lee Yangji (1955–92; Japanese: I Yanji), Yû Miri (1968–), and Hyeon Wol (1965–; Japanese: Gen Getsu). *See also* COLONIAL LITERATURE; FOREIGN AUTHORS WRITING IN JAPANESE; MILITARISM.

Bibliography

CONTENTS

INTRODUCTION

Japanese literature is written for Japanese readers. This has almost always been the case, meaning that the bulk of secondary studies is also in Japanese. From the later half of the 20th century onward, however, more and more Japanese literature has found its way into translation, primarily in English. Accordingly, some writers of international status or cosmopolitan outlook, such as Mishima Yukio, Ôe Kenzaburô, Murakami

Haruki, and Yoshimoto Banana, almost seem to take the foreign reader into consideration in their writings. The awarding of two Nobel Prizes to Japanese authors also suggests a waning of the insularity that characterized Japanese literature during the Tokugawa and Meiji periods.

Japan's tradition of literary criticism is long indeed, and literary scholarship enjoys a much broader readership in Japan than its counterpart does in the West, despite its focus on sometimes narrow or arcane issues in vogue among Japanese scholars. A few such studies have been translated into English, but the bulk of this work remains in Japanese.

However, since the opening of Japan to the West, non-Japanese have found Japan's literary traditions worthy of consideration, and since the late 19th century, a steady stream of studies and translations of Japanese literature has been written by scholars in English. This bibliography seeks to identify some of these studies and translations. Beginning in the 1950s, perhaps in response to the global popularity of Japanese films, Japanese works of literature began to find translators and publishers in English, and, from that time until the present, the number of English translations (and, in some cases, retranslations) of literature has proceeded apace.

The present select bibliography is divided into two major categories: General Scholarship and Select Bibliography of Authors and Translations, which are further subdivided. It is composed almost entirely of books, most of which were published during the past few decades; a vast array of journal articles on modern Japanese literature can be mined with a few keystrokes and an effective electronic reference service.

Specific studies and works of criticism are under the General Scholarship category, in which has also been included general Web resources dealing with modern Japanese literature. For those who wish a broad overview of modern Japanese literature, Donald Keene's two-volume *Dawn to the West: Japanese Literature of the Modern Era* (New York: Columbia University Press, 1981) provides both breadth and depth with a study of the primary genres as well as criticism. Another useful volume is J. Thomas Rimer's *A Reader's Guide to Japanese Literature* (New York: Kodansha International, 1988), a survey of both classical and modern literature with overviews of important authors and works. Insight into the workings of modern Japanese poetry is found in Makoto Ueda's *Modern Japanese Poets and the Nature of Literature* (Stanford,

Calif.: Stanford University Press, 1983), and Samuel Leiter's *Historical Dictionary of Japanese Traditional Theatre* (Lanham, Md.: Scarecrow Press, 2006) contains a number of entries discussing the continuity of theater into the modern period.

In terms of criticism, a large number of very good monographs and scholarly studies has appeared in recent years, reflecting the maturing of the discipline. Some are quite theoretical, others comparative in scope, and yet others thematic. Some of the important works dealing with narrative fiction include Irmela Hijiya-Kirschnereit's *Rituals of Self-Revelation: Shishôsetsu as Literary Genre and Socio-Cultural Phenomenon* (Cambridge, Mass.: Harvard University Asia Center, 1996), which is an important study of the I-Novel, and Dennis Washburn's *The Dilemma of the Modern in Japanese Fiction* (New Haven, Conn.: Yale University Press, 1995), which investigates the continuities that link classical with modern Japanese literature. Modern theater studies include both translations, such as David Goodman's *After Apocalypse: Four Japanese Plays of Hiroshima and Nagasaki* (New York: Columbia University Press, 1986), as well as critical-historical studies, such as Carol Fisher Sorgenfrei and Shûji Terayama's *Unspeakable Acts: The Avant-Garde Theatre of Terayama Shûji and Postwar Japan* (Honolulu: University of Hawai'i Press, 2005). Leith Morton has provided a valuable study of modern poetry in his overview *Modernism in Practice: An Introduction to Postwar Japanese Poetry* (Honolulu: University of Hawai'i Press, 2004).

Much of the scholarship taking place today in the field concerns specific movements or periods, and the Literary Histories section demonstrates both the variety of perspectives and approaches as well as the breadth of history represented in contemporary scholarship on modern Japanese literature. Historical studies include a panoply of topics, such as the emergence of the novel in the Meiji period (Janet Walker's *The Japanese Novel of the Meiji Period and the Ideal of Individualism* (Princeton, N.J.: Princeton University Press, 1979), the I-Novel (Edward Fowler's *The Rhetoric of Confession: Shishôsetsu in Early Twentieth-Century Japanese Fiction* (Berkeley: University of California Press, 1988), the war and its aftermath (Marlene J. Mayo, J. Thomas Rimer, and H. Eleanor Kerkham's *War, Occupation, and Creativity: Japan and East Asia, 1920–1960* [Honolulu: University of Hawai'i Press, 2001]), translation and adaptation (J. Scott Miller's *Adaptations of Western Literature in Meiji Japan* [New York: Palgrave, 2001]), and atomic bomb literature (John Whittier Treat's *Writing Ground Zero: Japanese Literature and the Atomic Bomb* (Chicago: University of Chicago Press, 1995).

Feminist approaches to the study of modern Japanese literature form a particularly strong area of English-language scholarship, and the bibliographical section Women and Literature includes a dozen studies that address aspects of women in modern literature, including women as subjects (Makoto Ueda's *The Mother of Dreams and Other Short Stories: Portrayals of Women in Modern Japanese Fiction* (New York: Kodansha International, 1986) and women as writers (Tomoko Kuribayashi and Mizuho Terasawa's *The Outsider Within: Ten Essays on Modern Japanese Women Writers* (Lanham, Md.: University Press of America, 2002).

Other topical areas of literary exploration expand our understanding beyond the usual scope. In Film and Literature this includes Keiko I. McDonald's *From Book to Screen: Modern Japanese Literature in Films* (Armonk, N.Y.: M.E. Sharpe, 2000), a work that examines over a dozen literary works and their film adaptations. Detective Fiction arose early in Japan and continues to be a popular genre, as Mark Silver outlines in his *Purloined Letters: Cultural Borrowing and Japanese Crime Literature* (Honolulu: University of Hawai'i Press, 2008). Peripheral literatures within Japan, such as that of minority Okinawans, are the focus of Michael S. Molasky and Steve Rabson in their book *Southern Exposure: Modern Japanese Literature from Okinawa* (Honolulu: University of Hawai'i Press, 2000) as well as Leith Morton in his work *The Alien Within: Representations of the Exotic in Twentieth-Century Japanese Literature* (Honolulu: University of Hawai'i Press, 2009).

A number of valuable Web resources are listed as well in this bibliography, although the nature of the Web makes it difficult to guarantee the longevity of the sites. The Japan Foundation Website (www.jpf.go.jp) is quite useful, both for information on contemporary scholarship but also for its fairly comprehensive online database listing works of Japanese literature in foreign translation. Mark Jewel's Japanese literature site (www.jlit.net) maintains an ongoing chronology and gives a wealth of details for both modern and classical Japanese literature. Specific author Web pages are too numerous, and varied in quality, to note, but *of Western Literature in Meiji Japan* (New York: Palgrave, 2001), and atomic bomb literature (John Whittier Treat's *Writing Ground Zero: Japanese Literature and the Atomic Bomb* (Chicago: University of Chicago Press, 1995).

Feminist approaches to the study of modern Japanese literature form a particularly strong area of English-language scholarship, and the bibliographical section Women and Literature includes a dozen studies that address aspects of women in modern literature, including women as subjects (Makoto Ueda's *The Mother of Dreams and Other Short Stories: Portrayals of Women in Modern Japanese Fiction* (New York: Kodansha International, 1986) and women as writers (Tomoko Kuribayashi and Mizuho Terasawa's *The Outsider Within: Ten Essays on Modern Japanese Women Writers* (Lanham, Md.: University Press of America, 2002).

Other topical areas of literary exploration expand our understanding beyond the usual scope. In Film and Literature this includes Keiko I. McDonald's *From Book to Screen: Modern Japanese Literature in Films* (Armonk, N.Y.: M.E. Sharpe, 2000), a work that examines over a dozen literary works and their film adaptations. Detective Fiction arose early in Japan and continues to be a popular genre, as Mark Silver outlines in his *Purloined Letters: Cultural Borrowing and Japanese Crime Literature* (Honolulu: University of Hawai'i Press, 2008). Peripheral literatures within Japan, such as that of minority Okinawans, are the focus of Michael S. Molasky and Steve Rabson in their book *Southern Exposure: Modern Japanese Literature from Okinawa* (Honolulu: University of Hawai'i Press, 2000) as well as Leith Morton in his work *The Alien Within: Representations of the Exotic in Twentieth-Century Japanese Literature* (Honolulu: University of Hawai'i Press, 2009).

A number of valuable Web resources are listed as well in this bibliography, although the nature of the Web makes it difficult to guarantee the longevity of the sites. The Japan Foundation Website (www.jpf.go.jp) is quite useful, both for information on contemporary scholarship but also for its fairly comprehensive online database listing works of Japanese literature in foreign translation. Mark Jewel's Japanese literature site (www.jlit.net) maintains an ongoing chronology and gives a wealth of details for both modern and classical Japanese literature. Specific author Web pages are too numerous, and varied in quality, to note, but a good search engine will yield a variety of Internet resources, many with English pages as well.

Works by and about specific authors are found in the Select Bibliography of Authors and Translations section, under either Anthologies, General Authors, or Specific Authors, depending upon whether the work is a broad anthology, focuses on a few authors, or treats one individual author, respectively. The Anthologies section reflects the rather young state of the field, but in recent years several important anthologies have made modern literature available to an increasing number of non-Japanese readers. Primary among them is a very recent two-volume set edited by Van C. Gessel and J. Thomas Rimer, *The Columbia Anthology of Modern Japanese Literature* (New York: Columbia University Press, 2005, 2007). This major anthology covers from the Meiji period to the 21st century and includes selections by major writers, poets, playwrights, and critics, many available for the first time in English translation. Two other more compact anthologies that have become classics are Van C. Gessel and Tomone Matsumoto's *The Shôwa Anthology: Modern Japanese Short Stories: 1929–1984* (New York: Kodansha International, 1989), and Hiroaki Sato, Burton Watson, and J. Thomas Rimer's *From the Country of Eight Islands: An Anthology of Japanese Poetry* (Garden City, N.Y.: Anchor Books, 1981).

As for journals of note, there are three primary periodicals that focus, in part, on the study of modern Japanese literature. *Monumenta Nipponica*, an interdisciplinary journal serving as an international forum for research on Japanese culture and society, is published semiannually by Sophia University, Tokyo. It carries both original scholarly contributions on history, literature, art history, religion, and thought, and translations of important Japanese literary and historical sources. *The Journal of Japanese Studies*, published semiannually by the Society for Japanese Studies and housed at the University of Washington, publishes broad, exploratory articles suggesting new analyses and interpretations, substantial book reviews, translations of Japanese articles of particular interest, and occasional symposia. *Japanese Language and Literature: Journal of the Association of Teachers of Japanese*, published semiannually by the Association of Teachers of Japanese, contains articles on Japanese language and literary topics as well as reviews of recent books.

In addition, the Library of Congress maintains a strong collection of scholarship on modern Japanese literature as well as works in translation, and major universities with programs in Japanese language usually have library resources devoted to modern literature.

GENERAL SCHOLARSHIP

Overviews

Beasley, W. G. *Modern Japan: Aspects of History, Literature, and Society.* Berkeley: University of California Press, 1975.

Gessel, Van C. *Japanese Fiction Writers since World War II.* Detroit, Mich.: Gale Research, 1997.

———. *Japanese Fiction Writers, 1868–1945.* Detroit, Mich.: Gale Research, 1997.

Hsu, Robert C. *Modern Japanese Writers.* New York: Scribner, 2001.

Isoda, Kôichi, and Japan P. E. N. Club. *A Survey of Japanese Literature Today.* Tokyo: Japan P.E.N. Club, 1984.

Katô, Shûichi. *A History of Japanese Literature.* 3 vols. London: Macmillan, 1979.

Keene, Donald. *Appreciations of Japanese Culture.* New York: Columbia University Press, 1981.

———. *Dawn to the West: Japanese Literature of the Modern Era.* 2 vols. New York: Holt, Rhinehart and Winston, 1984.

———. *The Pleasures of Japanese Literature.* New York: Columbia University Press, 1988.

Leiter, Samuel L. *Historical Dictionary of Japanese Traditional Theatre.* Lanham, Md.: Scarecrow Press, 2006.

Lewell, John. *Modern Japanese Novelists: A Biographical Dictionary.* New York: Kodansha International, 1993.

Mulhern, Chieko Irie. *Japanese Women Writers: A Bio-Critical Sourcebook.* Westport, Conn.: Greenwood Press, 1994.

Rimer, J. Thomas. *Modern Japanese Fiction and Its Traditions: An Introduction.* Princeton, N.J.: Princeton University Press, 1978.

———. *A Reader's Guide to Japanese Literature.* New York: Kodansha International, 1988.

Rimer, J. Thomas, and Robert E. Morrell. *Guide to Japanese Poetry.* Boston: G.K. Hall, 1984.

Schierbeck, Sachiko Shibata, and Marlene R. Edelstein. *Japanese Women Novelists in the 20th Century: 104 Biographies, 1900–1993.* Copenhagen: Museum Tusculanum Press, 1994.

Ueda, Makoto. *Modern Japanese Writers and the Nature of Literature.* Stanford, Calif.: Stanford University Press, 1976.

———. *Modern Japanese Poets and the Nature of Literature.* Stanford, Calif.: Stanford University Press, 1983.

——. *The Mother of Dreams and Other Short Stories: Portrayals of Women in Modern Japanese Fiction.* New York: Kodansha International, 1986.

——. *Literary and Art Theories in Japan.* Ann Arbor: Center for Japanese Studies, University of Michigan, 1991.

Critical Studies of Modern Japanese Literature and Theater

Narrative Fiction

Cohn, Joel R. *Studies in the Comic Spirit in Modern Japanese Fiction.* Cambridge, Mass.: Harvard University Asia Center, 1998.

Dodd, Stephen. *Writing Home: Representations of the Native Place in Modern Japanese Literature.* Cambridge, Mass.: Harvard University Asia Center, 2004.

Fujii, James A. *Complicit Fictions: The Subject in the Modern Japanese Prose Narrative.* Berkeley: University of California Press, 1993.

Hijiya-Kirschnereit, Irmela. *Rituals of Self-Revelation: Shishôsetsu as Literary Genre and Socio-Cultural Phenomenon.* Cambridge, Mass.: Harvard University Asia Center, 1996.

Hirata, Hosea. *Discourses of Seduction: History, Evil, Desire, and Modern Japanese Literature.* Cambridge, Mass.: Harvard University Asia Center, 2005.

Keene, Donald. *Modern Japanese Novels and the West.* Charlottesville: University of Virginia Press, 1961.

——. *Five Modern Japanese Novelists.* New York: Columbia University Press, 2002.

Kirkup, James. *Aspects of the Short Story. Six Modern Short Stories with Commentary.* Tokyo: Kaibunsha, 1969.

Miyoshi, Masao. *Accomplices of Silence; The Modern Japanese Novel.* Berkeley: University of California Press, 1974.

Murakami, Fuminobu. *Ideology and Narrative in Modern Japanese Literature.* Assen, The Netherlands: Van Gorcum, 1996.

Pollack, David. *Reading Against Culture: Ideology and Narrative in the Japanese Novel.* Ithaca, N.Y.: Cornell University Press, 1992.

Sakaki, Atsuko. *Recontextualizing Texts: Narrative Performance in Modern Japanese Fiction.* Cambridge, Mass.: Harvard University Asia Center, 1999.

——. *Obsessions with the Sino-Japanese Polarity in Japanese Literature.* Honolulu: University of Hawai'i Press, 2006.

Slaymaker, Douglas. *The Body in Postwar Japanese Fiction*. New York: Routledge-Curzon, 2004.

Suzuki, Tomi. *Narrating the Self: Fictions of Japanese Modernity*. Stanford, Calif.: Stanford University Press, 1996.

Tsukimura, Reiko. *Life, Death, and Age in Modern Japanese Fiction*. Toronto: University of Toronto-York University, Joint Centre on Modern East Asia, 1978.

Tsuruta, Kinya, and Thomas E. Swann. *Approaches to the Modern Japanese Novel*. Tokyo: Sophia University, 1976.

Washburn, Dennis C. *The Dilemma of the Modern in Japanese Fiction*. New Haven, Conn.: Yale University Press, 1995.

———. *Translating Mount Fuji: Modern Japanese Fiction and the Ethics of Identity*. New York: Columbia University Press, 2007.

Theater

Goodman, David G. *After Apocalypse: Four Japanese Plays of Hiroshima and Nagasaki*. New York: Columbia University Press, 1986.

Powell, Brian. *Kabuki in Modern Japan: Mayama Seika and His Plays*. Basingstoke, Hampshire: Macmillan in association with St. Antony's College, Oxford, 1990.

Rolf, Robert, and John K. Gillespie. *Alternative Japanese Drama: Ten Plays*. Honolulu: University of Hawai'i Press, 1992.

Sorgenfrei, Carol Fisher, and Shûji Terayama. *Unspeakable Acts: The Avant-Garde Theatre of Terayama Shûji and Postwar Japan*. Honolulu: University of Hawai'i Press, 2005.

Poetry

Kubota, Michiyo, and Joseph Hodnick. *A Forgotten Fan: Five Early 20th Century Japanese Poets*. Charlotte, N.C.: Pure Heart Press, 2003.

Morton, Leith. *Modernism in Practice: An Introduction to Postwar Japanese Poetry*. Honolulu: University of Hawai'i Press, 2004.

Sato, Hiroaki. *Ten Japanese Poets*. Hanover, N.H.: Granite Publications, 1973.

Ueda, Makoto. *Modern Japanese Poets and the Nature of Literature*. Stanford, Calif.: Stanford University Press, 1983.

Literary Histories

Bardsley, Jan. *The Bluestockings of Japan: New Woman Essays and Fiction from Seitô, 1911–16*. Ann Arbor: Center for Japanese Studies, University of Michigan, 2007.

Calichman, Richard. *Overcoming Modernity: Cultural Identity in Wartime Japan*. New York: Columbia University Press, 2008.

Colligan-Taylor, Karen. *The Emergence of Environmental Literature in Japan*. New York: Garland, 1990.

Fairbanks, Carol. *Japanese Women Fiction Writers: Their Culture and Society, 1890s to 1990s*. Lanham, Md.: Scarecrow Press, 2002.

Fowler, Edward. *The Rhetoric of Confession: Shishôsetsu in Early Twentieth-Century Japanese Fiction*. Berkeley: University of California Press, 1988.

Honma, Kenshirô. *The Literature of Naturalism: An East–West Comparative Study*. Kyoto: Yamaguchi Publishing House, 1983.

Kornicki, Peter F. *The Reform of Fiction in Meiji Japan*. London: Published by Ithaca Press for the Board of the Faculty of Oriental Studies, Oxford University, 1982.

Lippit, Seiji M. *Topographies of Japanese Modernism*. New York: Columbia University Press, 2002.

Maeda, Ai, and James A. Fujii. *Text and the City: Essays on Japanese Modernity*. Durham, N.C.: Duke University Press, 2004.

Matthew, Robert. *Japanese Science Fiction: A View of a Changing Society*. London: Routledge, 1989.

Mayo, Marlene J., J. Thomas Rimer, and H. Eleanor Kerkham. *War, Occupation, and Creativity: Japan and East Asia, 1920–1960*. Honolulu: University of Hawai'i Press, 2001.

Mertz, John Pierre. *Novel Japanese: Spaces of Nationhood in Early Meiji Narrative, 1870–88*. Ann Arbor: Center for Japanese Studies, University of Michigan, 2003.

Miller, J. Scott. *Adaptations of Western Literature in Meiji Japan*. New York: Palgrave, 2001.

Mortimer, Maya. *Meeting the Sensei: The Role of the Master in Shirakaba Writers*. Leiden: Brill, 2000.

Nakamura, Mitsuo, and Shinkôkai Kokusai Bunka. *Modern Japanese Fiction 1868–1926*. Tokyo: Kokusai Bunka Shinkôkai, 1968.

Napier, Susan Jolliffe. *From Impressionism to Anime: Japan as Fantasy and Fan Cult in the Mind of the West*. New York: Palgrave Macmillan, 2007.

Powell, Irena. *Writers and Society in Modern Japan*. New York: Kodansha International, 1983.

Rimer, J. Thomas, and Studies Joint Committee on Japanese. *Culture and Identity: Japanese Intellectuals During the Interwar Years*. Princeton, N.J.: Princeton University Press, 1990.

Rubin, Jay. *Injurious to Public Morals: Writers and the Meiji State*. Seattle, Wash.: University of Washington Press, 1984.

Sas, Miryam. *Fault Lines: Cultural Memory and Japanese Surrealism*. Stanford, Calif.: Stanford University Press, 1999.

Schlant, Ernestine, and J. Thomas Rimer. *Legacies and Ambiguities: Postwar Fiction and Culture in West Germany and Japan*. Washington, D.C.: Woodrow Wilson Center Press, 1991.

Shea, George Tyson. *Leftwing Literature in Japan: A Brief History of the Proletarian Literary Movement*. Tokyo: Hosei University Press, 1964.

Slaymaker, Douglas. *A Century of Popular Culture in Japan*. Lewiston, N.Y.: E. Mellen Press, 2000.

Tachibana, Reiko. *Narrative as Counter-Memory: A Half-Century of Postwar Writing in Germany and Japan*. New York: State University of New York Press, 1998.

Tanaka, Yukiko. *Women Writers of Meiji and Taishô Japan: Their Lives, Works, and Critical Reception, 1868–1926*. Jefferson, N.C.: McFarland, 2000.

Tansman, Alan. *The Aesthetics of Japanese Fascism*. Berkeley: University of California Press, 2009.

Treat, John Whittier. *Writing Ground Zero: Japanese Literature and the Atomic Bomb*. Chicago: University of Chicago Press, 1995.

Ueda, Atsuko. *Concealment of Politics, Politics of Concealment: The Production of "Literature" in Meiji Japan*. Stanford, Calif.: Stanford University Press, 2007.

Walker, Janet A. *The Japanese Novel of the Meiji Period and the Ideal of Individualism*. Princeton, N.J.: Princeton University Press, 1979.

Yamanouchi, Hisaaki. *The Search for Authenticity in Modern Japanese Literature*. Cambridge: Cambridge University Press, 1978.

Women and Literature

Bardsley, Jan. *The Bluestockings of Japan: New Woman Essays and Fiction from Seitô, 1911–16*. Ann Arbor: Center for Japanese Studies, University of Michigan, 2007.

Birnbaum, Phyllis. *Modern Girls, Shining Stars, the Skies of Tokyo: Five Japanese Women*. New York: Columbia University Press, 1999.

Copeland, Rebecca L., and Esperanza U. Ramirez-Christensen. *The Father-Daughter Plot: Japanese Literary Women and the Law of the Father*. Honolulu: University of Hawai'i Press, 2001.

Cornyetz, Nina. *Dangerous Women, Deadly Words: Phallic Fantasy and Modernity in Three Japanese Writers*. Stanford, Calif.: Stanford University Press, 1999.

Fairbanks, Carol. *Japanese Women Fiction Writers: Their Culture and Society, 1890s to 1990s*. Lanham, Md.: Scarecrow Press, 2002.

Kuribayashi, Tomoko, and Mizuho Terasawa. *The Outsider Within: Ten Essays on Modern Japanese Women Writers*. Lanham, Md.: University Press of America, 2002.

Russell, Catherine. *The Cinema of Naruse Mikio: Women and Japanese Modernity*. Durham, N.C.: Duke University Press, 2008.

Schalow, Paul Gordon, and Janet A. Walker. *The Woman's Hand: Gender and Theory in Japanese Women's Writing*. Stanford, Calif.: Stanford University Press, 1996.

Schierbeck, Sachiko Shibata, and Soren Egerod. *Postwar Japanese Women Writers: An Up-to-Date Bibliography with Biographical Sketches*. Copenhagen, Denmark: East Asian Institute, University of Copenhagen, 1989.

Tanaka, Yukiko. *Women Writers of Meiji and Taishô Japan: Their Lives, Works, and Critical Reception, 1868–1926*. Jefferson, N.C.: McFarland, 2000.

Ueda, Makoto. *The Mother of Dreams and Other Short Stories: Portrayals of Women in Modern Japanese Fiction*. New York: Kodansha International, 1986.

Vernon, Victoria V. *Daughters of the Moon: Wish, Will, and Social Constraint in Fiction by Modern Japanese Women*. Berkeley: Institute of East Asian Studies, University of California, 1988.

Film and Literature

Bernardi, Joanne. *Writing in Light: The Silent Scenario and the Japanese Pure Film Movement*. Detroit, Mich.: Wayne State University Press, 2001.

Dym, Jeffrey A. *Benshi, Japanese Silent Film Narrators, and Their Forgotten Narrative Art of Setsumei: A History of Japanese Silent Film Narration*. Lewiston, N.Y.: E. Mellen Press, 2003.

McDonald, Keiko I. *From Book to Screen: Modern Japanese Literature in Films*. Armonk, N.Y.: M.E. Sharpe, 2000.
Russell, Catherine. *The Cinema of Naruse Mikio: Women and Japanese Modernity*. Durham, N.C.: Duke University Press, 2008.

Detective Fiction

Kawana, Sari. *Murder Most Modern: Detective Fiction and Japanese Culture*. Minneapolis: University of Minnesota Press, 2008.
Silver, Mark. *Purloined Letters: Cultural Borrowing and Japanese Crime Literature, 1868–1937*. Honolulu: University of Hawai'i Press, 2008.

Other Topics

Heinrich, Amy Vladeck. *Currents in Japanese Culture: Translations and Transformations*. New York: Columbia University Press, 1997.
Keene, Donald, and Motoichi Izawa. *Some Japanese Portraits*. New York: Kodansha International, 1979.
Lifton, Robert Jay, Shûichi Katô, and Michael Reich. *Six Lives, Six Deaths: Portraits from Modern Japan*. New Haven, Conn.: Yale University Press, 1979.
Lippit, Noriko Mizuta. *Reality and Fiction in Modern Japanese Literature*. White Plains, N.Y.: M. E. Sharpe, 1980.
McClellan, Edwin, Dennis C. Washburn, and Alan Tansman. *Studies in Modern Japanese Literature: Essays and Translations in Honor of Edwin McClellan*. Ann Arbor: Center for Japanese Studies, University of Michigan, 1997.
Molasky, Michael S., and Steve Rabson. *Southern Exposure: Modern Japanese Literature from Okinawa*. Honolulu: University of Hawai'i Press, 2000.
Morton, Leith. *Modern Japanese Culture: The Insider View*. Oxford: Oxford University Press, 2003.
———. *The Alien Within: Representations of the Exotic in Twentieth-Century Japanese Literature*. Honolulu: University of Hawai'i Press, 2009.
Rimer, J. Thomas. *Pilgrimages: Aspects of Japanese Literature and Culture*. Honolulu: University of Hawai'i Press, 1988.
Saeki, Shôichi. *Hidden Dimensions in Modern Japanese Literature*. Tokyo: Japan Foundation, 1985.

Seidensticker, Edward, Aileen Patricia Gatten, and Anthony H. Chambers. *New Leaves: Studies and Translations of Japanese Literature in Honor of Edward Seidensticker*. Ann Arbor: Center for Japanese Studies, University of Michigan, 1993.

Tomonari, Noboru. *Constructing Subjectivities: Autobiographies in Modern Japan*. Lanham, Md.: Lexington Books, 2008.

Ueda, Makoto. *Literary and Art Theories in Japan*. Ann Arbor: Center for Japanese Studies, University of Michigan, 1991.

Web Resources

Japan Cultural Profile. Visiting Arts Cultural Profiles [cited 15 December 2008]. Available from http://www.culturalprofiles.net/japan.

Japan Foundation Web Site. Japan Foundation [cited 25 October 2008]. Available from http://www.jpf.go.jp/.

Japanese Literature. [cited 15 December 2008]. Mark Jewel, Waseda University. Available from http://www.jlit.net/index.html.

Japanese Literature Publishing Project. Japanese Government Agency for Cultural Affairs, Japanese Literature Publishing and Promotion Center [cited 24 October 2008]. Available from http://www.jlpp.jp/en/.

Japanese Text Initiative. Electronic Text Center, Japanese Text Initiative, University of Virginia Library [cited 24 October 2008]. Available from http://etext.lib.virginia.edu/japanese/.

Outline Chronology of Japanese Cultural History. John Pierre Mertz, North Carolina State University [cited 15 December 2008]. Available from http://www4.ncsu.edu/~fljpm/chron/jc01.outline.html.

SELECT BIBLIOGRAPHY OF AUTHORS AND TRANSLATIONS

Anthologies

Apostolou, John L., and Martin Harry Greenberg. *The Best Japanese Science Fiction Stories*. New York: Barricade Books, 1997.

Birnbaum, Alfred. *Monkey Brain Sushi: New Tastes in Japanese Fiction*. New York: Kodansha International, 1991.

Birnbaum, Phyllis. *Rabbits, Crabs, Etc.: Stories by Japanese Women*. Honolulu: University of Hawai'i Press, 1982.

Copeland, Rebecca L., and Melek Ortabasi. *The Modern Murasaki: Writing by Women of Meiji Japan*. New York: Columbia University Press, 2006.

Dunlop, Lane. *Autumn Wind and Other Stories.* Rutland, Vt.: Charles E. Tuttle, 1994.

Gessel, Van C., and Tomone Matsumoto. *The Shôwa Anthology: Modern Japanese Short Stories: 1929–1984.* New York: Kodansha International, 1989.

Goossen, Theodore William. *The Oxford Book of Japanese Short Stories.* New York: Oxford University Press, 1997.

Hibbett, Howard. *Contemporary Japanese Literature: An Anthology of Fiction, Film, and Other Writing Since 1945.* Boston: Cheng and Tsui, 2005.

Mitsios, Helen. *New Japanese Voices: The Best Contemporary Fiction from Japan.* New York: Atlantic Monthly Press, 1991.

Rimer, J. Thomas, and Van C. Gessel. *The Columbia Anthology of Modern Japanese Literature.* 2 vols. New York: Columbia University Press, 2005, 2007.

Rogers, Lawrence. *Tokyo Stories: A Literary Stroll.* Berkeley: University of California Press, 2002.

Sato, Hiroaki, Burton Watson, and J. Thomas Rimer. *From the Country of Eight Islands: An Anthology of Japanese Poetry.* Garden City, N.Y.: Anchor Books, 1981.

Scheiner, Irwin. *Modern Japan: An Interpretive Anthology.* New York: Macmillan, 1974.

Tanaka, Yukiko, and Elizabeth Hanson. *This Kind of Woman: Ten Stories by Japanese Women Writers, 1960–1976.* Stanford, Calif.: Stanford University Press, 1982.

General Authors

Bargen, Doris G. *Suicidal Honor: General Nogi and the Writings of Mori Ôgai and Natsume Sôseki.* Honolulu: University of Hawai'i Press, 2006.

Gessel, Van C. *Three Modern Novelists: Sôseki, Tanizaki, Kawabata.* New York: Kodansha International, 1993.

Keene, Dennis. *The Modern Japanese Prose Poem: An Anthology of Six Poets: Miyoshi Tatsuji, Anzai Fuyue, Tamura Ryûichi, Yoshioka Minoru, Tanikawa Shuntarô, Inoue Yasushi.* Princeton, N.J.: Princeton University Press, 1980.

Murakami, Fuminobu. *Postmodern, Feminist and Postcolonial Currents in Contemporary Japanese Culture: A Reading of Murakami Haruki, Yoshimoto Banana, Yoshimoto Takaaki and Karatani Kojin.* New York: Routledge, 2005.

Napier, Susan Jolliffe. *Escape from the Wasteland: Romanticism and Realism in the Fiction of Mishima Yukio and Oe Kenzaburo*. Cambridge, Mass.: Harvard University Asia Center, 1991.

Petersen, Gwenn Boardman. *The Moon in the Water: Understanding Tanizaki, Kawabata, and Mishima*. Honolulu: University of Hawai'i Press, 1979.

Snyder, Stephen, and Philip Gabriel. *Ôe and Beyond: Fiction in Contemporary Japan*. Honolulu: University of Hawai'i Press, 1999.

Takahashi, Tsutomu. *Parallelisms in the Literary Vision of Sin: Double-Readings of Natsume Soseki and Nathaniel Hawthorne, Akutagawa Ryunosuke and Ambrose Bierce, and Hagiwara Sakutaro and Stephen Crane*. New York: P. Lang, 1996.

Specific Authors (in alphabetical order, SURNAME in capitals; works *by* the author listed first, followed by works *about* the author)

ABE Kôbô

Abe, Kôbô. *Friends*. Rutland, Vt.: Charles E. Tuttle, 1971.

———. *The Woman in the Dunes*. New York: Vintage Books, 1972.

———. *The Box Man. Translated from the Japanese by E. Dale Saunders*. New York: Alfred A. Knopf, 1974.

———. *The Man Who Turned into a Stick: Three Related Plays*. Tokyo: University of Tokyo Press, 1975.

———. *Secret Rendezvous*. New York: Alfred A. Knopf, 1979.

———. *The Ruined Map*. New York: Perigee Books, 1980.

———. *The Ark Sakura*. New York: Alfred A. Knopf, 1988.

———. *Beyond the Curve*. New York: Kodansha International, 1991.

———. *Three Plays*. New York: Columbia University Press, 1993.

Abe, Kôbô, and Machi Abe. *Inter Ice Age 4*. New York, N.Y.: Perigee Books, 1981.

Abe, Kôbô, and Maryellen Toman Mori. *Kangaroo Notebook: A Novel*. New York: Alfred A. Knopf, 1996.

Iles, Timothy. *Abe Kôbô: An Exploration of His Prose, Drama and Theatre*. Fucecchio (Firenze), Italy: European Press Academic Publishing, 2000.

Shields, Nancy K. *Fake Fish: The Theater of Kobo Abe*. New York: Weatherhill, 1996.

AGAWA Hiroyuki

Agawa, Hiroyuki. *Devil's Heritage*. Tokyo: Hokuseido Press, 1957.

———. *The Reluctant Admiral: Yamamoto and the Imperial Navy*. New York: Kodansha International, 1979.

Agawa, Hiroyuki, and Teruyo Shimizu. *Burial in the Clouds*. Rutland, Vt.: Charles E. Tuttle, 2006.

AKUTAGAWA Ryûnosuke

Akutagawa, Ryûnosuke. *Japanese Short Stories*. New York: Liveright Publishing, 1961.

———. *Exotic Japanese Stories*. New York: Liveright Publishing, 1964.

———. *Hell Screen. Cogwheels. A Fool's Life*. Hygiene, Colo.: Eridanos Press, 1987.

Akutagawa, Ryûnosuke, and Geoffrey Bownas. *Kappa: A Novel*. Boston: Tuttle Publishing, 2000.

Akutagawa, Ryûnosuke, and Glenn W. Shaw. *Tales Grotesque and Curious*. Tokyo: Hokuseido Press, 1938.

ARISHIMA Takeo

Arishima, Takeo. *The Agony of Coming into the World*. Tokyo: Hokuseido Press, 1955.

———. *A Certain Woman*. Tokyo: University of Tokyo Press, 1978.

———. *Labyrinth*. Lanham, Md.: Madison Books, 1992.

Anderer, Paul. *Other Worlds: Arishima Takeo and the Bounds of Modern Japanese Fiction*. New York: Columbia University Press, 1984.

ARIYOSHI Sawako

Ariyoshi, Sawako. *The Doctor's Wife*. New York: Kodansha International, 1978.

———. *The River Ki*. New York: Kodansha International, 1980.

———. *The Twilight Years*. New York: Kodansha International, 1984.

Ariyoshi, Sawako, and James R. Brandon. *Kabuki Dancer*. New York: Kodansha International, 1994.

ATÔDA Takashi

Atôda, Takashi. *The Square Persimmon, and Other Stories*. Rutland, Vt.: C.E. Tuttle, 1991.

DAZAI Osamu

Dazai, Osamu. *The Setting Sun*. Norfolk, Conn.: J. Laughlin, 1956.

———. *No Longer Human*. Norfolk, Conn.: New Directions, 1958.

———. *Crackling Mountain and Other Stories*. Rutland, Vt.: Charles E. Tuttle, 1989.

———. *Return to Tsugaru: Travels of a Purple Tramp*. Tokyo: Kodansha International, 1985.

———. *Self Portraits: Tales from the Life of Japan's Great Decadent Romantic*. New York: Kodansha International, 1991.

——. *Blue Bamboo: Tales of Fantasy and Romance*. New York: Kodansha International, 1993.

O'Brien, James A. *Dazai Osamu*. New York: Twayne Publishers, 1975.

Lyons, Phyllis I., and Osamu Dazai. *The Saga of Dazai Osamu: A Critical Study with Translations*. Stanford, Calif.: Stanford University Press, 1985.

Wolfe, Alan Stephen. *Suicidal Narrative in Modern Japan: The Case of Dazai Osamu*. Princeton, N.J.: Princeton University Press, 1990.

ENCHI Fumiko

Enchi, Fumiko. *The Waiting Years*. New York: Kodansha International, 1971.

——. *Masks*. New York: Alfred A. Knopf, 1983.

Enchi, Fumiko, and Roger K. Thomas. *A Tale of False Fortunes*. Honolulu: University of Hawai'i Press, 2000.

Ericson, Joan E., and Fumiko Hayashi. *Be a Woman: Hayashi Fumiko and Modern Japanese Women's Literature*. Honolulu: University of Hawai'i Press, 1997.

Fessler, Susanna. *Wandering Heart: The Work and Method of Hayashi Fumiko*. Albany: State University of New York Press, 1998.

ENDÔ Shûsaku

Endô, Shûsaku. *The Golden Country: A Play*. Rutland, Vt.: C.E. Tuttle, 1970.

——. *Silence*. New York: Taplinger Publishing, 1979.

——. *When I Whistle: A Novel*. New York: Taplinger Publishing, 1979.

——. *Samurai*. New York: Kodansha International, 1982.

——. *Wonderful Fool: A Novel*. New York: Harper and Row, 1983.

——. *Stained Glass Elegies*. New York: Dodd, Mead, 1985.

——. *Scandal: A Novel*. New York: Dodd, Mead, 1988.

——. *Foreign Studies*. London: P. Owen, 1989.

Endô, Shûsaku, and Van C. Gessel. *Deep River*. New York: New Directons, 1994.

Endô, Shûsaku, and Mark Williams. *The Girl I Left Behind*. New York: New Directions, 1995.

Bussie, Jacqueline Aileen. *The Laughter of the Oppressed: Ethical and Theological Resistance in Wiesel, Morrison, and Endo*. New York: T and T Clark International, 2007.

Williams, Mark. *Endô Shûsaku: A Literature of Reconciliations*. London: Routledge, 1999.

FUJIMORI Seikichi

Fujimori, Seikichi. *On Watanabe-Kazan as a Painter, with Particular Reference to His Sketches and Dessins.* Tokyo: Central Federation of Nippon Culture, 1939.

FUKUZAWA Yukichi

Fukuzawa, Yukichi, and Eiichi Kiyooka. *Autobiography.* New York: Columbia University Press, 1966.

——. *An Outline of a Theory of Civilization.* Tokyo: Sophia University, 1973.

——. *Preface to the Collected Works of Fukuzawa.* Tokyo: Published for Fukuzawa Yukichi Society, 1980.

——. *Fukuzawa Yukichi on Education: Selected Works.* Tokyo: University of Tokyo Press, 1985.

——. *The Autobiography of Fukuzawa Yukichi.* Lanham, Md.: Madison Books, 1992.

Fukuzawa, Yukichi, Eiichi Kiyooka, and Keiko Fujiwara, 1992.

——. *Fukuzawa Yukichi on Japanese Women: Selected Works.* Tokyo: University of Tokyo Press, 1988.

Blacker, Carmen. *The Japanese Enlightenment; a Study of the Writings of Fukuzawa Yukichi.* Cambridge: Cambridge University Press, 1964.

Craig, Albert M. *Civilization and Enlightenment: The Early Thought of Fukuzawa Yukichi.* Cambridge, Mass.: Harvard University Press, 2009.

Hopper, Helen M. *Fukuzawa Yukichi: From Samurai to Capitalist.* New York: Pearson/Longman, 2004.

Macfarlane, Alan. *The Making of the Modern World: Visions from the West and East.* New York: Palgrave, 2002.

Miwa, Kimitada. *Fukuzawa Yukichi, Essays on Division of Power.* Tokyo: Sophia University, 1983.

Scheiner, Irwin. *Modern Japan: An Interpretive Anthology.* New York: Macmillan, 1974.

FURUI Yoshikichi

Furui, Yoshikichi, and Donna George Storey. *Child of Darkness: Yôko and Other Stories.* Ann Arbor: Center for Japanese Studies, University of Michigan, 1997.

Furui, Yoshikichi, and Meredith McKinney. *Ravine and Other Stories.* Berkeley, Calif.: Stone Bridge Press, 1997.

——. *White-Haired Melody*. Ann Arbor: Center for Japanese Studies, University of Michigan, 2008.

FUTABATEI Shimei

Futabatei, Shimei. *An Adopted Husband.* New York: Greenwood Press, 1969.

Futabatei, Shimei, and Marleigh Grayer Ryan. *Japan's First Modern Novel: Ukigumo of Futabatei Shimei.* Westport, Conn.: Greenwood Press, 1983.

Cockerill, Hiroko. *Style and Narrative in Translations: The Contribution of Futabatei Shimei.* Manchester, UK: St. Jerome Publishers, 2006.

HAGIWARA Sakutarô

Hagiwara, Sakutarô. *Cat Town.* Tokyo: Jûjiya Press, 1948.

——. *Howling at the Moon: Poems of Hagiwara Sakutarô; Translated and with an Introduction by Hiroaki Sato.* Tokyo: University of Tokyo Press, 1978.

——. *Rats' Nests: The Collected Poetry of Hagiwara Sakutarô.* Stanwood, Wash.: Yakusha, 1993.

Hagiwara, Sakutarô, Robert Epp, and Gakuji Iida. *His Psychic Spoor: One Hundred Fifty Annotated Hagiwara Sakutarô Poems.* Stanwood, Wash.: Yakusha, 2005.

Hagiwara, Sakutarô, and Graeme Wilson. *Face at the Bottom of the World and Other Poems.* Rutland, Vt.: Charles E. Tuttle, 1969.

Kurth, Frederick, Robert Epp, and Sakutarô Hagiwara. *Howling with Sakutarô: Cries of a Cosmic Waif.* Los Angeles: ZamaZama Press, 2004.

HAYASHI Fumiko

Hayashi, Fumiko, and Lane Dunlop. *Floating Clouds.* New York: Columbia University Press, 2006.

Ericson, Joan E., and Fumiko Hayashi. *Be a Woman: Hayashi Fumiko and Modern Japanese Women's Literature.* Honolulu: University of Hawai'i Press, 1997.

Lafcadio HEARN

Hearn, Lafcadio. *Japan, an Attempt at Interpretation.* New York: Macmillan, 1904.

——. *Japanese Lyrics.* Boston: Houghton Mifflin, 1915.

——. *A Japanese Miscellany.* Boston: Little, Brown, 1919.

——. *Kwaidan: Stories and Studies of Strange Things.* Tokyo: Shimbi Shoin, 1932.

——. *Lands and Seas.* Tokyo: Hokuseido Press, 1939.
——. *Manuscripts.* New York: AMS Press, 1975.
——. *Memoranda for the Lectures at Tokyo Imperial University.* New York: AMS Press, 1975.
——. *Glimpses of Unfamiliar Japan.* Rutland, Vt.: Charles E. Tuttle, 1976.
Hearn, Lafcadio, and Donald Richie. *Lafcadio Hearn's Japan: An Anthology of His Writings on the Country and Its People.* Rutland, Vt.: Charles E. Tuttle, 1997.
Hearn, Lafcadio, and Elizabeth Bisland. *The Writings of Lafcadio Hearn.* New York: Houghton Mifflin, 1922.
Hearn, Lafcadio, and John Erskine. *Books and Habits.* New York: Dodd, Mead, 1921.
Hearn, Lafcadio, Louis Allen, and Jean Wilson. *Lafcadio Hearn: Japan's Great Interpreter: A New Anthology of His Writings, 1894–1904.* Folkestone, Kent: Japan Library, 1992.
Hearn, Lafcadio, and Masakazu Kuwata. *Earless Ho-Ichi: A Classic Japanese Tale of Mystery.* New York: Kodansha International, 1966.
Hearn, Lafcadio, and Milton Bronner. *Letters from the Raven.* New York: Brentano's, 1907.
Hearn, Lafcadio, and Yuko Green. *The Boy Who Drew Cats and Other Japanese Fairy Tales.* Mineola, N.Y.: Dover Publications, 1998.
Cott, Jonathan, and Lafcadio Hearn. *Wandering Ghost: The Odyssey of Lafcadio Hearn.* New York: Alfred A. Knopf, 1991.

HIGUCHI Ichiyô

Danly, Robert Lyons, and Ichiyô Higuchi. *In the Shade of Spring Leaves: The Life and Writings of Higuchi Ichiyô, a Woman of Letters in Meiji Japan.* New Haven, Conn.: Yale University Press, 1981.

HINO Ashihei

Hino, Ashihei. *Wheat and Soldiers.* New York: Farrar and Rinehart, 1939.
——. *Flower and Soldiers.* Tokyo: Kenkyûsha, 1940.
——. *War and Soldiers.* London: Putnam, 1940.
Rosenfeld, David M. *Unhappy Soldier: Hino Ashihei and Japanese World War II Literature.* Lanham, Md.: Lexington Books, 2002.

HORIGUCHI Daigaku

Horiguchi, Daigaku, and Robert Epp. *Rainbows: Selected Poetry of Horiguchi Daigaku.* Stanwood, Wash.: Yakusha, 1994.

HOTTA Yoshie

Hotta, Yoshie, and Nobuko Tsukui. *Judgment.* Osaka: Intercultural Research Institute, Kansai Gaidai University, 1963.

IBUSE Masuji

Ibuse, Masuji. *Black Rain.* New York: Kodansha, 1979.

———. *Salamander and Other Stories.* New York: Kodansha International, 1981.

———. *Waves: Two Short Novels.* New York: Kodansha International, 1986.

———. *Castaways: Two Short Novels.* New York: Kodansha International, 1987.

Liman, Anthony V. *A Critical Study of the Literary Style of Ibuse Masuji: As Sensitive as Waters.* Lewiston, N.Y.: E. Mellen Press, 1992.

Tachibana, Reiko. *Narrative as Counter-Memory: A Half-Century of Postwar Writing in Germany and Japan.* New York: State University of New York Press, 1998.

Treat, John Whittier. *Pools of Water, Pillars of Fire: The Literature of Ibuse Masuji.* Seattle, Wash.: University of Washington Press, 1988.

INOUE Yasushi

Inoue, Yasushi. *The Roof Tile of Tempyô.* Tokyo: University of Tokyo Press, 1975.

———. *Tun-Huang: A Novel.* New York: Kodansha International, 1978.

———. *Lou-Lan and Other Stories.* New York: Kodansha International, 1979.

———. *Chronicle of My Mother.* New York: Kodansha International, 1982.

———. *Wind and Waves: A Novel.* Honolulu: University of Hawai'i Press, 1989.

Inoue, Yasushi, and Kyôko Yukawa. *Selected Poems of Inoue Yasushi.* Tokyo: Hokuseido Press, 1979.

Kazuo ISHIGURO

Ishiguro, Kazuo. *A Pale View of Hills.* New York: Putnam, 1982.

———. *An Artist of the Floating World.* London: Faber and Faber, 1986.

———. *The Remains of the Day.* New York: Alfred A. Knopf, 1990.

———. *The Unconsoled.* New York: Alfred A. Knopf, 1995.

———. *When We Were Orphans.* New York: Alfred A. Knopf, 2000.

———. *Never Let Me Go.* New York: Alfred A. Knopf, 2005.

Ishiguro, Kazuo, Brian W. Shaffer, and Cynthia F. Wong. *Conversations with Kazuo Ishiguro*. Jackson: University Press of Mississippi, 2008.

Burton, Robert Stacey. *Artists of the Floating World: Contemporary Writers between Cultures*. Lanham, Md.: University Press of America, 2007.

ISHIHARA Shintarô

Ishihara, Shintarô. *The Japan That Can Say 'No'!* New York: Simon and Schuster, 1991.

ISHIKAWA Jun

Ishikawa, Jun. *The Bodhisattva, or, Samantabhadra: A Novel*. New York: Columbia University Press, 1990.

Ishikawa, Jun, and William Jefferson Tyler. *The Legend of Gold and Other Stories*. Honolulu: University of Hawai'i Press, 1998.

ISHIKAWA Takuboku

Ishikawa, Takuboku. *The Poetry of Ishikawa Takuboku*. Tokyo: Hokuseido Press, 1959.

———. *A Handful of Sand*. Westport, Conn.: Greenwood Press, 1976.

Ishikawa, Takuboku, and Carl Gordon Sesar. *Poems to Eat*. New York: Kodansha International, 1966.

Ishikawa, Takuboku, Sanford Goldstein, and Seishi Shinoda. *Sad Toys*. West Lafayette, Ind.: Purdue University Press, 1977.

Ishikawa, Takuboku, and Tomo Endô. *A Broken Toy. Kanashiki Gangu: a Collection of Poems*. Osaka: Baika Women's College Library, 1967.

Hijiya, Yukihito. *Ishikawa Takuboku*. Boston: Twayne Publishers, 1979.

ISHIKAWA Tatsuzô

Ishikawa, Tatsuzô. *Resistance at Forty-Eight: A Japanese Novel*. Tokyo: Hokuseido Press, 1960.

———. *Evil for Pleasure*. Tokyo: Yohan Publications, 1972.

———. *Soldiers Alive*. Honolulu: University of Hawai'i Press, 2003.

ITÔ Sachio

Itô, Sachio, and Shio Sakanishi. *Songs of a Cowherd; Translated from the Works of Sachio Itô*. Boston: Marshall Jones, 1936.

IWANO Hômei

Nagashima, Yôichi. *Objective Description of the Self: A Study of Iwano Hômei's Literary Theory*. Aarhus, Denmark: Aarhus University Press, 1997.

IZUMI Kyôka

Izumi, Kyôka. *The Saint of Mt. Koya*; *The Song of the Troubadour*. Kanazawa, Japan: Committee for the Translation of the Works of Izumi Kyôka, 1990.

Izumi, Kyôka, and Charles Shirô Inouye. *Japanese Gothic Tales*. Honolulu: University of Hawai'i Press, 1996.

———. *In Light of Shadows: More Gothic Tales by Izumi Kyôka*. Honolulu: University of Hawai'i Press, 2005.

Inouye, Charles Shirô. *The Similitude of Blossoms: A Critical Biography of Izumi Kyôka (1873–1939), Japanese Novelist and Playwright*. Cambridge, Mass.: Harvard University Asia Center, 1998.

Poulton, M. Cody. *Spirits of Another Sort: The Plays of Izumi Kyoka*. Ann Arbor: Center for Japanese Studies, University of Michigan, 2001.

KAIKÔ Takeshi

Kaikô, Takeshi. *Darkness in Summer*. New York: Alfred A. Knopf, 1973.

———. *Panic and the Runaway: Two Stories*. Tokyo: University of Tokyo Press, 1977.

———. *Into a Black Sun*. New York: Kodansha International, 1980.

———. *Five Thousand Runaways*. New York: Dodd, Mead, 1987.

KANEKO Mitsuharu

Morita, James R. *Kaneko Mitsuharu*. Boston: Twayne Publishers, 1980.

KARATANI Kôjin

Karatani, Kôjin. *Origins of Modern Japanese Literature*. Durham, N.C.: Duke University Press, 1993.

KATÔ Shûichi

Katô, Shûichi. *Form, Style, Tradition; Reflections on Japanese Art and Society*. Berkeley: University of California Press, 1971.

———. *A History of Japanese Literature*. New York: Kodansha International, 1979.

Katô, Shûichi, and Chia-ning Chang. *A Sheep's Song: A Writer's Reminiscences of Japan and the World*. Berkeley: University of California Press, 1999.

Katô, Shûichi, Junko Abe, and Leza Lowitz. *Japan, Spirit and Form*. Rutland, Vt.: C.E. Tuttle, 1994.

Lifton, Robert Jay, Shûichi Katô, and Michael Reich. *Six Lives, Six Deaths: Portraits from Modern Japan*. New Haven, Conn.: Yale University Press, 1979.

KAWABATA Yasunari

Kawabata, Yasunari. *The House of the Sleeping Beauties and Other Stories.* New York: Kodansha International, 1969.

——. *The Lake.* New York: Kodansha International, 1974.

——. *The Sound of the Mountain.* Harmondsworth, UK: Penguin, 1974.

——. *Japan the Beautiful and Myself.* New York: Kodansha International, 1981.

——. *Thousand Cranes.* New York: Perigee Books, 1981.

——. *The Old Capital.* San Francisco: North Point Press, 1987.

——. *Palm-of-the-Hand Stories.* San Francisco: North Point Press, 1988.

——. *Beauty and Sadness.* New York: Vintage International, 1996.

Kawabata, Yasunari, Alisa Freedman, Donald Richie, and Samurô Ôta. *The Scarlet Gang of Asakusa.* Berkeley: University of California Press, 2005.

Kawabata, Yasunari, and Edward Seidensticker. *Snow Country.* New York: Vintage Books, 1996.

Kawabata, Yasunari, and J. Martin Holman. *The Dancing Girl of Izu and Other Stories.* Washington, D.C.: Counterpoint, 1998.

Kawabata, Yasunari, and Michael Emmerich. *First Snow on Fuji.* Washington, D.C.: Counterpoint, 1999.

Kawabata, Yasunari, and Peter Metevelis. *Tales with Two Souls: A Variety in Time and Culture.* Pittsburgh, Pa.: Dorrance Publishing, 1999.

KIKUCHI Kan (Hiroshi)

Kikuchi, Hiroshi, and Kiichi Nishi. *Victory or Defeat.* Tokyo: The Kairyûdô, 1934.

Kikuchi, Hiroshi, Perry Jishô, and Kimiko Vago. *Beyond the Pale of Vengeance.* Mt. Shasta, Calif.: Shasta Abbey Press, 1998.

KINOSHITA Junji

Kinoshita, Junji. *Between God and Man: A Judgment on War Crimes: A Play in Two Parts.* Tokyo: University of Tokyo Press, 1979.

KINOSHITA Naoe

Kinoshita, Naoe. *Pillar of Fire.* London: Allen and Unwin, 1972.

KISHIDA Kunio

Kishida, Kunio. *Five Plays.* Ithaca, N.Y.: East Asia Program, Cornell University, 1989.

Rimer, J. Thomas. *Toward a Modern Japanese Theatre: Kishida Kunio.* Princeton, N.J.: Princeton University Press, 1974.

KITA Morio

Kita, Morio. *The House of Nire.* New York: Kodansha, 1984.

———. *Ghosts.* New York: Kodansha International, 1991.

KOBAYASHI Hideo

Kobayashi, Hideo, and Paul Anderer. *Literature of the Lost Home: Kobayashi Hideo—Literary Criticism, 1924–1939.* Stanford, Calif.: Stanford University Press, 1995.

KOBAYASHI Takiji

Kobayashi, Takiji. *The Cannery Boat, and Other Japanese Short Stories.* New York: Greenwood Press, 1968.

———. *The Factory Ship and the Absentee Landlord.* Tokyo: University of Tokyo Press, 1973.

KÔDA Rohan

Kôda, Rohan. *Leaving the Hermitage.* London: Allen and Unwin, 1925.

Kôda, Rohan, and Chieko Irie Mulhern. *Pagoda, Skull, and Samurai: Three Stories.* Ithaca, N.Y.: China-Japan Program, Cornell University, 1982.

Mulhern, Chieko Irie. *Kôda Rohan.* Boston: Twayne Publishers, 1977.

KOJIMA Nobuo

Kojima, Nobuo. *Embracing Family.* Champaign, Ill.: Dalkey Archive Press, 2005.

KÔNO Taeko

Kôno, Taeko, Lucy North, and Lucy Lower. *Toddler-Hunting and Other Stories.* New York: New Directions, 1996.

KUBO Sakae

Kubo, Sakae, and David G. Goodman. *Land of Volcanic Ash: A Play in Two Parts, Cornell University East Asia Papers.* Ithaca, N.Y.: China-Japan Program, Cornell University, 1986.

KURAHASHI Yumiko

Kurahashi, Yumiko. *The Adventures of Sumiyakist Q.* St. Lucia, Australia: University of Queensland Press, 1979.

Kurahashi, Yumiko, and Atsuko Sakaki. *The Woman with the Flying Head and Other Stories.* Armonk, N.Y.: M.E. Sharpe, 1998.

KURATA Hyakuzô

Kurata, Hyakuzô. *Shinran.* Tokyo: Cultural Interchange Institute for Buddhists, 1964.

Kurata, Hyakuzô, and Glenn W. Shaw. *The Priest and His Disciples: A Play*. London: E. Benn, 1927.

KUROI Senji

Kuroi, Senji, and Philip Gabriel. *Life in the Cul-De-Sac*. Berkeley, Calif.: Stone Bridge Press, 2001.

KUROSHIMA Denji

Kuroshima, Denji, and Zeljko Cipris. *A Flock of Swirling Crows and Other Proletarian Writings*. Honolulu: University of Hawai'i Press, 2005.

KUWABARA Takeo

Kuwabara, Takeo, and Hidetoshi Katô. *Japan and Western Civilization: Essays on Comparative Culture*. Tokyo: University of Tokyo Press, 1983.

MARUYA Saiichi

Maruya, Saiichi. *Singular Rebellion*. New York: Kodansha International, 1986.

———. *Rain in the Wind: Four Stories*. New York: Kodansha International, 1990.

———. *Grass for My Pillow*. New York: Columbia University Press, 2002.

Maruya, Saiichi, and Dennis Keene. *A Mature Woman*. London: Andre Deutsch, 1995.

MARUYAMA Kaoru

Maruyama, Kaoru, and Robert Epp. *Self-Righting Lamp: Selected Poems*. Rochester, Mich.: Katydid Books, 1990.

———. *That Far-Off Self: The Collected Poetry of Maruyama*. Stanwood, Wash.: Yakusha, 1992.

MASAMUNE Hakuchô

Rolf, Robert. *Masamune Hakuchô*. Boston: Twayne Publishers, 1979.

MASAOKA Shiki

Masaoka, Shiki, and Harold J. Isaacson. *Peonies Kana: Haiku*. London: Allen and Unwin, 1973.

Masaoka, Shiki, and Sanford Goldstein. *Songs from a Bamboo Village: Selected Tanka from* Takenosato Uta *by Shiki Masaoka*. Rutland, Vt.: Charles E. Tuttle, 1998.

Beichman, Janine. *Masaoka Shiki*. Boston: Twayne Publishers, 1982.

Miner, Earl Roy. *Japanese Poetic Diaries*. Berkeley: University of California Press, 1969.

MATSUMOTO Seichô

Matsumoto, Seichô. *Points and Lines*. New York: Kodansha International, 1970.

———. *The Voice and Other Stories*. New York: Kodansha International, 1989.

———. *Inspector Imanishi Investigates*. New York: Soho Press, 1989.

MINAKAMI Tsutomu

Minakami, Tsutomu, and Dennis C. Washburn. *The Temple of the Wild Geese and Bamboo Dolls of Echizen: Two Novellas*. Champaign, Ill.: Dalkey Archive Press, 2008.

MISHIMA Yukio

Mishima, Yukio. *Death in Midsummer and Other Stories*. New York: New Directions, 1966.

———. *Forbidden Colors*. New York: Alfred A. Knopf, 1968.

———. *Thirst for Love*. New York: Alfred A. Knopf, 1969.

———. *Sun and Steel*. London: Secker and Warburg, 1971.

———. *Spring Snow*. London: Secker and Warburg, 1972.

———. *The Temple of Dawn*. New York: Alfred A. Knopf, 1973.

———. *Five Modern Nô Plays*. New York: Vintage Books, 1973.

———. *Runaway Horses*. New York: Alfred A. Knopf, 1973.

———. *The Decay of the Angel*. New York: Alfred A. Knopf, 1974.

———. *Madame De Sade*. New York: Grove Press, 1977.

———. *After the Banquet*. New York: Perigee Books, 1980.

———. *The Temple of the Golden Pavilion*. New York: Perigee Books, 1980.

———. *The Sailor Who Fell from Grace with the Sea*. New York: Perigee Books, 1980.

Mishima, Yukio, and Geoffrey W. Sargent. *Patriotism*. New York: New Directions Books, 1995.

Mishima, Yukio, and Hiroaki Sato. *Silk and Insight: A Novel*. Armonk, N.Y.: M.E. Sharpe, 1998.

Mishima, Yukio, and John Bester. *Acts of Worship: Seven Stories*. New York: Kodansha International, 1989.

Mishima, Yukio, and Tsunetomo Yamamoto. *The Way of the Samurai: Yukio Mishima on Hagakure in Modern Life*. New York: Basic Books, 1977.

Starrs, Roy. *Deadly Dialectics: Sex, Violence, and Nihilism in the World of Yukio Mishima*. Honolulu: University of Hawai'i Press, 1994.

——. *Soundings in Time: The Fictive Art of Kawabata Yasunari.* Richmond, Surrey, UK: Japan Library, 1998.

MIURA Ayako

Miura, Ayako. *Shiokari Pass.* London: OMF Books, 1974.

——. *The Wind Is Howling.* Downers Grove, Ill.: Inter Varsity Press, 1977.

MIYAMOTO Teru

Miyamoto, Teru, and Roger K. Thomas. *Autumn Brocade.* New York: New Directions Book, 2005.

MIYAZAWA Kenji

Miyazawa, Kenji. *Winds and Wildcat Places.* New York: Kodansha International, 1967.

——. *Winds from Afar.* New York: Kodansha International, 1972.

——. *Spring and Asura; Poems of Kenji Miyazawa.* Chicago: Chicago Review Press, 1973.

——. *Night of the Milky Way Railway.* Armonk, N.Y.: M.E. Sharpe, 1991.

——. *Milky Way Railroad.* Berkeley, Calif.: Stone Bridge Press, 1996.

Miyazawa, Kenji, and Hiroaki Sato. *A Future of Ice: Poems and Stories of a Japanese Buddhist.* San Francisco: North Point Press, 1989.

——. *Miyazawa Kenji: Selections.* Berkeley: University of California Press, 2007.

Miyazawa, Kenji, and John Bester. *Once and Forever: The Tales of Kenji Miyazawa.* New York: Kodansha International, 2007 (original 1993).

Miyazawa, Kenji, and Roger Pulvers. *Strong in the Rain: Selected Poems.* Tarset, Northumberland, UK: Bloodaxe Books, 2007.

Strong, Sarah Mehlop, and Karen Colligan-Taylor. *Masterworks of Kenji Miyazawa*, Tokyo: International Foundation for the Promotion of Languages and Culture, 1984.

MORI Ôgai

Mori, Ôgai. *The Incident at Sakai and Other Stories.* Honolulu: University of Hawai'i Press, 1977.

——. *Saiki Kôi and Other Stories.* Honolulu: University of Hawai'i Press, 1977.

——. *The Historical Literature of Mori Ôgai.* Honolulu: University of Hawai'i Press, 1977.

Mori, Ôgai, and Burton Watson. *The Wild Goose.* Ann Arbor: Center for Japanese Studies, University of Michigan, 1995.

Mori, Ôgai, David A. Dilworth, and J. Thomas Rimer. *The Historical Fiction of Mori Ôgai.* Honolulu: University of Hawai'i Press, 1991.

Mori, Ôgai, and Doppo Kunikida. *Sanshô-Dayû and Other Short Stories: Pathos in Japanese Literature.* Tokyo: Hokuseido Press, 1970.

Mori, Ôgai, and J. Thomas Rimer. *Youth and Other Stories.* Honolulu: University of Hawai'i Press, 1994.

———. *Not a Song Like Any Other: An Anthology of Writings by Mori Ogai.* Honolulu: University of Hawai'i Press, 2004.

Bowring, Richard John. *Mori Ôgai and the Modernization of Japanese Culture.* Cambridge: Cambridge University Press, 1979.

Rimer, J. Thomas. *Mori Ôgai.* New York: Twayne Publishers, 1975.

MURAKAMI Haruki

Murakami, Haruki. *A Wild Sheep Chase: A Novel.* New York: Penguin Books, 1990.

———. *Hard-Boiled Wonderland and the End of the World: A Novel.* New York: Vintage Books, 1993.

———. *Dance Dance Dance: A Novel.* New York: Kodansha International, 1994.

———. *The Elephant Vanishes.* New York: Vintage Books, 1994.

———. *The Wind-up Bird Chronicle.* New York: Alfred A. Knopf, 1997.

———. *South of the Border, West of the Sun.* New York: Alfred A. Knopf, 1999.

———. *Birthday Stories.* London: Harvill, 2004.

———. *Vintage Murakami.* New York: Vintage Books, 2004.

———. *Kafka on the Shore.* New York: Alfred A. Knopf, 2005.

———. *After Dark.* New York: Alfred A. Knopf, 2007.

Murakami, Haruki, Alfred Birnbaum, and Philip Gabriel. *Underground.* New York: Vintage International, 2001.

Murakami, Haruki, and Jay Rubin. *Norwegian Wood.* New York: Vintage International, 2000.

———. *After the Quake: Stories.* New York: Alfred A. Knopf, 2002.

Murakami, Haruki, and Philip Gabriel. *The Sputnik Sweetheart: A Novel.* New York: Alfred A. Knopf, 2001.

Murakami, Haruki, Philip Gabriel, and Jay Rubin. *Blind Willow, Sleeping Woman: Twenty-Four Stories.* New York: Alfred A. Knopf, 2006.

Japan Foundation. *A Wild Haruki Chase: Reading Murakami Around the World.* Berkeley, Calif.: Stone Bridge Press, 2008.

Seats, Michael. *Murakami Haruki: The Simulacrum in Contemporary Japanese Culture.* Lanham, Md.: Lexington Books, 2006.

Strecher, Matthew. *Dances with Sheep: The Quest for Identity in the Fiction of Murakami Haruki.* Ann Arbor: Center for Japanese Studies/University of Michigan, 2002.

Suter, Rebecca. *The Japanization of Modernity: Murakami Haruki Between Japan and the United States.* Cambridge, Mass.: Harvard University Asia Center, 2008.

MURAKAMI Ryû

Murakami, Ryû. *Almost Transparent Blue.* New York: Kodansha International, 1981.

——. *69: Sixty-Nine.* New York: Kodansha International, 1993.

——. *Coin Locker Babies.* New York: Kodansha International, 1995.

Murakami, Ryû, and Ralph F. McCarthy. *In the Miso Soup.* New York: Penguin Books, 2006.

——. *Piercing.* New York: Penguin Books, 2007.

MURÔ Saisei

Murô, Saisei. *Murô Saisei: Three Works.* Ithaca, N.Y.: Cornell University, 1985.

NAGAI Kafû

Nagai, Kafû. *A Strange Tale from East of the River and Other Stories.* Rutland, Vt.: Charles E. Tuttle, 1972.

——. *During the Rains and Flowers in the Shade: Two Novellas.* Stanford, Calif.: Stanford University Press, 1994.

Nagai, Kafû, and Mitsuko Iriye. *American Stories, Pacific Basin Institute Book.* New York: Columbia University Press, 2000.

Nagai, Kafû, and Stephen Snyder. *Rivalry: A Geisha's Tale.* New York: Columbia University Press, 2007.

Seidensticker, Edward. *Kafû, the Scribbler; the Life and Writings of Nagai Kafû, 1879–1959.* Stanford, Calif.: Stanford University Press, 1965.

NAGATSUKA Takashi

Nagatsuka, Takashi, and Ann Waswo. *The Soil: A Portrait of Rural Life in Meiji Japan.* Berkeley, Calif.: University of California Press, 1989.

NAKA Kansuke

Naka, Kansuke. *The Silver Spoon.* Chicago: Chicago Review Press, 1976.

NAKAE Chômin

Nakae, Chômin, and Margaret B. Dardess. *A Discourse on Government: Nakae Chômin and His Sansuijin Keirin Mondô: An Essay and Introduction.*

Bellingham, Wash.: Program in East Asian Studies, Western Washington State College, 1977.

Nakae, Chômin, Nobuko Tsukui, and Jeffrey Hammond. *A Discourse by Three Drunkards on Government*. New York: Weatherhill, 1984.

NAKAGAMI Kenji

Nakagami, Kenji. *The Cape and Other Stories from the Japanese Ghetto*. Berkeley, Calif.: Stone Bridge Press, 1999.

Zimmerman, Eve. *Out of the Alleyway: Nakagami Kenji and the Poetics of Outcaste Fiction*. Cambridge, Mass.: Harvard University Asia Center, 2007.

NAKAHARA Chûya

Nakahara, Chûya, and Ry Beville. *Poems of the Goat*. Richmond, Va.: American Book, 2002.

Nakahara, Chûya, Paul St. John Mackintosh, and Maki Sugiyama. *The Poems of Nakahara Chûya*. Leominster, Herfordshire, UK: Gracewing, 1993.

Nakahara, Chûya, Kenneth L. Richard, and J. L. Riley. *Depilautumn: The Poetry of Nakahara Chuya*. Toronto: University of Toronto-York University Joint Centre on Modern East Asia, 1981.

NAKAJIMA Atsushi

Nakajima, Atsushi. *Light, Wind, and Dreams; an Interpretation of the Life and Mind of Robert Louis Stevenson*. Tokyo: Hokuseido Press, 1962.

NAKAMURA Mitsuo

Nakamura, Mitsuo. *Japanese Fiction in the Meiji Era*. Tokyo: Kokusai Bunka Shinkokai, 1966.

———. *Contemporary Japanese Fiction, 1926–1968*. Tokyo: Kokusai Bunka Shinkokai, 1969.

NAKANO Shigeharu

Nakano, Shigeharu. *Three Works*. Ithaca, N.Y.: Cornell China-Japan Program, 1979.

Silverberg, Miriam Rom. *Changing Song: The Marxist Manifestos of Nakano Shigeharu*. Princeton, N.J.: Princeton University Press, 1990.

NATSUME Sôseki

Natsume, Sôseki. *Grass on the Wayside: A Novel*. Chicago: University of Chicago Press, 1969.

———. *Kokoro: A Novel*. Rutland, Vt.: Charles E. Tuttle, 1969.

——. *Botchan.* New York: Kodansha International, 1972.
——. *Ten Nights of Dream, Hearing Things, the Heredity of Taste.* Rutland, Vt.: Charles E. Tuttle, 1974.
——. *The Gate.* New York: Putnam, 1982.
——. *The Three-Cornered World.* New York: Putnam, 1982.
——. *The Wayfarer.* New York: Putnam, 1982.
——. *I Am a Cat.* Boston: Tuttle Publishing, 2002.
Natsume, Sôseki, and Ikuo Tsunematsu. *The Heredity of Taste.* Boston: Tuttle Publishing, 2004.
Natsume, Sôseki, Ikuo Tsunematsu, and Inger Sigrun Brodey. *My Individualism, and, the Philosophical Foundations of Literature.* Boston: Tuttle Publishing, 2004.
Natsume, Sôseki, Ikuo Tsunematsu, and Marvin Marcus. *Inside My Glass Doors.* Boston: Tuttle Publishing, 2002.
——. *The 210th Day.* Boston: Tuttle Publishing, 2002.
Natsume, Sôseki, and Jay Rubin. *Sanshiro: A Novel.* New York: Putnam, 1982.
Natsume, Sôseki, Kingo Ochiai, and Sanford Goldstein. *To the Spring Equinox and Beyond.* Rutland, Vt.: Charles E. Tuttle, 1985.
Natsume, Sôseki, and Meredith McKinney. *Kusamakura.* New York: Penguin Books, 2008.
Natsume, Sôseki, Michael K. Bourdaghs, Atsuko Ueda, and Joseph A. Murphy. *Theory of Literature and Other Writings.* New York: Columbia University Press, 2009.
Natsume, Sôseki, Peter Milward, and Kii Nakano. *The Tower of London.* Brighton, U.K.: In Print Publishers, 1992.
Natsume, Sôseki, and Soiku Shigematsu. *Zen Haiku: Poems and Letters of Natsume Soseki.* New York: Weatherhill, 1994.
Natsume, Sôseki, and V. H. Viglielmo. *Light and Darkness: An Unfinished Novel.* New York: Putnam, 1982.
Auestad, Reiko Abe. *Rereading Sôseki: Three Early Twentieth-Century Japanese Novels.* Wiesbaden: Harrassowitz, 1998.
Doi, Takeo. *The Psychological World of Natsume Sôseki.* Cambridge, Mass.: Harvard University Asia Center, 1976.

NISHIWAKI Junzaburô

Nishiwaki, Junzaburô, and Hosea Hirata. *The Poetry and Poetics of Nishiwaki Junzaburô: Modernism in Translation.* Princeton, N.J.: Princeton University Press, 1993.

NIWA Fumio

Niwa, Fumio. *The Buddha Tree: A Novel.* Rutland, Vt.: Charles E. Tuttle, 1971.

NOGAMI Yaeko

Nogami, Yaeko. *The Neptune, The Foxes.* Tokyo: Kenkyûsha, 1957.

NOMA Hiroshi

Noma, Hiroshi, and James Raeside. *"Dark Pictures" and Other Stories.* Ann Arbor: Center for Japanese Studies, University of Michigan, 2000.

ÔBA Minako

Ôba, Minako, Michiko N. Wilson, and Michael K. Wilson. *Birds Crying.* Norwalk, Conn.: Eastbridge, 2005.

Ôba, Minako, and Janice Brown. *Tarnished Words: The Poetry of Ôba Minako.* Norwalk, Conn.: Eastbridge, 2006.

Wilson, Michiko N. *Gender Is Fair Game: (Re)thinking the (Fe)male in the Works of Ôba Minako, Japanese Women Writing.* Armonk, N.Y.: M.E. Sharpe, 1999.

ODA Sakunosuke

Oda, Sakunosuke. *Stories of Osaka Life.* New York: Columbia University Press, 1990.

ÔE Kenzaburô

Ôe, Kenzaburô. *The Silent Cry.* New York: Kodansha International, 1974.

——. *Teach Us to Outgrow Our Madness: Four Short Novels.* New York: Grove Press, 1977.

——. *A Personal Matter.* New York: Grove Press, 1982.

——. *The Crazy Iris and Other Stories of the Atomic Aftermath.* New York: Grove Press, 1985.

——. *Fire from the Ashes: Short Stories about Hiroshima and Nagasaki.* London: Readers International, 1985.

——. *The Pinch Runner Memorandum.* Armonk, N.Y.: M.E. Sharpe, 1993.

——. *Japan, the Ambiguous, and Myself: The Nobel Prize Speech and Other Lectures.* New York: Kodansha International, 1995.

——. *A Healing Family.* New York: Kodansha International, 1996.

——. *An Echo of Heaven.* New York: Kodansha International, 1996.

——. *Rouse Up, O Young Men of the New Age.* New York: Grove Press, 2002.

Ôe, Kenzaburô, and David L. Swain. *Hiroshima Notes.* Tokyo: YMCA Press, 1981.

Ôe, Kenzaburô, and J. Philip Gabriel. *Somersault: A Novel.* New York: Grove Press, 2003.

Ôe, Kenzaburô, Kunioki Yanagishita, and William Wetherall. *A Quiet Life.* New York: Grove Press, 1996.

Ôe, Kenzaburô, Paul St. John Mackintosh, and Maki Sugiyama. *Nip the Buds, Shoot the Kids.* New York: Marion Boyars, 1995.

Ôe, Kenzaburô, and Shôichi Saeki. *The Catch and Other War Stories.* New York: Kodansha International, 1981.

Wilson, Michiko N. *The Marginal World of Ôe Kenzaburô: A Study in Themes and Techniques.* Armonk, N.Y.: M.E. Sharpe, 1986.

OGUMA Hideo

Oguma, Hideo, and David G. Goodman. *Long, Long Autumn Nights: Selected Poems of Oguma Hideo, 1901–1940.* Ann Arbor: Center for Japanese Studies, University of Michigan, 1989.

OKAMOTO Kanoko

Okamoto, Kanoko, and Kazuko Sugisaki. *The House Spirit, and Other Stories.* Santa Barbara, Calif.: Capra Press, 1995.

OKAMOTO Kidô

Okamoto, Kidô, and Masanao Inouye. *The American Envoy.* Kobe: J.L. Thompson, 1931.

Okamoto, Kidô, Zoè Kincaid, and Hanso Tarao. *The Mask-Make: A Drama in Three Acts.* New York: S. French, 1928.

ÔOKA Shohei

Ôoka, Shôhei. *Fires on the Plain.* Westport, Conn.: Greenwood Press, 1978.

Ôoka, Shôhei, and Wayne P. Lammers. *Taken Captive: A Japanese POW's Story.* New York: J. Wiley and Sons, 1996.

Ôoka, Shôhei, and Dennis C. Washburn. *The Shade of Blossoms.* Ann Arbor: Center for Japanese Studies, University of Michigan, 1998.

——. *A Wife in Musashino.* Ann Arbor: Center for Japanese Studies, University of Michigan, 2004.

Stahl, David C. *The Burdens of Survival: Ôoka Shôhei's Writings on the Pacific War.* Honolulu: University of Hawai'i Press, 2003.

OZAKI Kôyô

Ozaki, Kôyô, and Arthur Lloyd. *The Gold Demon.* Tokyo: Seibundo, 1917.

SAITÔ Mokichi

Saitô, Mokichi, Seichi Shinoda, and Sanford Goldstein. *Red Lights: Selected Tanka Sequences from Shakkô.* West Lafayette, Ind.: Purdue Research Foundation, 1989.

Heinrich, Amy Vladeck. *Fragments of Rainbows: The Life and Poetry of Saitô Mokichi, 1882–1953*. New York: Columbia University Press, 1983.

SATÔ Haruo

Satô, Haruo, and Francis B. Tenny. *The Sick Rose: A Pastoral Elegy*. Honolulu: University of Hawai'i Press, 1993.

——. *Beautiful Town: Stories and Essays*. Honolulu: University of Hawai'i Press, 1996.

SHIBA Ryôtarô

Shiba, Ryôtarô, and Eileen Katô. *The Heart Remembers Home*. Tokyo: Japan Echo, 1979.

——. *Drunk as a Lord*. New York: Kodansha International, 2001.

Shiba, Ryôtarô, and Akiko Takemoto. *Kukai the Universal: Scenes from His Life*. New York: ICG Muse, 2003.

Shiba, Ryôtarô, and Juliet Winters Carpenter. *The Last Shogun: The Life of Tokugawa Yoshinobu*. New York: Kodansha International, 1998.

SHIGA Naoya

Shiga, Naoya. *A Dark Night's Passing*. New York: Kodansha International, 1976.

——. *Morning Glories*. Berkeley, Calif.: Oyez, 1977.

——. *The Paper Door and Other Stories*. San Francisco, Calif.: North Point Press, 1987.

Sibley, William F., and Naoya Shiga. *The Shiga Hero*. Chicago: University of Chicago Press, 1979.

Starrs, Roy, and Naoya Shiga. *An Artless Art: The Zen Aesthetic of Shiga Naoya: A Critical Study with Selected Translations*. Richmond, Surrey: Japan Library, 1998.

SHIMAMURA Hôgetsu

Tomasi, Massimiliano. *The Literary Theory of Shimamura Hôgetsu (1871–1918) and the Development of Feminist Discourse in Modern Japan*. Lewiston, N.Y.: E. Mellen Press, 2008.

SHIMAO Toshio

Shimao, Toshio, and Kathryn Sparling. *"The Sting of Death" and Other Stories*. Ann Arbor: Center for Japanese Studies, University of Michigan, 1985.

Gabriel, Philip. *Mad Wives and Island Dreams: Shimao Toshio and the Margins of Japanese Literature*. Honolulu: University of Hawai'i Press, 1999.

SHIMAZAKI Tôson

Shimazaki, Tôson. *The Broken Commandment.* Tokyo: University of Tokyo Press, 1974.

———. *The Family.* Tokyo: University of Tokyo Press, 1976.

———. *Chikuma River Sketches.* Honolulu: University of Hawai'i Press, 1991.

Shimazaki, Tôson, and William E. Naff, 1987. *Before the Dawn.* Honolulu: University of Hawai'i Press, 1991.

Andersson, Renée. *Burakumin and Shimazaki Tôson's Hakai: Images of Discrimination in Modern Japanese Literature.* Lund, Sweden: Department of East Asian Languages, Lund University, 2000.

Bourdaghs, Michael. *The Dawn That Never Comes: Shimazaki Tôson and Japanese Nationalism.* New York: Columbia University Press, 2003.

SHÔNO Junzô

Shôno, Junzô, and Wayne P. Lammers. *Still Life and Other Stories.* Berkeley, Calif.: Stone Bridge Press, 1992.

———. *Evening Clouds: A Novel.* Berkeley, Calif.: Stone Bridge Press, 2000.

SONO Ayako

Sono, Ayako. *Watcher from the Shore: A Novel.* New York: Kodansha International, 1990.

SUEHIRO Tetchô

Kyoko, Kurita. "Meiji Japan's Y23 Crisis and the Discovery of the Future: Suehiro Tetcho's Nijusan-nen mirai-ki." *Harvard Journal of Asiatic Studies* 60 (1):5–43, 2000.

TACHIHARA Masaaki

Tachihara, Masaaki. *Wind and Stone: A Novel.* Berkeley, Calif.: Stone Bridge Press, 1992.

Tachihara, Masaaki, and Clark Malcolm. *Cliff's Edge, and Other Stories.* Ann Arbor, Mich.: Midwest Publishers, International, 1980.

TACHIHARA Michizô

Tachihara, Michizô, Gakuji Iida, and Robert Epp. *Of Dawn, of Dusk: The Poetry of Tachihara Michizô, 1914–1939.* Stanwood, Wash.: Yakusha, 2001.

TADA Chimako

Tada, Chimako. *Moonstone Woman: Selected Poems and Prose.* Rochester, Mich.: Katydid Books, 1990.

TAKAHASHI Takako

Takahashi, Takako, and Maryellen Toman Mori. *Lonely Woman*. New York: Columbia University Press, 2004.

TAKAMURA Kôtarô

Takamura, Kôtarô. *Chieko's Sky*. New York: Kodansha International, 1978.

———. *Chieko and Other Poems of Takamura Kôtarô*. Honolulu: University of Hawai'i Press, 1980.

———. *The Chieko Poems*. Copenhagen: Green Integer Books, 2007.

Takamura, Kôtarô, and Hiroaki Sato. *A Brief History of Imbecility: Poetry and Prose of Takamura Kotarô*. Honolulu: University of Hawai'i Press, 1992.

TAKEDA Taijun

Takeda, Taijun. *This Outcast Generation: Luminous Moss*. Rutland, Vt.: C.E. Tuttle, 1967.

TANIZAKI Jun'ichirô

Tanizaki, Jun'ichirô. *Ashikari and the Story of Shunkin: Modern Japanese Novels*. Westport, Conn.: Greenwood Press, 1970.

———. *The Key*. New York: Perigee Books, 1981.

———. *The Secret History of the Lord of Musashi, and, Arrowroot*. New York: Alfred A. Knopf, 1982.

———. *Naomi*. New York: Putnam, 1986.

———. *Childhood Years: A Memoir*. New York: Kodansha International, 1989.

———. *Diary of a Mad Old Man*. New York: Vintage Books, 1991.

———. *Quicksand*. New York: Alfred A. Knopf, 1994.

Tanizaki, Jun'ichirô, Anthony H. Chambers, and Paul McCarthy. *The Gourmet Club: A Sextet*. New York: Kodansha International, 2001.

Tanizaki, Jun'ichirô, and Edward Seidensticker. *The Makioka Sisters*. New York: Vintage Books, 1995.

———. *Some Prefer Nettles*. New York: Vintage Books, 1995.

Tanizaki, Jun'ichirô, and Howard Hibbett. *Seven Japanese Tales*. New York: Vintage Books, 1996.

Chambers, Anthony H. *The Secret Window: Ideal Worlds in Tanizaki's Fiction*. Cambridge, Mass.: Harvard University Asia Center, 1994.

LaMarre, Thomas. *Shadows on the Screen: Tanizaki Jun'ichirô on Cinema and "Oriental" Aesthetics*. Ann Arbor: Center for Japanese Studies, University of Michigan, 2005.

TAWARA Machi

Tawara, Machi, and Juliet Winters Carpenter. *Salad Anniversary*. New York: Kodansha International, 1989.

TAYAMA Katai

Tayama, Katai. *Country Teacher: A Novel.* Honolulu: University of Hawai'i Press, 1984.

Tayama, Katai, and Kenneth G. Henshall. *The Quilt and Other Stories.* Tokyo: University of Tokyo Press, 1981.

——. *Literary Life in Tôkyô, 1885–1915: Tayama Katai's Memoirs.* Leiden: Brill, 1987.

Tayama, Katai, and Yoko Fukano. *Futon.* Brisbane: Department of Japanese, University of Queensland, 1987 (original publication 1978).

TERAYAMA Shûji

Sorgenfrei, Carol Fisher, and Shûji Terayama. *Unspeakable Acts: The Avant-Garde Theatre of Terayama Shûji and Postwar Japan.* Honolulu: University of Hawai'i Press, 2005.

TOKUDA Shûsei

Tokuda, Shûsei, and Richard Torrance. *Rough Living.* Honolulu: University of Hawai'i Press, 2001.

Torrance, Richard. *The Fiction of Tokuda Shusei, and the Emergence of Japan's New Middle Class.* Seattle, Wash.: University of Washington Press, 1994.

TOKUTOMI Sohô

Tokutomi, Sohô, and Sinh Vinh. *The Future Japan.* Edmonton, Canada: University of Alberta Press, 1989.

Pierson, John D. *Tokutomi Sohô, 1863–1957, a Journalist for Modern Japan.* Princeton, N.J.: Princeton University Press, 1980.

TOMIOKA Taeko

Tomioka, Taeko, Noriko Mizuta Lippit, and Kyoko Iriye Selden. *Funeral of a Giraffe: Seven Stories.* Armonk, N.Y.: M.E. Sharpe, 2000.

TSUBOI Sakae

Tsuboi, Sakae. *Twenty-Four Eyes.* Rutland, Vt.: C.E. Tuttle, 1983.

TSUBOI Shigeji

Tsuboi, Shigeji. *Egg in My Palm: Selected Poetry of Tsuboi Shigeji.* Stanwood, Wash.: Yakusha, 1993.

TSUBOUCHI Shôyô

Ryan, Marleigh Grayer. *The Development of Realism in the Fiction of Tsubouchi Shôyô.* Seattle, Wash.: University of Washington Press, 1975.

TSUJI Kunio

Tsuji, Kunio. *The Signore: Shogun of the Warring States.* New York: Kodansha International, 1989.

TSUSHIMA Yûko

Tsushima, Yûko. *Child of Fortune.* New York: Kodansha International, 1983.

———. *Woman Running in the Mountains: A Novel.* New York: Pantheon Books, 1991.

Tsushima, Yûko, and Geraldine Harcourt. *The Shooting Gallery.* New York: Pantheon Books, 1988.

UMEZAKI Haruo

Umezaki, Haruo. *Occurrences of an Old Dilapidated House.* New York: Kobunsha, 1968.

UNO Chiyo

Uno, Chiyo. *Confessions of Love.* Honolulu: University of Hawai'i Press, 1989.

Uno, Chiyo, and Rebecca L. Copeland. *The Story of a Single Woman.* London: P. Owen, 1992.

Copeland, Rebecca L., and Chiyo Uno. *The Sound of the Wind: The Life and Works of Uno Chiyo.* Honolulu: University of Hawai'i Press, 1992.

UNO Kôji

Uno, Kôji, and Elaine Tashiro Gerbert. *Love of Mountains: Two Stories.* Honolulu: University of Hawai'i Press, 1997.

YAMADA Eimi

Yamada, Eimi, and Sonya Johnson. *Trash.* New York: Kodansha International, 1994.

Yamada, Eimi, Yumi Gunji, and Marc Jardine. *Bedtime Eyes.* New York: St. Martin's Press, 2006.

YAMAMOTO Michiko

Yamamoto, Michiko. *Betty-San: Stories.* New York: Kodansha International, 1983.

YAMAMOTO Shûgorô

Yamamoto, Shûgorô. *Another View of Bushido.* Tokyo: Senjo Publishing, 1985.

———. *The Flower Mat.* Rutland, Vt.: Charles E. Tuttle, 1977.

YAMAMOTO Yûzô

Yamamoto, Yuzô, and Glenn W. Shaw. *Three Plays*. Tokyo: Hokuseido Press, 1935.

YAMAZAKI Masakazu

Yamazaki, Masakazu. *Mask and Sword: Two Plays for the Contemporary Japanese Theater*. New York: Columbia University Press, 1980.

YASUOKA Shôtarô

Yasuoka, Shôtarô. *A View by the Sea*. New York: Columbia University Press, 1984.

Yasuoka, Shôtarô, and Royall Tyler. *The Glass Slipper and Other Stories*. Champaign, Ill.: Dalkey Archive Press, 2008.

YOKOMITSU Riichi

Yokomitsu, Riichi. *Love and Other Stories of Yokomitsu Riichi*. Tokyo: University of Tokyo Press, 1974.

Yokomitsu, Riichi, and Dennis C. Washburn. *Shanghai: A Novel*. Ann Arbor: Center for Japanese Studies, University of Michigan, 2001.

YOSANO Akiko

Yosano, Akiko, Sam Hamill, and Keiko Matsui Gibson. *River of Stars: Selected Poems of Yosano Akiko*. Boston: Shambhala Publications, 1996.

Yosano, Akiko, Sanford Goldstein, and Seishi Shinoda. *Tangled Hair: Selected Tanka from Midaregami*. Rutland, Vt.: Charles E. Tuttle, 1987.

Takeda, Noriko. *A Flowering Word: The Modernist Expression in Stephane Mallarme, T.S. Eliot, and Yosano Akiko*. New York: P. Lang, 2000.

YOSHIKAWA Eiji

Yoshikawa, Eiji. New York: Alfred A. Knopf, 1956.

——. *Musashi*. New York: Kodansha International, 1981.

——. *Taiko: An Epic Novel of War and Glory in Feudal Japan*. New York: Kodansha International, 1992.

YOSHIMOTO Banana

Yoshimoto, Banana, and Ann Sherif. *N.P.: A Novel*. New York: Grove Press, 1994.

——. *Lizard*. New York: Washington Square Press, 1996.

Yoshimoto, Banana, and Megan Backus. *Kitchen*. Tokyo: Fukutake Shoten, 1993.

Miller, J. Scott. 1993. Teaching *The Tale of Genji* with Saikaku's *Life of an Amorous Man*. In: *Approaches to Teaching Murasaki Shikibu's* The Tale of Genji, edited by E. Kamens. New York: Modern Language Association of America.

YOSHIYUKI Junnosuke

Yoshiyuki, Junnosuke. *The Dark Room*. New York: Kodansha International, 1975.

About the Author

J. Scott Miller is a professor of Japanese and comparative literature at Brigham Young University in Provo, Utah, whose faculty he joined in 1994. He received his undergraduate degree in comparative literature from BYU, studied at Tsukuba University as a Japanese Government Ministry of Education Fellow, and earned his M.A. and Ph.D. in East Asian Studies from Princeton University. He has spent a combined total of seven years in residence in Japan, has written books and articles on Japanese literature, and has taught Japanese literature at Colgate University and BYU. His research interests include Japanese literature from the 19th century onward, oral narrative, translation theory, and early Japanese sound recordings. Among his publications are *Adaptations of Western Literature in Meiji Japan* (New York: Palgrave, 2001) and "Teaching *The Tale of Genji* with Saikaku's *Life of an Amorous Man*," in *Approaches to Teaching Murasaki Shikibu's* The Tale of Genji (New York: Modern Language Association of America, 1993). Reference books to which he has contributed include the *Encyclopedia of Asian History* (New York: Charles Scribner's Sons, 1988), *Japan: An Illustrated Encyclopedia* (New York: Kodansha International, 1993), and the volumes *Japanese Fiction Writers, 1868–1945* and *Japanese Fiction Writers since World War II* in the "Dictionary of Literary Biography" series (Detroit, Mich.: Gale Research, 1997).

Lightning Source UK Ltd.
Milton Keynes UK
UKOW040605140312

188940UK00002B/2/P